THE PERSISTENCE OF MYTH:
Psychoanalytic and Structuralist Perspectives

EDITED BY
PETER L. RUDNYTSKY

© 1988 The Guilford Press
A Division of Guilford Publications, Inc.
72 Spring Street, New York, NY 10012

Printed in the United States of America

Last digit is print number: 9 8 7 6 5 4 3 2 1

ISBN 0-89862-584-X

THE PERSISTENCE OF MYTH:
Psychoanalytic and Structuralist Perspectives

This journal combines The Psychoanalytic Review (founded 1913) and Psychoanalysis (founded 1952). Former editors of Psychoanalysis: John C. Gustin, Clement Staff. Former editors of The Psychoanalytic Review: William A. White, Smith Ely Jelliffe, Nolan D. C. Lewis, Marie Coleman Nelson, Murray Sherman. A PUBLICATION OF THE NATIONAL PSYCHOLOGICAL ASSOCIATION FOR PSYCHOANALYSIS, INC.

THE GUILFORD PRESS
NEW YORK   LONDON

PREFACE

Peter L. Rudnytsky

The word "mythic" is often used pejoratively in common parlance as a synonym for "untrue." But, considered more profoundly, myths are the shaping fictions of an individual, a culture, or even the human race as a whole. As such, far from being "falsehoods," myths may be the repositories of the most enduring truths.

Psychoanalysis and structuralism, arguably the two most powerful intellectual movements of the twentieth century, have at once shed critical light on the understanding of myths and themselves sought to appropriate the explanatory power of myths for their own purposes. Freud opened new vistas for the study of art and literature through his concept of the Oedipus complex even as he capitalized on the prestige of Sophocles's *Oedipus the King* as a cultural touchstone. Lévi-Strauss's theory of myths as a system of mediations designed to overcome contradictions coexists with his recognition that structuralism is itself a "myth of mythology." But this mythic dimension, far from invalidating the scientific standing of structuralism or psychoanalysis—as positivistic critics contend—is a sign of hermeneutic self-awareness in disciplines that take human beings themselves as their objects of scrutiny.

As Lévi-Strauss's elaboration of Freud's hypothesis of the universality of the incest taboo attests, psychoanalysis and structuralism are fundamentally compatible in their outlooks. To be sure, there are divergences on some points. Psychoanalysis is a dynamic individual psychology; structuralism is grounded in the anthropological study of cultures. And whereas psychoanalysis takes for granted the primacy of instinctual drives in behavior, structuralism places more emphasis on cognitive processes. But these are relatively minor differences of emphasis. Above all, as far as the study of myth is concerned, both psychoanalysis and structuralism share the positivistic conviction that, in Edmund Leach's (1971) words, "serious scientific inquiry should not search for ultimate causes deriving from some outside source but must confine itself to the study of relations existing between facts which are directly accessible to observation" (p. 86). Thus, all myths are to be treated with "equal philosophical respect," and the stories of the Bible, for instance, are to be considered neither more nor less true than the fables of any other culture.

The essays in this volume are unified by their theoretical focus and by a historical progression. John Kerr's "*The Devil's Elixirs*, Jung's 'Theology,' and the Dissolution of Freud's 'Poisoning Complex'" provides an introduction by examining the role played in the history of psychoanalysis by E. T. A. Hoffmann's novel. Kerr situates Jung's 1909 reading of the work in the context of the upheaval wrought by his contemporaneous involvement with Sabina Spielrein and the pressure this brought to bear on his relationship with Freud. He traces parallels between the involutions of Hoffmann's plot and Jung's own personal circumstances and shows Jung's theory of archetypes to be adumbrated in the work. In a concluding section, Kerr treats Freud's discussion of Hoffmann in "The 'Uncanny'" as a rebuttal to Jung and brings to the fore Freud's briefly held conception of love as a dangerous potion. Psychoanalysis itself emerges from Kerr's prismatic exploration as a "devil's elixir" uncannily imbued with Romanticism.

Since its inception, psychoanalysis has been shadowed by the myth of Oedipus, and it is therefore appropriate that the historical sequence of essays should begin by returning us to this literary double. In "The Riddle of the Riddle of the Sphinx," Theodore Lidz interrogates the symbolism of the riddle confronted by Oedipus. Addressing the views of both Freud and Lévi-Strauss, which variously understand the myth's subject to be human origins, Lidz proffers his own interpretation that the riddle has to do with the denial of the importance of the mother.

In the course of his essay, Lidz remarks that Oedipus's feet were needlessly fettered when he was exposed as an infant to die on Mount Cithaeron. Precisely this gratuitous detail provides the point of departure for Lowell Edmunds's anatomy lesson in "The Body of Oedipus." Utilizing the approaches both of comparative mythology and psychoanalysis, Edmunds breaks down his subject into a tripartite relation: between feet and genitals, between eyes and genitals, and between eyes and feet. Because Oedipus's mutilated feet belong "to an order of signification independent of the narrative," he treats them as "signifiers in a synchronic dimension of the myth."

Whereas the Oedipus myth, as Edmunds points out, did not begin with Sophocles, Daniel Rubey shows us that its influence persisted from the classical through the medieval period. His exemplary essay, "The Troubled House of Oedipus and Chrétien's *Néo-Tristan*: Re-writing the Mythologies of Desire," traces an awareness of the social implications of the Oedipus myth to at least the twelfth century, when vernacular literature first arose in France in the romances of Chrétien de Troyes. Focusing on *Cligés*, Chrétien's second romance and the least known of his works, Rubey disentangles the interlinked strands of the Oedipus, Tristan, and Arthur legends and anchors their meaning in the actual social, political, and dynastic struggles of the period.

A second foray into the medieval period is Edmund Leach's "Late Medieval Representations of Saint Mary Magdalene." Agreeing with Lévi-Strauss that myths must be viewed as "elements in a corpus which adds up to a cosmological system," Leach brings his masterful touch to bear on the biblical and non-biblical stories about the "repentant sinner" Mary Magdalene, and proves them to be permutations of apparently unrelated stories about the "sinless" Virgin Mary. If the Virgin enables God to become Man, her flamboyant double—as the first to behold the resurrected Christ—is the "mother" of the second birth of Man made into God.

Leach founds his analysis not only on literary but also on visual evidence. In "The Artistic Image and the Inward Gaze: Toward a Merging of Perspectives," Ellen Handler Spitz guides the reader on a tour of Italian Renaissance painting to defend the proposition that artistic images are "primary and irreducible" sources of psychoanalytic knowledge. Her phenomenological lens brings into view changing theories of the countertransference and analogies between restoration of works of art and the difficult therapeutic choices faced by analysts. Above all, however, Spitz returns us to the images themselves and challenges us to emulate the daring Florentines by becoming "risk-takers in the art of interpretation."

The final two essays take up major works of English Renaissance literature. Dianne Hunter's feminist contribution, "Doubling, Mythic Difference, and the Scapegoating of Female Power in *Mac-*

beth," deploys both structuralist and psychoanalytic strategies to read Shakespeare's play as "mediating unwelcome contradictions attendant on the transfer of power from the Tudor to the Stuart line." My own "'Here Only Weak': Sexuality and the Structure of Trauma in *Paradise Lost*" moves in three parts from the concept of "deferred action" as a model for the Fall, to Milton's patriarchal equation between femininity and sexuality, to an analysis of narcissism and incest as forms of self-love in the epic. Citing the allegory of Satan, Sin, and Death, I conclude that a violation of the incest taboo is at the root of Milton's depiction of the Fall.

As befits a collection featuring structuralist as well as psychoanalytic perspectives, many unifying threads emerge synchronically, as it were, among the various essays. Leach's emphasis on myths as belonging to a "cosmological system," for example, is shared by both Lidz and Edmunds. Like Rubey, Hunter grounds her reading of *Macbeth* in contemporaneous political conflicts. Hunter's feminism, in turn, finds a responsive chord in Leach's use of gnostic sources concerning Mary Magdalene and in my assessment of Milton's patriarchalism. In highlighting the subjective origins of psychoanalytic theory, Kerr concurs with Spitz's awareness of "the dialectic between beholder and image" and her plea for a more tolerant view of countertransference.

The positivistic and demystifying tendencies of both psychoanalysis and structuralism are too deeply ingrained in our contributors to permit a naive idealization of myth. The invisible realities that myths seek to embody, after all, may serve to legitimate an unjust society. But if a political analysis reminds us of the ease with which mythology shades into ideology, the persistence of ancient legends to our own day is sufficient proof that they also contain abiding truths about the human condition. The myths of Oedipus and the Fall may not tell us the way things *were*; but they do teach us the way they *are*.

I am grateful to Leila Lerner for inviting me to serve as Guest Editor of *The Psychoanalytic Review* and to Ruth Kaye for her steadfast collaboration in planning this issue.

REFERENCE

LEACH, E. (1971) *Genesis as Myth and Other Essays*. London: Jonanthan Cape.

THE DEVIL'S ELIXIRS, JUNG'S "THEOLOGY," AND THE DISSOLUTION OF FREUD'S "POISONING COMPLEX"

John Kerr

Psychoanalysis and literature have from the beginning stood in the uneasy relationship of half-brothers unsure of their shares in a single estate. These half-brothers have at times acted as though their own claims were best served by invoking ties of the closest kinship between them. Then again, at other times, they have abruptly reversed themselves and each has insisted, with renewed vigor, that his lineage needs to be distinguished from the other's, that his is a different paternity. Accordingly, one enters into any arrangement with the two brothers with a certain apprehension: What was gladly agreed to today may be tomorrow's point of contention.

Let us begin, then, with the gentlest of discriminations: One of these half-brothers is clearly the elder, and though the younger may protest his greater acuity, the claims of the first-born should be heard first. Thus, we should note, with Ellenberger (1970), Holt (1978), and Rudnytsky (1987), that the literature and philosophy of the Romantic movement, both in Germany and elsewhere, provided the first dynamic psychiatry with many of its themes and issues, and that these then subsequently made their way into psychoanalysis. The literary motif of the *doppelgänger*, to take but one example, appears to have rematerialized in French psychopathology as "multiple personality," and to have subsequently come down to us in the form of "splitting," that most disturbing concept which has lately been seen haunting the clinical imagination.

In what follows, I shall focus on the impact exerted on the history of psychoanalysis by a single work from the Romantic tradition, E. T. A. Hoffmann's *The Devil's Elixirs* (1816). Owing to the wealth of historical documents now available, it is possible to state with considerable precision how this particular novel came to be one of the foci of the dialogue between Freud and Jung, this moreover at a particularly critical point in the evolution of their friendship. Principally, I propose to argue that the novel had a formative role in shaping both Jung's incipient disaffection with the Freudian paradigm and his own later theories. As well, I will offer a tentative suggestion concerning the novel's impact on Freud's ongoing theorizing both at the time and subsequently.

A DIFFICULT TIME

To understand the pivotal role of *The Devil's Elixirs* in the dialogue between Freud and Jung, we first have to grasp the unusual circumstances in which Jung read the book during the first week of March, 1909. The early spring of 1909 was a time of spectacular difficulty for Carl Jung, and his difficulties were inextricably linked to his involvement with the new field of psychoanalysis. Jung had only recently enjoyed a meteoric rise to psychiatric prominence. From the moment he set foot in the Burghölzli hospital at the end of 1900, it was clear that he was a true intellectual aristocrat — he hailed from a distinguished Basel family — and that he was uniquely gifted to pursue a career in psychiatry. Jung proceeded to win an international reputation at the astonishingly young age of 31, this on the strength of two extraordinary contributions to medical psychology — his volume on the association experiment and his *Psychology of Dementia Praecox* — both of which were published in 1906. For a variety of reasons both personal and theoretical, Jung had elected to give his achievements an unusual caste by unilaterally taking on the burden of appearing in print as a supporter of the controversial Viennese neurologist, Sigmund Freud. Jung's decision, in some ways a benighted one, had led first to a correspondence and then to a friendship with Freud, who could only wonder at his good fortune at securing the support of this unsolicited champion. In short order, Jung made good on the promise of his overtures. In the fall of 1907, he became the first psychiatrist to make a public defense of Freud's theories at an international congress. In the spring of 1908, he took it upon himself to call a Congress for Freudian Psychology, the first such Congress ever held. And, at that Congress, or rather at a private enclave that met immediately afterwards, Jung also agreed to serve as the executive editor of a new journal devoted principally to psychoanalysis, the *Jahrbuch für Psychoanalytische und Psychopathologische Forschungen*. Then things began to come apart.

By making himself Freud's spokesman, Jung had also made himself the target for the anti-Freud sentiment that was just then, in the wake of the scandalous Dora case, beginning to become virulent in German psychiatry and neurology. In Switzerland, where a web of personal and institutional affiliations linked the nation's psychiatrists and neurologists into a close-knit community, interest in psychotherapy and medical psychology was burgeoning. In deference to Jung's position, and that of his mentor Eugen Bleuler as well, the anti-Freud campaign in Switzerland was conducted largely in private. In the fall of 1908, however, the dean of Swiss psychiatrists, the distinguished Auguste Forel, gave the signal for a more trenchant public discussion. Though Jung was not specifically named in Forel's (1908) brief review of the state of contemporary psychotherapy, it was clear that he was the target of remarks that questioned the propriety, and the possible suggestive effect, of inquiring too persistently after sexual complexes. And in case Jung had missed the allusion in Forel's article, Freud thoughtfully pointed it out to him in his letter of November 8, 1908: "Forel's attacks are chiefly on you, probably out of ignorance" (McGuire, 1974, p. 175).

Unfortunately, Jung was at this very time engaged in secret meetings with a former patient, Sabina Spielrein. The Jung–Spielrein relationship is far too complex and far too intimately connected with the events just reviewed for a brief summary. It will suffice to say that the relationship had evolved slowly, with frequent changes of meaning, and that it constituted for Jung a very personal and a very private complement to his public career as Freud's spokesman. We cannot be certain that the relationship was ever consummated; we can be certain, however, that by the late fall of 1908 it had already gone beyond the bounds of Swiss propriety.

At this juncture, either Jung or his wife took the necessary first step toward saving his career by communicating privately with Spielrein's mother. What happened next is well documented in Carotenuto's volume (1982). For our purposes, the crucial event occurred in late February 1909, when disaster struck. Spielrein was unwilling to return to the role of patient. She attacked Jung physically and with sufficient vehemence to draw blood. Jung was now in a position of uncertainty and dread. In the absence of any further communication from the young woman (he would have none until the end of May), Jung did not know whether he would be publicly unmasked and effectively ruined. Worse still, such was the nature of his transgression that a public unmasking would have simultaneously brought the new science of psychoanalysis into instant disrepute, most certainly in Switzerland and quite possibly throughout the German-speaking medical world. Freud, no doubt, would have to disown him. And, as if by a malevolent play of chance, within a matter of days after Spielrein angrily quit his office, the very first issue of the *Jahrbuch*, with Jung, Freud, and Bleuler on the masthead, came rolling off the presses.

If one examines closely Jung's correspondence with Freud during the months of March and April in 1909, the evidence of Jung's terrible predicament is everywhere to be found, beginning with his letter of March 7, 1909. Though he is less than straightforward as to the actual facts of the Spielrein affair, Jung does take the gentlemanly step of warning Freud that a scandal may be brewing. The letters that follow pitch and yaw terribly as Jung struggles to maintain his composure, while he waits to see what revenge, if any, Spielrein would take. And it is in these very same letters that a resurgent mystical tendency makes its presence felt to a degree unprecedented in the correspondence to date. This mystical tendency reached its climax in the famous "spookery" (McGuire, 1974, p. 216) incident in Freud's home at the end of March when, to Freud's absolute astonishment, Jung correctly predicted that a second loud retort would come resounding from the bookcase. In the letters that immediately followed this incident, moreover, Jung remained largely unrepentant, seemingly determined to see what he called "psychosynthesis" (McGuire, 1974, p. 216) through to the end.

All this is well documented in the Freud-Jung correspondence, in the Carotenuto volume, and in Jung's memoirs (1962). Here let us confine ourselves to a few points with which to round out the context. First, even before disaster had struck and Spielrein had quit his office, Jung had begun trying to contain the potential damage to his reputation by softening his heretofore stringent psychoanalytic line. To Ernest Jones, with whom he was friendly, Jung had written on February 25, 1909:

We should do well not to burst out with the theory of sexuality in the foreground. I have many thoughts about that, especially on the ethical aspects of the question. I believe that in publicly announcing certain things one would saw off the branch on which civilization rests; one undermines the impulse to sublimation. . . . Both with students and with patients I get on further by not making the theme of sexuality prominent. (cited in Jones, 1955, p. 139)

Second, both before and after the disaster struck, Jung sought to preserve his own options by assiduously courting the friendship of men other than Freud. These men, in turn, seem to have been used by Jung as a sounding board for those ideas with which he would blanket himself in the cold days after his imagined expulsion from psychoanalysis. The Reverend Oskar Pfister was one such person. Jung's letter to Freud (on January 19, 1909) says of Pfister, "Oddly enough, I find this mixture of medicine and theology to my liking" (McGuire, 1974, p. 197). The young philosopher Paul Häberlin was another new acquaintance. Jung's letter to Freud (March 21, 1909) goes so far as to say of Häberlin: "He tops Pfister by a head in psychological acuity and biological knowledge, and he has studied theology as well as philosophy and natural science. Nor does he lack a certain mystical streak, on which account I set special store by him, since it guarantees a deepening of thought beyond the ordinary and a grasp of far-reaching syntheses" (McGuire, 1974, p. 214). But the most important of Jung's new acquaintances went unmentioned in the Freud correspondence — Theodore Flournoy. Jung first met Flournoy during this period (Hannah, 1976, p. 98). Flournoy was the grand old man of Geneva psychology and the author of a celebrated work on mediumship that had inspired Jung's own medical dissertation. It was from Flournoy that Jung derived the perspectives that would later inform his mature criticisms of Freud.

It is tempting to see Jung as behaving with a certain panicky calculation in these various maneuvers. And, indeed, there was much in his behavior that a more diligent conscience might have prohibited. But Jung's turn to other men, and most especially his turn to a "mixture of medicine and theology," might perhaps better be seen as a return. With some justice, Jung could say in his own defense that he had strayed too far in Freud's direction and was returning home to views he had held earlier in his career. As well, he could say with some justice — this point must be left undefended here — that he was also championing views held by none other than the young woman whom he had lately been so eager to be rid of, Sabina Spielrein.

As the reader undoubtedly already knows, however, Freud and Jung did *not* break off their relationship at this time. Following his visit to Vienna at the end of March, Jung quit the Burghölzli, vacationed in Italy during mid-April, then returned to Switzerland to establish himself in private practice in the new residence at Kussnacht. During the second week of April, he had a noteworthy dream that helped him clarify, first, his relationship to Freud and, second, the theoretical differences that lay between them. Then in May, to the astonishment of all, Spielrein took the extraordinary step of communicating directly with Freud. By the end of June, to the relief of all, the matter had been finally, and discreetly, settled. By Jung's lights, Freud had earned both his gratitude and his loyalty by standing by him during this difficult time and Jung was moved to continue their personal and political affiliation. Their theoretical differences, meanwhile, went underground, not to surface for another two and a half years.

In the long run, of course, the theoretical differences between the two men were not to be reconciled and the rupture of their friendship had not been prevented, only postponed. But what is principally interesting here is what further light can be shed on Jung's behavior during March and April of 1909 by a consideration of his reading *The Devil's Elixirs*. For it was in early March, during the most acute phase of the crisis, that Hoffmann's novel came into Jung's hands and thence made its appearance in the correspondence with Freud. In reply to Jung's desperate, not quite honest letter of March 7, 1909, warning of a possible scandal involving a patient, Freud had replied in a letter (March 9, 1909) with brave sentiments designed to buck up Jung's courage: "To be slandered and scorched by the love with which we operate — such are the perils of our trade, which we are certainly not going to abandon on their account" (McGuire, 1974, p. 210). But Freud's patience had been tried by Jung's sorry confession — full of references to the Devil — and in the next paragraph he went on to chide Jung for cutting a poor figure. A Jung family legend had it that their line had been begun by an illegitimate child of Goethe three generations before and Freud,

knowledgeable of the legend if not quite attuned to the exact genealogical fact, appealed to Goethe-as-ancestor in his rebuke:

> And another thing: "In league with the Devil and yet you fear fire?"
> Your grandfather [*sic*] said something like that. I bring up this quota-
> tion because you definitely lapse into the theological style in relating
> this experience. (McGuire, 1974, p. 211)

The Spielrein affair was still well short of settled, and would remain
that way for three more months, but Jung was understandably re-
lieved by Freud's reply and wrote back quickly on March 11, 1909 to
thank him for his support. In passing, Jung defended the tone of his
confession, "You mustn't take on about my 'theological' style, I just
felt that way" (McGuire, 1974, p. 212). In the paragraphs that follow
in the letter, one can almost feel Jung regaining his confidence as he
mentions his various plans for the future. And, in the process, he
returns to the theme of "theology," this time giving it a more whimsical turn:

> I have made a nice discovery in Hoffmann's *The Devil's Elixir* (a good
> deal of my "theology" evidently comes from there). I am thinking of
> writing something on it for your *Papers*. A whole tangle of neurotic
> problems, but all palpably real. Altogether, I have endless plans for
> work next year, and I look forward so much to the new era of outer
> (and inner) independence that is so important for me. (McGuire,
> 1974, pp. 212–213)

In point of fact, Jung never did write up his thoughts on *The Devil's
Elixirs* for Freud's monograph series. The reader will have to decide,
after reading further, to what extent Jung's later career might be seen
as a gloss on Hoffmann. First, a look at the novel itself is in order so
that we can see what Jung found so "palpably real."

BROTHER MEDARDUS AND THE ARCHETYPES

E. T. A. Hoffmann (1776–1822) was a man of many accomplish-
ments. A jurist by training and profession, he was also a *Kappelmeister*
and theatrical producer, as well as a music critic whose essays influenced Wagner and others. His own belief was that he would make his
mark on the world as a composer and he left behind a symphony,
nine operas, two masses, and numerous shorter compositions. But it
is for his idiosyncratic, almost incidental literary output that the

world now remembers him. Beginning in 1909, and continuing until his death 13 years later, working entirely in his leisure, Hoffmann produced a succession of short stories and novels that have since come to define a whole strand of the Romantic movement. His name has become synonymous with the grotesque, the chilling, and the macabre; his influence can be detected in such diverse descendants as Gogol, Poe, and Dostoevsky.

For the English reader unfamiliar with his work, Hoffmann can perhaps best be located somewhere between the Gothic novel and the work of Poe: He is a scion of the Gothic tradition, insofar as the fantastic and the metaphysical are allowed free play in the action, but a worthy ancestor to Poe insofar as each of his creations is informed by an urgently real psychological tension. The reader knows from the outset that what happens in a Hoffmann tale could never have happened; the reader does not for a moment doubt that what is felt in a Hoffmann tale has been felt many times before and will be felt again many times hence.

Hoffmann's themes were ideally suited to be taken up in turn by the first dynamic psychiatry and again by psychoanalysis. Nor was this accidental. Hoffmann familiarized himself with the psychiatry of his day and, among other things, made frequent visits to a nearby asylum in search of inspiration. The intersection with psychiatry shows in his work; as Taylor has put it in his introduction to the English translation (1963) of *The Devil's Elixirs*: "Hypnotism, somnambulism and telepathy are the phenomena which fascinated him; delirium, persecution mania and schizophrenia are the mental states with which he invested his characters; fright, fear and terror are the emotions released by these forces and experiences" (p. vii). To be sure, the category of the "uncanny" pre-existed Hoffmann's works, but it was Hoffman who gave the uncanny its quintessentially horrible expression, and it was to Hoffmann that Freud turned in 1919 when he thought it necessary to give the definitive psychoanalytic statement on the uncanny.

Die Elixire des Teufels is not thought to be Hoffmann's masterpiece; it is merely the work that fate placed in Jung's hands in March of 1909. Hoffmann wrote the book in two separate parts, the first in 1814, the second in 1815, and the novel reads that way. The first half describes the adventures of one Brother Medardus while the second half, which begins with a meditation on the afternoon of life, is chiefly concerned with clarifying the mysterious events of the first half and with describing Medardus's reflections on his deeds and his ultimate repentance.

The novel begins with a conceit as the author takes on the guise of an editor presenting a collection of manuscripts he has found. The central manuscript in this collection purports to be the autobiographical confession of an eighteenth-century Capuchin monk, one Brother Medardus. The initial segment of Medardus's account is exquisitely concerned with temptation, especially sexual temptation, and the devices of a tortured conscience. Brother Medardus tells us how he was raised in a monastery, how he mastered a disturbing attraction to the choirmaster's daughter by deciding precipitously to become a monk, and how a serendipitous talent for oratory spread his reputation as a preacher far and wide. Medardus's new-found security is momentarily shattered when a beautiful young woman, unknown to him but the living image of St. Rosalia, whose picture hangs in the chapel, comes to him in the confessional and announces that she is in love with him. While he is trying to regain his composure following this incident, Medardus is given as one of his tasks the care of the monastery's relics. Among these relics is a casket of Syracusan wine, said to have been wrested from the devil by St. Anthony, and before long Medardus is secretly sampling it. Such are the effects of the elixir, that Medardus finds new eloquence and even greater fame. But the head of the monastery is increasingly displeased — vanity, not piety, is what he hears from the pulpit — and although Medardus feels that he is the victim of jealousy, it is soon plain to all that his position is untenable. Accordingly, he is chosen to take a message to Rome and, with his bottle of the Devil's Syracusan with him, he steps out into the world. Inwardly, he has already planned to go his own way.

Almost at once, Medardus is plunged into a dangerous game of double impersonation. On his way through the mountains he comes across a nobleman resting on a precipice; he startles the man, who promptly falls to his apparent death. Proceeding further, Medardus comes to the castle of a Baron F. Here he discovers that he is taken for the dead nobleman, Count Victor. It had been Victor's plan to pose as a Capuchin so that he could pursue a secret liason with the Baron's wife, Euphemia. Medardus takes Victor's place in Euphemia's arms, but inwardly he has designs on the Baron's daughter,

Aurelia, who is the living image of the woman who had earlier surprised him in the confessional. In a rage of arrogance, Medardus eventually humiliates Euphemia by revealing his true identity, then kills her with the poison she meant for him. He attempts to rape Aurelia, but is surprised by her brother Hermogenes. He kills Hermogenes and flees into the night.

After an interlude in which he stays with a forester, who is boarding a mad monk whom he has found wandering in the forest, Medardus takes up life in a town. He obtains a new wardrobe and a new haircut, largely due to the ministrations of a comic figure, the barber Peter Schönfeld. But just as he has begun to accustom himself to his new life, he is publicly accused of Hermogenes's murder by a mysterious figure, the Old Painter. The Old Painter has appeared before in the story and will appear again — it is plain at this point that he is an apparition and it will be plain shortly that he holds the key to all the strange events that are unfolding.

Helped by Schönfeld, Medardus again makes his escape. Next he comes to a city where he quickly enters the court of the Prince. Here, too, there has been intrigue, but events go well until a new arrival at the court: Aurelia. She is both frightened and attracted by this man who so resembles her brother's murderer. They fall in love and their marriage is planned. In a double reversal, Medardus is suddenly unmasked, put in prison, and there visited by both the Old Painter and a mysterious double of himself. Then, equally suddenly, he is acquitted. Another man, the mad monk who had previously appeared at the forester's cabin, has confessed to Medardus's crimes. The real Medardus, however, cannot tolerate his own guilt and in another fit stabs himself in Aurelia's presence. In his delirium he believes he has killed her and again he flees. In the forest, he is attacked by the mad monk, who has also escaped, and the barber Schönfeld finds him in a catatonic state and deposits him in an asylum run by his order outside Rome.

Now Medardus enters into a cycle of repentance, self-chastisement, and sanctimoniousness. He becomes caught up in murderous intrigues at the court of the Pope, but makes his escape, and the rest of the novel concerns his journey back through the landscape of his earlier adventures. At each step of the way, he finds more pieces of the puzzle. It becomes clear that Count Victor did not die in the fall from the precipice and that, having gone mad, he has taken up

Medardus's identity: Victor is the mad monk who has been pursuing Medardus and confessing to his crimes. Eventually, the real Medardus returns to his original monastery and resumes his former life. By now he has come into possession of a manuscript written by the Old Painter that explains the web of destiny in which he, Count Victor, and Aurelia are all caught up. The Old Painter is a wraith. A student of Leonardo's who turned to paganism, he was in his own life bewitched by the very Syracusan that began this tale. It was he who painted the portrait of St. Rosalia that hangs in the chapel, but his model for the saint was an apparition of Venus. Then, he sired a child by a witch, herself a double of Venus–St. Rosalia, and though he subsequently repented he is condemned to walk the earth until the last of his line has also obtained salvation — or died. The story of the Old Painter's line, contained in his manuscript, is a tale of incest and repentance constantly repeated in each new generation. Victor, Medardus, and Aurelia are the last of the Old Painter's line.

The climax of the novel comes with the appearance of Aurelia at the monastery. Out of repentance for her own sins — the love of a monk — she has decided to enter the convent. But on the day of her investiture, she is murdered by Count Victor, who is intent on completing his criminal career as Medardus's delusional double. Aurelia's death is accompanied by a miracle: The smell of roses, the saint's flower, fills the church. A year later to the day, Medardus, now reconciled to God, himself dies.

Stepping back from the plot, several points are worth addressing. The novel suffers, at least so far as the modern sensibility is concerned, from Hoffmann's determination to keep track of every subsidiary theme and to weave them together at the end. The intent, no doubt, is musical, but the result is that side issues sometimes blot out the main action. And, while some of the revelations of the second half of the book work effectively to clear up the mysteries of the first half, many of them do not. With the figure of the Old Painter, moreover, Hoffmann has irretrievably broken the bounds of reality right from the start; there is thus a limit to the satisfaction the reader can take in the subsequent realistic clarifications of the uncanny, seemingly mad, coincidences that dominate the initial action. And for this reason, the central theme of the novel — the mysterious interconnections of chance, fate, and divine plan — makes less of an impression than Hoffmann intended.

This said, we should hasten to add that the psychological tensions of the novel are surprisingly effective. The myriad juxtapositions of passion and lust on the one hand and pure transcendental love on the other work far better than the reader may suppose from the plot summary. Here Hoffmann was borrowing from his own life and the quality of lived experience comes through clearly. If one has forgotten what it is to conceive a guilty, desperate love, *The Devil's Elixirs* will bring the experience back. Equally effective is Hoffmann's handling of guilt in all its terrible ramifications: pride, posturing, self-destructiveness, and paranoia.

It is not hard to appreciate why this novel appealed to Jung and why he found its problems "palpably real." Himself the son of a Pastor, Jung too had strayed far into the wider world, there to encounter both fame and fantasies of incest. A guilty conscience and a string of evil coincidences were his lot no less than that of Brother Medardus. Moreover, the general outlook of the novel, its mixture of religion, philosophy, and the occult, resembles nothing so much as the point of view Jung had espoused more than a decade earlier in his lectures of 1896–1899 to the Zofingia, a student association, during his years at the University of Basel. The voice was more than amicable — it was familiar.

In one further respect, Hoffmann spoke far more trenchantly to Jung on these subjects than he does to the modern reader. For an essential aspect of the novel, one that tends to elude the modern reader completely, is the multi-generational nature of sin. Count Victor, Medardus, and Aurelia are equally trapped in a web of familial guilt that precedes their own actions. The most they can hope for is that by righteousness they will atone for the sins of their line. The possibilities of ordinary human happiness are denied to them by virtue of the Old Painter's misdeeds generations before. In his way, Hoffmann had anticipated by 40 years the doctrine of hereditary degeneration that was to dominate psychiatry for the second half of the nineteenth century. His characters, like those patients who would later be diagnosed as having hereditary taint, are prone to exotic mental states and thus required to observe more stringent moral regimens in their lives than are ordinary people. But here let us observe that Jung had made his entry into the medical world with a work advancing a new perspective on the very issue of hereditary degeneration. Jung's medical dissertation (1902) is principally concerned with the case description of his cousin, who fancied herself to be a medium and incarnated various past lives of herself and of Jung in their séances together. But in the dissertation, he also makes the daring suggestion that perhaps some of the consequences of hereditary degeneration are benign and even desirable.

Specifically, Jung had suggested that one consequence of a psychopathic constitution was a greater psychic sensitivity. This sensitivity typically manifested itself in pathological states, such as the mediumistic trance, but it might also come to the aid of development by allowing the afflicted a glimpse into future adaptations. Thus, Jung implied, the medium's trance-personality, "Ivenes," prefigured her adult identity. This claim is handled gingerly in Jung's text, in part because Jung was mixing French and German sources with regard to the degeneration issue and in part because he had elected to conceal the role of hypnotism in inducing the trance state — an omission that, if discovered, would cast serious doubts on his claim. However, given the nature of the claim, and the fact that, as is now known, the medium was Jung's first cousin, it should not escape notice that Jung partially shared the same inherited tendencies and thus, potentially, the same putative precognitive abilities. Indeed, claims for a special psychic sensitivity, modestly decorated with genial disclaimers, can be found scattered throughout Jung's memoirs.

Beyond the issue of inherited sensitivity, the matter of lineage had other personal meanings for Jung. As his memoirs (1962) make repeatedly clear, Jung had long felt both a mysterious connection with previous generations and a sense that his own personality would necessarily remain incomplete so long as he could not locate his biography in the fabric of history. Thus, to take but one example, not only did he inwardly subscribe to the fancy that Goethe was his great-grandfather, but he also secretly believed, as Ellenberger (1970, p. 378, n. 20) has noted, that his own second self was a veritable incarnation of this forebear. As he wrestled with his terrible predicament in the spring of 1909, then, Jung was undoubtedly tempted by the thought that his great-grandfather's sins were repeating themselves in him. (Freud knew Jung's propensities in this regard — they can be readily deduced from a close reading of his dissertation — and it was undoubtedly for this reason that he elected to quote Goethe in his mild rebuke of March 9, 1909.) How reassuring, then, for Jung to find such exculpating passages as the following in Hoffmann's tale:

The Pope was silent for a few moments. Then he continued with a serious expression:

"What if Nature were to follow in the realm of the spirit the physical law by which an organism can only reproduce its own kind; if propensity and desire, like the in-dwelling power which makes the leaves green, were to be handed down from father to son, obliterating free will? There are whole families of robbers and murderers. This would then be the original sin, an eternal, ineradicable curse on a guilty house, for which no sacrifice could atone." (Taylor trans., p. 273)

In the matter of guilt, Hoffmann's nefarious Pope is proposing just that shift of focus—from the individual to the collective—with which Jung himself was later to be associated. Nor should it escape our notice that in March of 1909 such a shift of emphasis served a crucial organizing function for Jung as he wrestled with the persecutions of his "rather too sensitive conscience" (McGuire, 1974, p. 207). What for the individual must be confronted in terms of responsibility and guilt, for the collective can be addressed in terms of the fundamental nature of the psyche, of the inherited structure of "propensity and desire."

Thus Hoffmann crystallized for Jung the manner in which his previous concerns, as manifested in his dissertation, could be resurrected in such a way that he might regain both his composure and the objectivity that is indispensable for a psychotherapeutic viewpoint. By shifting his focus to the realm of the collective, Jung could begin to understand what was typical in his predicament. This is what Freud (who, to be sure, was still ignorant of the facts) was asking him to do; but it was also what he had to do, if he were to survive. Yet, for Jung, such a multi-generational perspective had always been associated with "psychosynthesis," with the subconscious apprehension of future possibilities.[1] And so the uncanny coincidences of the *The Devil's Elixirs*, which Hoffmann consistently explains by reference to past events with only the merest hint of an unconscious telepathic collaboration between characters, were metabolized by Jung's pre-existent prejudices to generate his own brand of multi-generational tendencies toward precognition. Thus did it happen that, for invoking "grandfather" Goethe in his letter, Freud was soon thereafter rewarded with "spookery" right in his own home.

Again, Jung could be accused of using a shift to the realm of the collective to wall up the moral significance of his own transgressions, but let us remember that the relation of moral responsibility to any objective appraisal of the psyche is a bedeviling topic for anyone. And, let us also remind ourselves, Jung chose to make his career not as a moralist but as a psychologist. This said, it should be noted that when Hoffmann's novel subsequently appeared in Jung's published writings, it was typically in the context of a generalized statement on the relationship of guilt to the unconscious. In Jung's special terminology of the archetypes, that which one wishes to conceal or repress typically becomes personified in dreams as a shadowy companion — the "shadow" in Jung's nomenclature. Of the four later citations of Hoffmann's novel in Jung's work, three are in explicit reference to the archetype of the shadow and the fourth makes essentially the same point. This last citation, which is the first chronologically, occurs in Jung's essay "On the Psychology of the Unconscious" (1943).[2] In this essay, which underwent several revisions as it kept pace with the further evolution of Jung's views, a case description of a hysterical woman serves as the fulcrum for distinguishing between the views of Adler and Freud. Brother Medardus and his *doppelgänger* put in their appearance during the course of an analysis of one of the patient's symptoms:

> The patient, then, had a laughing fit at the death of her father — she had finally arrived on top. It was an hysterical laughter, a psychogenic symptom, something that sprang from unconscious motives and not from those of the conscious ego. That is a difference not to be made light of, and one that also tells us whence and how certain human virtues arise. Their opposites went down to hell — or, in modern parlance, into the unconscious — where the counterparts of our conscious virtues have long been accumulating. Hence for every virtue we wish to know nothing of the unconscious; indeed it is the acme of virtuous sagacity to declare that there is no such thing as the unconscious. But alas! it fares with us all as with Brother Medardus in Hoffmann's tale *The Devil's Elixirs:* somewhere we have a sinister and frightful brother, our own flesh-and-blood counterpart, who holds and maliciously hoards everything that we would so willingly hide under the table. (1943, p. 39)

But Jung's long-term debt to Hoffmann would seem to go far beyond an occasional citation. Here we must leap ahead to Jung's later work. It took nearly a decade for Jung to resolve the painful feelings brought about by his eventual break with Freud at the end of 1912, and while most of his scientific work during that decade was devoted to the problem of psychological types, by far the greater part of his energy was spent in intensive self-study. It was only in the 1920s that Jung began publishing the fruits of that self-analysis: the theory of the archetypes. And here we can only report the astonishing fact that *all the major archetypes discovered by Jung in his self-analysis appear in Hoffmann's novel.* In the figure of Aurelia–St. Rosalia–Venus we have a clear adumbration of the "anima." The Old Painter can readily be seen behind the archetype of the "wise old man." The archetype of the "persona" has never been better depicted than by Medardus's self-presentation in the court of Baron F., where he was publicly Medardus, but privately, in his joint intrigue with Euphemia, Count Victor pretending to be Medardus. Or rather, Medardus pretending to be Victor pretending to be Medardus. And the complementary archetype of the "shadow" is so well exemplified by the mad monk (Victor) pursuing Medardus that, as mentioned above, Jung three times cited the book specifically as an exemplar of the "shadow" motif. Here let us add that in two of these three citations Jung's reference is ambiguous, as though Brother Medardus, and not the mad monk (Victor), were the pursuing shadow. This, no doubt, reflects simple carelessness of expression, but an unconscious truth may be suspected as well: Jung experienced Medardus, and behind Medardus, the novel as a whole, as *his* "shadow," the first time he read it.

In the matter of archetypes, perhaps we should note the one figure who appears in Hoffmann, but is missing in Jung: the barber Peter Schönfeld. Schönfeld, who repeatedly comes to Medardus's rescue, is a personification of Folly in the best sense — as that whimsical capacity of human nature that is redemptive. Jung's archetypal world lacks an equivalent figure and thus is somewhat staid in comparison to Hoffmann's.[3] And, going beyond the archetypes proper for a moment, there are two other areas where Jung may be indebted to Hoffmann. Jung's later notion of "synchronicity" would appear to owe much to the tangled web of chance and fate that was Hoffmann's main theme. And, as well, Jung's subsequent contention that, following the "afternoon of life," man turns to spiritual issues is explicitly and repeatedly stated as a premise in Part 2 of *The Devil's Elixirs*.

To be sure, Jung's later theory of the archetypes was the fruit of an involved and circuitous intellectual evolution. There is no reason to doubt the sincerity of Jung's own account of his experiences during his self-analysis, and these bear directly on the later theory. Moreover, the general idea of the archetype — the *Ur-Typus* — was not new; as a scientific formulation, it derived from Romantic biology and predated Jung's psychological version by a full century. As for the specific archetypes of Jung's theory, these, too, clearly reflect an interweaving of multiple experiences, intellectual as well as personal. To take but one example, one can find Jung speaking of man's "shadow side," specifically in reference to sexuality, as early as his 1910 review of Wittels's book, *The Sexual Need*. And, if one looks further back, one can find an equivalent phrase, "the psychic shadow side," in an early 1903 paper, "On Simulated Insanity," where it is attributed to Binet as a synonym for the subconscious generally. There can thus be no question of Jung having cribbed his theory from Hoffmann wholesale. Hoffmann was certainly a major influence on him. It is tempting to say that *The Devil's Elixirs* provided the unconscious scaffolding around which the later experiences of the self-analysis, and the theories derived from these experiences, were constructed. But before making such a claim it is important to know just how deeply the novel embedded itself in Jung's psyche when he read it in the spring of 1909. On this last point, there survives one important clue.

A DREAM IN TWO PARTS

After visiting Freud at the end of March, 1909, Jung and his wife returned to Zurich and cleaned out his flat at the Burghölzli. Then, in the second week in April, as he planned a bicycle trip to Italy, Jung had a dream that, as he tells us in his memoirs, clarified the essential differences between his outlook and Freud's. The first part of the dream "had its scene in a mountainous region on the Swiss-Austrian border":

> It was toward evening, and I saw an elderly man in the uniform of an Imperial Austrian customs official. He walked past, somewhat stooped, without paying any attention to me. His expression was peevish, rather melancholic and vexed. There were other persons present, and someone informed me that the old man was not really there, but was the ghost of a customs official who had died years ago. "He is one of those who still couldn't die properly. . . ."
>   I set about analyzing this dream. In connection with "customs" I at once thought of the word "censorship." In connection with "border" I thought of the border between consciousness and the unconscious on

the one hand, and between Freud's views and mine on the other hand. . . . As for the old customs official, his work had obviously brought him so little that was pleasurable and satisfactory that he took a sour view of the world. I could not refuse to see the analogy with Freud. (1962, p. 163)

This part of the dream was followed by "a second and far more remarkable part":

I was in an Italian city, and it was around noon, between twelve and one o'clock. A fierce sun was beating down upon the narrow streets. . . . A crowd came streaming toward me, and I knew that the shops were closing and people were on their way home to dinner. In the midst of this stream of people walked a knight in full armor. He mounted the steps toward me. He wore a helmet of the kind that is called a basinet, with eye slits, and chain armor. Over this was a white tunic into which was woven, front and back, a large red cross.
    One can easily imagine how I felt: suddenly to see in a modern city, during the noonday rush hour, a crusader coming toward me. What struck me as particularly odd was that none of the many persons walking about seemed to notice him. No one turned his head or gazed after him. It was as though he were completely invisible to everyone but me. I asked myself what this apparition meant, and then it was as if someone answered me — but there was no one there to speak: "Yes, this is a regular apparition. The knight always passes by here between twelve and one o'clock and has been doing so for a very long time (for centuries, I gathered) and everyone knows about it." (1962, p. 165)

With regard to the knight, Jung did not fail to see the analogy to himself. In his memoirs he goes on to contrast the two figures, the one moribund, the other "full of life and completely real" (p. 165). Unlike Freud, he tells us, he was not content with a psychology that "succeeded in finding nothing more in the depths of the psyche than the all too familiar and 'all-too-human' limitations" (p. 166). He wanted a psychology that allowed for a certain numinous potential within the unconscious, allowed for something that would give meaning to life. This contrast in theoretical orientation, according to his memoirs, is reflected in the differing figures of the customs official and the knight.

Certainly the two dream figures are to be contrasted. But the contrast given in the memoirs has been drawn too sharply. Omitted entirely is a detail that Jung reported to a seminar group in 1925 as the single most disturbing element in the dream: the fact that *both the knight and the customs official were dead and didn't know it.* Not only was Jung puzzled by this parallelism, but he pointedly consulted Freud for his interpretation during their trip together to America during the fall of 1909. Freud, however, as Jung informed his seminar in 1925, could make nothing of this detail either. (Another point revealed to the seminar, to which we will return later, was that the customs official not only reminded Jung of Freud, he *was* Freud. In addition, Jung informed his seminar that the knight was a Crusader, while in the memoirs he allows only that the knight reminded him of stories he'd read in childhood about the search for the Holy Grail.) The theme of "dying but not dying" had multiple references in Jung's life to date — to his father, to Spielrein, to the Old Painter — and they cannot all be sorted out here. Let it be clear, however, that contrary to the overly sharp contrast drawn in the memoirs, the figure of the knight was in his own way as "dead" as that of the customs official. Both figures are superfluous. With respect to the knight, this is clear enough in the dream itself: the knight is a throwback, and he is strikingly out of place amid the bustling commercial life of a modern city.

Here it is important to recall two things. First, Jung was himself an aristocrat of distinguished, even legendary, descent. Jung's ancestry had been one of the traits that had initially impressed Bleuler, himself descended from a peasant background, and thus had contributed to Jung's meteoric rise in the Burghölzli. Second, in April of 1909 Jung was in the precarious position of having given Freud an incomplete account of the Spielrein affair; he was still in considerable danger of being unmasked by the young woman, with unknown consequences to himself and to the new science of psychoanalysis. With these points in mind, the following passage in *The Devil's Elixirs* especially stands out. The action takes place in the court of the Prince. Medardus, posing as a Polish nobleman, has just been miraculously acquitted of Hermogenes's murder; he has not yet convicted himself in a guilty fit before the unsuspecting Aurelia. During the interlude between these two events, he is accosted by the court physician, who thinks it appropriate to deliver a lecture on the declining status of the nobleman in today's society:

> In this age when intellectual values are assuming more and more importance, ancestral and family pride has become a quaint, almost ludicrous phenomenon. Starting in the days of chivalry and with the

profession of arms, a class arose whose sole task was to defend the
other classes, and the subordinated relationship of protected to protector followed naturally. . . .

But the use of brute force is fast diminishing, and the power of
the mind is asserting itself in every realm. . . . Each person is thrown
back on to his own resources and forced to justify himself in the eyes
of the world by his own intellectual achievement, whatever superficial
brilliance may attend his position in the state. Ancestral pride, derived from chivalry, reflects a fundamentally opposite ideal, namely
my ancestors were heroes, therefore I, too, am a hero. . . .

Where the power of the mind is concerned, things are not like
this. Wise fathers often produce stupid sons, and because our age
ascribes a nobility of intellect to those who have a nobility of lineage,
it is probably more worrying to be descended from Leibniz than from
Amadis of Gaul or some ancient knight of the Round Table. The age
is moving irrevocably forwards, and the situation of our noble classes
is rapidly deteriorating. This may well explain their tactless behaviour
towards highly cultured commoners; a mixture of appreciative respect
and intolerable condescension, the product of a deep despair that the
triviality of their past glory will be exposed to the knowing gaze of the
wise, and their insufficiencies held up to ridicule. (Taylor translation,
pp. 209–210)

I believe that this passage in Hoffmann impressed Jung suffi-
ciently in March that it then informed the dream-thoughts and
dream-images of April. Medardus's situation at this point in the
novel mirrored Jung's own predicament — temporarily acquitted of a
charge when really he was guilty. And the physician's speech to
Medardus on the precarious state of the nobility would seem to
speak to a dawning sense in Jung that his own lineage, no matter
how distinguished, was going to be little protection against the impending storm. The sense of this part of the dream, then, is that
while he might be different from Freud, and glad of the difference,
Jung was still in grave danger of being held up to ridicule by the
knowing gaze of the wise.

The connection between the passage just quoted and the Crusader of Jung's dream may seem tenuous at best. But Jung's dream
had two parts. There is no customs official *per se* in *The Devil's Elixirs*.
There is, however, the following monologue on the subject of "awareness" by the comic barber Peter Schönfeld. Medardus has just regained his sanity at the asylum outside Rome. Schönfeld, who had
brought him there, is recounting to him the particulars of his con-

fused state when Medardus interrupts by saying that he counts himself glad to now be sane and wants to hear no more. Schönfeld
protests:

> Now what is the good of that, reverend Sir? . . . I mean, of that
> peculiar mental function known as awareness? It is nothing but the
> miserable activity of some pettifogging toll-keeper, or customs-officer,
> or assistant chief controller, who sets up a poky little office in his mind
> and says, whenever any goods are to be sent out: "Oh, no! Export
> prohibited. They must remain here." The finest jewels are buried in
> the ground like worthless seeds, and the most that comes up is beet-
> root, from which, with practice, a quarter of an ounce of foul-tasting
> sugar can be squeezed by applying a pressure of a thousand tons.
> Well, well, well. And yet this pitiful exportation is supposed to lay the
> foundation for trade with the heavenly city, where all is magnificence
> and splendour. . . . (Taylor trans., p. 231)

If we grant that this passage in *The Devil's Elixirs* exerted a
decisive influence in shaping the dream of the customs official, we
can see more clearly the close relation of Jung's "theology" to Hoffmann's. Jung, as he all but tells the reader of his memoirs, was intent
on storming the "heavenly city" of the unconscious. He wanted direct
access, unencumbered by the limitations of an "all-too-human" re-
ductionism. For Jung, furthermore, such a direct access meant going
beyond mere "awareness." It meant finding in the subliminal combi-
nations of the subconscious mind a glimpse into the future. Earlier, I
outlined how Hoffmann's multi-generational portrait of fate was red-
olent for Jung with implicit possibilities of "psychosynthesis." Now I
shall go farther and juxtapose Jung's dream of the knight and the
customs official with the same theme of "psychosynthesis." Transparently, the knight, construed as either a Crusader or a seeker after
the Holy Grail, is someone who wishes to go beyond the humdrum
and ordinary, but this of itself does not necessarily imply the "beyond" of precognition. For Jung, however, it did, or at least that is
the only conclusion that can be drawn from his letter to Freud a few
days after he had the dream.

The letter in question was tentatively begun April 2, but not
finished and mailed until April 12, 1909. As it was his first letter to
Freud following the visit to Vienna, Jung thought it appropriate to
offer his apologies for the incident during his last evening in Freud's
home: "When I left Vienna I was afflicted with some *sentiments d'in-*

completude because of the last evening I spent with you. It seemed to me that my spookery struck you as altogether too stupid . . ." (McGuire, 1974, p. 216). But one paragraph later, the letter turns unrepentant and Jung adds ominously: "That last evening with you has, most happily, freed me inwardly from the oppressive sense of your paternal authority. My unconscious celebrated this impression with a great dream which has preoccupied me for some days and which I have just finished analysing" (McGuire, 1974, p. 217). Beyond a doubt, this "great dream" was the dream in two parts depicting the customs official and the knight.[4] The rest of the letter makes it clear that Jung's "theology" is decidedly on the upswing and "psychosynthesis" is more in evidence than ever before. Principally, the letter describes two patients, one new and one old. Of his new patient Jung writes, "First rate spiritualistic phenomena occur in this case, though so far only once in my presence" (pp. 215-216). Of his old patient, who had been discussed with Freud and who had a penchant for repeatedly falling in love with schizophrenic men, Jung writes:

> I had the feeling that under it all there must be some quite special complex, a universal one having to do with the prospective tendencies in man. If there is a "psychanalysis" [*sic*] there must also be a "psychosynthesis" which creates future events according to the same laws. (I see I am writing rather as if I had a flight of ideas.) The leap towards psychosynthesis proceeds via the person of my patient, whose unconscious is right now preparing, apparently with nothing to stop it, a new stereotype into which everything from outside, as it were, fits in conformity with the complex. (Hence the idea of the objective effect of the prospective tendency!) (McGuire, 1974, pp. 216-217)

To make the matter explicit, no sooner had Jung finished analyzing his "great dream" than he was sallying forth with the banner of "psychosynthesis." There was more Hoffmann than Freud in these sentiments, which was as it should have been. For lately there had been more Hoffmann than Freud in Jung's dreams. Spielrein had yet to be heard from at this point, and the ultimate denouement of the Freud–Jung relationship was still years away. But, transparently, the fateful event had already occurred: Jung had drunk very deeply indeed from *The Devil's Elixirs*.

THE ECLIPSE OF THE "POISONING COMPLEX"

It would appear to be scarcely accidental that Freud himself took his examples from Hoffmann when, long after the rupture with Jung, he elected to make his own statement on the subject of the "uncanny." What is striking about Freud's (1919) treatment of the subject is how strongly he emphasizes the element of the past. To be sure, Freud's theoretical inclination had always been to emphasize the significance of the personal past, but in "The Uncanny" this inclination hardens into a new theoretical principle. For it is here that Freud introduces his "death instinct" as an instinctive compulsion to repeat earlier events. The past is thus armed with its own terrible power in this revamping of Freud's system; the future is ignored. This makes the strongest possible contrast to Jung's future-oriented views. In the universe of discourse that Freud sets out in "The Uncanny," and again in *Beyond the Pleasure Principle*, such novelties as "psychosynthesis" and "prospective tendency" are systematically rendered impossible. Which, we may suspect, is an essential aspect of the latent polemical intent underlying both works.

For thematic reasons alone one might argue that Jung and *The Devil's Elixirs* were quite probably on Freud's mind when he sat down to work on "The Uncanny." But, as it happens, it is possible to go farther than this and in the process clear up a tiny mystery. For, as Freud warms up for his critique of the "uncanny" as the "constant recurrence of the same thing" (1919, p. 234), he does in fact begin by making reference to *The Devil's Elixirs*, much as though he intended to make it the centerpiece of his study. Shortly, however, in the manner of someone reporting a recent rereading of a work, Freud informs the reader that the plot is too intricate for a short summary and that the accumulation of mysterious repetitions and doublings is aesthetically unsatisfactory, even if it does help one grasp the essential mechanism of repetition. In passing, and somewhat dubiously, Freud alleges that the novel depicts instances of "telepathy," this while making it clear that "telepathy" excites him not at all. Overall, the page and a half on *The Devil's Elixirs* in Freud's essay is cursory to the point where one wonders why it is there at all. Seemingly, all Freud gets for his trouble is to give the reader the tentative impression that the figure of the "double" involves a recurrence of something past.

But Strachey has added a footnote to Freud's discussion of *The*

Devil's Elixirs that merits our attention. The note speaks for Strachey's meticulous scholarship—another editor would have missed it
entirely—so let us not here complain that the translation (presumably Strachey's own) of a passage from Hoffmann contained within
goes unidentified. The note reads in its entirety:

> Under the rubric "Varia" in one of the issues of the *Internationale Zeit-
> schrift für Psychoanalyse* for 1919 (5, 308), the year in which the present
> paper was first published, there appears over the initials "S. F." a short
> note which it is not unreasonable to attribute to Freud. Its insertion
> here, though strictly irrelevant, may perhaps be excused. The note is
> headed: "E. T. A. Hoffmann on the Function of Consciousness" and it
> proceeds: "In *Die Elixire des Teufels* (Part II, p. 210, in Hesse's edi-
> tion)—a novel rich in pathological mental states—Schönfeld comforts
> the hero, whose consciousness is temporarily disturbed, with the fol-
> lowing words: 'And what do you get out of it? I mean out of the
> particular mental function which we call consciousness, and which is
> nothing but the confounded activity of a damned toll-collector—ex-
> cise-man—deputy-chief customs officer, who has set up his infamous
> bureau in our top storey and who exclaims, whenever any goods try to
> get out: "Hi! hi! exports are prohibited . . . they must stay here . . .
> here, in this country."'" (1919, pp. 233–234)

Freud's gloss is discrepant with the actual situation in the novel.
Medardus has regained his sanity, not momentarily lost it; and
Schönfeld is not comforting him, but rebuking him for putting so
much emphasis on awareness. Let us observe further that Freud
breaks off the quotation before the reader would find out that what
cannot be exported are the goods of the "heavenly city" of the unconscious. And, stepping back from the text itself, let us add what
Strachey was not in a position to know, or rather, to guess. As he
warmed up to his study on "The Uncanny," Freud naturally returned
to the scene of the crime, to *The Devil's Elixirs*, to see what he could
make of it. What he found, as he tells us straightforwardly in his
essay, was a novel so intricate and dense that it was not really suitable
material for a short discursive essay. In the process of reading the
novel, however, Freud came across the passage on consciousness and
apparently saw—this is the ostensible point of his note in the *Zeitschrift*—a literary foreshadowing of his own doctrine of the censor.
But, I would submit, Freud saw something else as well: the source of
Jung's dream image. Freud knew Jung's dream, knew that he had
appeared in it, and knew that he had been frustrated in his own

attempt to analyze it. Now, just in case Jung was still reading the *Zeitschrift*, Freud made a small point of his recent discovery.

But it is not Freud's later writings on the uncanny with which I wish to concern the reader here. Rather, I would like to offer a tentative suggestion as to the initial impact on him of Jung's invocation of Hoffmann's novel in March of 1909. Freud, of course, had long been familiar with Hoffmann's work in general, and we can take it as given that he had some acquaintance with *The Devil's Elixirs* in particular, though, in point of fact, there is no specific reference to it in any of his writings prior to 1919.[5] Nonetheless, assuming that in 1909 Freud did have some familiarity with the novel's content from a prior reading, he was most likely concerned with that mysterious bottle of Syracusan, the elixir itself, and what it forebode about Jung's investigations into the "core complex."

Some background is in order here. In the spring of 1909, Freud was approximately one third of the way through a three-year development in which, in collaboration with a small group of favorites, he gradually arrived at a definitive formulation of what he called the "core" or "nuclear" complex. This "core" or "nuclear" complex was to perform two important heuristic functions. It was to unify the burgeoning field of complexes in general and it was to serve as a point of departure for the psychoanalytic investigation of mythology and folktales. Incidentally, either English word faithfully reflects the German *"kerncomplex,"* but "core" is perhaps preferable to "nuclear" if only because the alternative translation prejudices the English reader to suppose that right from the start there was an intimate connection with the nuclear family, and thus with the triangular nature of the oedipal conflicts. As Forrester (1980, Ch. 3) has shown in some detail, however, it was only very gradually that Freud came to the oedipal and triangular formulation of the "core complex," even if in retrospect this particular version would seem to have been anticipated by his discussion of Sophocles's *Oedipus Rex* in *The Interpretation of Dreams*. During the years 1908–1909, then, the "core complex" was not yet synonymous with the Oedipus complex; it was still an essentially elastic concept that could accommodate a number of subsidiary themes. In particular, a point somewhat minimized by Forrester, Freud consistently supposed that children's sexual researches necessarily played an important role in determining both the timing and the specific content of the "core complex" in any individual's development. The specific theoretical utility of the theme of infantile sexual research is beyond the scope of this paper, but among its virtues was its ready application to the content of various folktales. Toward the end of 1908, Freud repeatedly drew Jung's attention to the theme of children's sexual researches, and Jung responded by undertaking to observe the reactions of his eldest daughter to the birth of her baby brother. Both men understood that whatever Jung discovered through these observations might potentially bear on the doctrine of the "core complex."

What concerns us here is that among the variants of the "core complex" with which Freud was experimenting at the time was one he called the "poisoning complex" (McGuire, 1974, p. 186). Indeed, this particular complex is mentioned in his letter to Jung of December 11, 1908, which is also the first occasion in the Jung correspondence in which the phrase "core complex" (p. 186) occurs. Freud's statement is quite brief and altogether clinical: "A recent observation tempted me to trace the poisoning complex, when it is present, back to the infant's interpretation of its mother's morning sickness" (p. 186). From the remark, one would suspect that no more was in the offing than an interpretation of fears of being poisoned as a fear of sexuality and of pregnancy, the latter being mediated by the infant's perception of its mother's morning sickness. Nonetheless, we know that the idea of the "poisoning complex" was more general still and had lately been much on Freud's mind. On December 8, 1909, three days before this letter to Jung, while discussing a slip of one of Stekel's patients in a Wednesday night meeting, Freud had brought up the idea of "basic complexes" (Nunberg and Federn, 1967, p. 76) and then gone into the specific idea of poisoning. And a month earlier, while discussing Karl Abraham's recent paper on alcoholism and sexuality during the Wednesday night meeting of November 4, 1908, Freud had specifically brought up the "toxic" conception of love and had applied it to his own concept of the libido: "We simply transform the 'love potion' of legend into science. Things of such magnitude can only be rediscovered" (Nunberg and Federn, 1967, pp. 36–37). To be sure, at this time alcoholism was a major psychiatric preoccupation and Freud had good reasons for wishing to link up his theories with this topic. But as his last remark indicates, Freud had also realized by this time that the "toxic" conception of love as a poison bore on his own theory of the libido. The "poisoning complex" thus had the unusual property that it constituted, along the lines of an implicit self-analysis, Freud's comment on his more general theory of the chemical basis of the libido.

Some further background is in order here. Freud had long been persuaded, and had said so repeatedly in his various writings to date, that his concept of the "libido" would eventually be mapped exactly on the action of an endogenous sexual chemical in the brain. In an instructive paper that deserves wider circulation, Swales (1983) has contended that the model for this putative sexual chemical was cocaine. To Swales's detailed argumentation, let me add the thought that it was by virtue of Freud's experiences with this drug that he was readily prepared to outline a "metapsychology" in the emphatic sense that he went beyond the "psychology" of his mentor in these matters, Franz Brentano. This seminal philosopher, as is well known, had no place in his system for an "unconscious" *per se*; for Brentano, the method of psychology was the direct perception of mental states and its object necessarily had to be the product of consciousness. In contradicting the alternative view of Maudsley and others, Brentano noted in passing that although there were physiological processes in the brain that had psychological effects, these effects were readily, if indirectly, detectable by the evidence of conscious awareness. And as an example of such psychologically detectable physiological processes, Brentano (1874, p. 59) listed among other things the effect of "intoxicating beverages." It was, I would contend, the instructive example of cocaine that allowed Freud to extend Brentano's philosophy and make out of it a uniquely profitable new system that made room for unconscious sexual processes, presumed to be physiological, on the basis that their effects were analogously detectable through direct perception.

By conceiving of his libido as essentially a toxic process within the brain, Freud was locating his theory solidly within the traditions of late nineteenth- and early twentieth-century neurology and psychology. But his theory acquired a peculiar epicycle when first Riklin (1908) and then Abraham (1909), the latter working under Freud's direct editorial supervision, began pointing out the frequent recurrence of love-potions in both folktales and the motifs of ancient mythology. Love, it now appeared, had long been conceived of by an analogy to a potent elixir, perhaps derived from the gods. (As Freud put it to Abraham in his letter of June 7, 1908: "the legend of the

Soma potion contains the highly important presentiment that all our intoxicating liquors and stimulating alkaloids are merely a substitute for the unique, still unattained toxin of the libido that rouses the ecstasy of love" [Abraham and Freud, 1965, p. 40].) The overall logic of the "core complex," however, demanded that all such mythical conceptions be derived from the conflicts of early childhood, including those arising out of infantile sexual researches. And thus, by this roundabout but quite compelling route, Freud had begun to conceive of something new, the "poisoning complex," with which he would explain the toxic conception of love as a dangerous potion.

The essence of the "poisoning complex" can be stated succinctly. The child watches his mother's morning sickness with perplexity; he is told that a baby is coming and that this is good as it is the result of the "love" between his parents. The child, whose sexual researches are only beginning, thus comes to the conception that "love" is somehow toxic, that it makes people sick in the way poisons do. In this way, the child early comes to formulate the fantasy of a dangerous elixir, precisely the conception that animates countless myths and folktales. Also — an ingenious piece of self-analysis has potentially been constructed here — such a conception, suitably modified to square with nineteenth-century brain physiology, could be found at the heart of Freud's own theory. Nor was the complex without clinical relevance — both fears of being poisoned and the use of substitute poisons such as alcohol and other intoxicants could be meaningfully approached under this interpretive rubric.[6]

Notwithstanding this promising beginning, the "poisoning complex" was not destined for great things in the evolution of psychoanalysis and most readers have undoubtedly never heard of it. Freud was quite serious about it during the period from mid-1908 through May of 1909, only to drop the subject thereafter. Just how serious Freud was can be gauged from his letters to two of Jung's Swiss compatriots, the Reverend Oskar Pfister and Ludwig Binswanger. To Pfister, Freud sent along a critique of a recent contribution on March 18, 1909. The essence of Freud's position is that owing to the "indissoluble connection between death and sexuality" (Freud and Meng, 1963, p. 20) the methods of suicide are always symbolic of sexuality. And among the alternatives in the suicidal endeavor Freud specifically mentions "taking poison" as equivalent to "becom[ing] pregnant" and adds as an explanation, "Poisoning as a consequence of morning sickness is equivalent to pregnancy" (p. 20). The critique sent to Pfister was followed in May by a similar letter to Binswanger commenting on a case report that Binswanger was publishing in two parts in the *Jahrbuch*. In his letter of May 17, 1909 Freud specifically pointed out the lack of any reference to infantile nuclear complexes in Binswanger's report (Binswanger, 1957, p. 11) and then went on to offer his own analysis of the patient's symptoms. Again, among other suggestions, the formula "poisoning = pregnancy" (p. 17) is offered, though here Freud elaborates the concomitant idea that pregnancy may also be symbolized as an infection. In a subsequent letter a week later, Freud suggested that Binswanger publish these glosses as an appendix to the case. Had Binswanger accepted the suggestion, this particular version of the core complex would have gone into print as the first published instance in which the psychopathology of an adult was analyzed through the focusing lens of the doctrine of the "core complex."

But after Freud's attempt to induce Binswanger to publish glosses partially derived from this conception failed, the "poisoning complex" as an important component of the "core complex" rapidly disappeared from sight. It was one of the few ideas that Freud seems to have simply discarded altogether. And here I think the delayed impact of Jung's letter of March 11, 1909 makes itself felt. Initially, after his receipt of the letter, in which Jung promised to write his own study on Hoffmann's novel, Freud's interest in the topic seems to have accelerated. His March critique to Pfister was mailed within a week after Jung's letter arrived and the glosses to Binswanger were sent out a little more than two months later. But gradually, as he was confronted first by the full flower of Jung's "theology," and then by the revelations of Spielrein in her unsolicited communications of late May and early June, Freud began to realize he was potentially undercutting his own overall theory. As Spielrein's revelations made abundantly clear, the tendency in Zurich was to interpret the new doctrines along rather mystical lines, with mythic personifications and telepathic phenomena in abundance. In such a climate, a view of the libido theory as having been anticipated by ancient myths and folktales, and as being foreshadowed in individual development by a fortuitous conception of childhood, did little to stem the tide of "theology." For, in truth, Freud's idea of the "poisoning complex" was implicitly teleological — the child early gained a conception of love as a dangerous potion that would become highly meaningful later in life. With only a little tinkering, the "poisoning complex" could be given a Romantic twist, as though Nature were preparing the child for its fate by schooling it early in a central myth of mankind.

The matter was especially critical when one understands that Freud's sexual chemistry was the basis of his predominantly reductive view of the psyche, and hence also the basis of his aversion to the kind of teleological conceptions that Jung wanted to introduce. What mattered most here was the general view that a putative sexual chemical was responsible for all significant alterations of consciousness, even if these alterations might disguise themselves with the trappings of the supernatural. Put another way, Freud wanted first of all to make sure that the Devil's elixir was understood as libido in his sense. So long as this was in contention, it did not matter whether or not certain mythic conceptions of love potions were fashioned in childhood by each new generation. The libido theory was the main issue. The niceties of the "poisoning complex," however much they appealed to the systematic nature of Freud's mind, and however much they might accord with the fruits of his own self-analysis, were trivial in comparison. Henceforth, Freud resisted this particular temptation.

NOTES

1. The term "subconscious," derived from French psychopathology, is to be preferred here and elsewhere with regard to Jung's nascent theory of "psychosynthesis." In this regard, it is not to be confused with the distinction between "unconscious" and "preconscious" which occurs in Freudian theory.
2. This essay is not to be confused with a number of other essays by Jung with similar titles nor with the first English translation of his *Transformations and Symbols of the Libido* (1911–1912), which was retitled in 1916 by his American translator Beatrice Hinkle as *Psychology of the Unconscious*. Making matters worse, the particular essay at issue began life in 1912 with an altogether different title, "New Paths in Psychology," and only acquired its present title, and the illustrative citation of Brother Medardus, during its first revision in 1916–1917. For a lucid account of the perplexities of Jung's texts, see Homans's "How to read Jung" (1979, Ch. 2).
3. Hoffmann's Schönfeld has another aspect as well and this may partially explain his failure to win archetypal status. Schönfeld also goes by an Italian name, Pietro Belcampo, and he is as comfortable in the landscape of Rome during the second part of the book as he is in the North German landscape of the first part. No doubt, Hoffmann wished his character to bridge the gulf between the Mediterranean and Teutonic worlds, perhaps with Goethe's *Italian Journey* in the back of his mind. This aspect of the Schönfeld character, as a symbol for that part of the

German soul with a penchant for things Italian, would have struck a disquieting note for Jung who, in apparent imitation of Freud, had developed his own Rome neurosis (See McGuire, 1974, p. 346 and Jung, 1962, pp. 287–288). Jung, in fact, never did get to Rome, and when late in life he resolved finally to do so, he became faint at the train station and had to return home. All of which is to say that Schönfeld/Belcampo has achieved a synthesis that Jung could only envy.

4. The dating of Jung's dream to this particular point in time presents some difficulties in light of Jung's statement (1962, p. 163) that he had this dream while he was working on the manuscript of *Transformations and Symbols of the Libido*. As it is clear that Jung only began work on this project in October 1909, the necessary implication is that the dream came either late in 1909 or else during the years 1910–1911. Compounding matters, to his seminar group in 1925, Jung made the same statement — the dream came while he worked on the book — and then went farther and specifically dated the dream to 1912. My supposition in the text, that this is the "great dream" reported in the letter of April 2–12, flies in the face of these statements by Jung.

Nonetheless, there are good reasons for supposing that the supposition in the text is correct and that Jung's dating is wrong. To begin with, both the memoirs and the account given to the seminar group in 1925 contain numerous mistakes with regards to dates. (Frequently, they are the exact same mistakes as the memoirs repeat the faulty recollections of the seminar.) In the seminar notes Jung's first visit to Vienna is dated to 1906, instead of 1907; in the memoirs his second visit is dated to 1910, instead of 1909; and, also in the memoirs, an important bicycle trip to the northern part of Italy is dated to 1911, instead of 1910. In general, a close scrutiny of the memoirs, the more complete of the two sources with regard to the relationship with Freud, shows it to be a composite of several different accounts, which have been thrown together with only a passing glance at chronology.

5. Freud's prior acquaintance with Hoffmann is attested to by his letter to Martha Bernays of June 26, 1885: "I have been reading off and on a few things by the 'mad' Hoffmann, mad, fantastic stuff, here and there a brilliant thought" (E. Freud, 1960, p. 158).

6. There was another way in which the toxic conception of love figures in. At the Salzburg Congress in the spring of 1908, Jung had read a paper in which he advanced his own conception of a non-specific brain toxin in schizophrenia. Against Jung's view, shared in a less constricted form by his mentor Bleuler, Karl Abraham read a paper arguing that the key aspect of schizophrenia was auto-eroticism. Thus began several years of tension between Jung and Abraham. Freud's discussions of the Soma myth, and of love potions generally, in his letters to Abraham has this dispute with Jung as part of their context. Specifically, Freud and Abraham continued to hold the view that Jung's hypothetical toxin is nothing else but their sexual chemical by another, wrong, name.

REFERENCES

ABRAHAM, H., & FREUD, E. (Eds.). (1965) *A Psycho-Analytic Dialogue: The Letters of Sigmund Freud and Karl Abraham*. (B. Marsh & H. Abraham, Trans.) New York: Basic Books.

ABRAHAM, K. (1909) *Dreams and Myths*. (H. Abraham, Trans.) In *Selected Papers of*

Karl Abraham: Clinical Papers and Essays on Psychoanalysis. New York: Basic Books, 1955.

BINSWANGER, L. (1957) *Sigmund Freud: Reminiscences of a Friendship*. (N. Guterman, Trans.) New York: Grune & Stratton.

BRENTANO, F. (1874) *Psychology from an Empirical Standpoint*. (L. McAlister, Trans.) London: Routledge & Kegan Paul, 1973.

CAROTENUTO, A. (1982) *A Secret Symmetry: Sabina Spielrein between Jung and Freud*. (A. Pomerans, J. Shepley, & K. Winston, Trans.) New York: Pantheon.

ELLENBERGER, H. (1970) *The Discovery of the Unconscious: The History and Evolution of Dynamic Psychiatry*. New York: Basic Books.

FOREL, A. (1908) Zum heutigen Stand der Psychotherapie: Ein Vorschlag. *Journal für Psychologie und Neurologie*, 11.

FORRESTER, J. (1980) *Language and the Origins of Psychoanalysis*. New York: Columbia University Press.

FREUD, E. (1960) *The Letters of Sigmund Freud*. (T. Stern & J. Stern, Trans.) New York: Basic Books.

———— & MENG, H. (1963) *Psycho-Analysis and Faith: The Letters of Sigmund Freud and Oskar Pfister* (E. Mosbacher, Trans.) New York: Basic Books.

FREUD, S. (1919) The "Uncanny." *Standard Edition*, 17:218-256.

———— (1920) *Beyond the Pleasure Principle*. *Standard Edition*, 18:3-64.

HANNAH, B. (1976) *Jung His Life and Work: A Biographical Memoir*. New York: Putnam's.

HOFFMANN, E. T. A. (1816) *The Devil's Elixirs*. (R. Taylor, Trans.) London: John Calder, 1963.

HOLT, R. (1978) Ideological and Thematic Conflicts in the Structure of Freud's Theories. In S. Smith, *The Human Mind Revisited: Essays in Honor of Karl A. Menninger*. New York: International Universities Press.

HOMANS, P. (1979) *Jung in Context: Modernity and the Making of a Psychology*. Chicago: University of Chicago Press.

JONES, E. (1955) *The Life and Work of Sigmund Freud* (Vol. 2). New York: Basic Books.

JUNG, C. G. (1896-1899) *The Zofingia Lectures*. Princeton: Princeton University Press, 1983.

———— (1903) On Simulated Insanity. In *The Collected Works*, 1:159-187. Princeton: Princeton University Press, 1970.

———— (1910) Marginal Notes on Wittels: *Die Sexuelle Not*. In *The Collected Works*, 18: 393-396. Princeton: Princeton University Press, 1975.

———— (1911-1912) *Transformations and Symbols of the Libido*. (B. Hinkle, Trans.) New York: Dodd, Mead, 1947.

———— (1925) *[Analytic Psychology] Notes on the Seminar in Analytic Psychology*. (Compiled by C. de Angulo & Approved by C. G. Jung.) Zurich: multigraphed typescript.

———— (1943) On the Psychology of the Unconscious. In *The Collected Works* 7:1-119. Princeton: Princeton University Press, 1972.

———— (1962) *Memories, Dreams, Reflections*. (R. & C. Winston, Trans.) New York: Vintage, 1965.

McGUIRE, W. (1974) *The Freud/Jung Lettters*. (R. Mannheim & R. F. C. Hull, Trans.) Princeton: Princeton University Press.

NUNBERG, H., & FEDERN, E. (Eds.). (1967) *Minutes of the Vienna Psychoanalytic Society (Vol. 2): 1908-1910*. (H. Nunberg, Trans.) New York: International Universities Press.

RIKLIN, F. (1908) *Wish Fulfillment and Symbolism in Fairy Tales*. (W. White, Trans.) New York: Journal of Mental and Nervous Disease Monograph Series, 1915.

RUDNYTSKY, P. L. (1987) *Freud and Oedipus*. New York: Columbia University Press.
SWALES, P. J. (1983) Freud, Cocaine, Sexual Chemistry; The Role of Cocaine in Freud's Conception of the Libido. Privately published by author, New York.

225 Carroll St.
Brooklyn, New York 11231

THE RIDDLE OF THE RIDDLE OF THE SPHINX

Theodore Lidz

The riddle of the Sphinx has for millennia remained one of the best known and significant riddles of the Western world. Though its importance is itself something of a riddle, other riddles are also involved: Why was it necessary for Oedipus to solve the riddle before he could enter Thebes and inadvertently marry his mother? Why could no one but Oedipus solve the riddle? What does the Sphinx symbolize? Why was the riddle so difficult to solve for it does not seem especially perplexing in either of the forms in which it has been handed down to us (though, of course, most riddles do not seem difficult after we have been provided the answer)?

The riddle gained and retained its importance largely because of the power of Sophocles's play *Oedipus the King*; and because of Freud's use of the Oedipus myth, as recounted in the play, to symbolize what he considered to be a universal, though usually unconscious, wish of all men to kill their fathers and marry their mothers. The Oedipus complex has virtually been at the core of classical psychoanalysis, and its consequences and variations have been central to psychoanalytic practice. Nevertheless, the actual riddle that Oedipus solved to vanquish the Sphinx is not given by Sophocles, and when Freud (1900) cited the myth to introduce his theory in *The Interpretation of Dreams* he simply wrote that Oedipus "solved the riddle set him by the Sphinx who barred his way" (p. 261). Both Sophocles and Freud left the riddle unstated though mythologists and psychologists have subsequently suggested that the riddle is critical to the understanding of what the myth implies.

What were the circumstances that led Oedipus to the Sphinx? Oedipus had been raised by the rulers of Corinth, Polybus and Periboa (or Merope, according to Sophocles), as the heir to the throne. Teased that he did not resemble his parents, or told that he had been adopted, Oedipus became concerned and went to consult the Delphic Oracle. The Oracle, instead of responding to his query, prophesied that he would kill his father and marry his mother. Horrified, Oedipus decided never to return to Corinth lest the prophecy be fulfilled. Knowingly or unknowingly he headed toward Thebes. In a narrow pass where three roads converged, he encountered a group headed in the opposite direction. The leader, who was being driven in a chariot, ordered Oedipus off the road and to give way to his betters. When Oedipus responded that he had no betters other than his parents and the gods, the leader struck him with a goad. Oedipus in his fury killed the leader and all of his attendants, save one who escaped. Then, as Oedipus approached Thebes he was confronted by the Sphinx perched on a rock on Mount Pictus.

The Sphinx had been sent by the goddess Hera, the protector of marriages, to besiege Thebes because its King Laius had, according to some versions of the myth, refused to have sexual relations with Jocasta and presumably the fertility of the land depended on the fertility of Jocasta, its Queen-Priestess. The Sphinx, which had the face of a woman, the body of a lion, and the wings of an eagle, placed a riddle to anyone who wished to pass and enter Thebes, and strangled and devoured those who could not solve it. The riddle has come down to us in two related forms. The common form is "What that has but one voice goes on four legs in the morning, on two at noon, and three in the evening?" The other version goes "What of all that goes on land, flies through the air, and swims the ocean and has but one shape goes on two legs, four, and even three, and is weakest when it goes on four?" When Oedipus replied "Man," the Sphinx jumped from its perch on the mountain and plunged to its death on the rocks below. The riddle, even in its more complex form, does not seem so difficult that only the hero Oedipus was capable of solving it and abolishing the Sphinx.[1]

Oedipus, as we well know, was actually the son of Laius and Jocasta, but a curse — that if he had a son, his son would kill him — had been placed upon Laius by Pelops. Pelops placed the curse because Laius as a child or youth had taken refuge in the court of Pelops when Amphion and Zethus had invaded Thebes and killed the regent ruling for him. Laius who, according to some myths, had introduced sodomy into Attica, had fallen in love with Chrysippus, Pelops's favorite child who was his son by a nymph. When Laius returned to Thebes to become its king, he abducted Chrysippus, thus infuriating Pelops.

When Laius married Jocasta and became king, he refused to consummate the marriage out of fear of the curse (or because of his homosexuality?). However, Jocasta seduced him to her bed by getting him intoxicated. Oedipus was the result of this single cohabitation, but Laius insisted that the infant who was a threat to his life be exposed and Jocasta agreed. They gave the infant to a herdsman-servant so that he could abandon the child on Mount Cithaeron after immobilizing the baby by placing a spike through his ankles. The shepherd, unable to carry out the cruel order, gave the infant to another shepherd who was tending the flocks of the rulers of Corinth. The shepherd brought the child to Polybus and Periboa,[2] who, being childless, were happy to adopt him and raise him as their heir. They named him Oedipus because of his swollen feet.

Oedipus, fleeing Corinth to avoid the fate the Delphic Oracle had predicted, was meeting his fate as he approached Thebes; and, one should not forget, fulfilling the curse placed on his father. The Sphinx had barred his way, but her riddle did not stop his progress toward marrying his mother.[3] We surmise that Oedipus was able to give the correct answer because he had survived as an infant without a mother; then as a young man without parents he was able to make his own way and overcome obstacles, even his father; and, as would happen, would use a staff as a third foot when an old man. The riddle and its solution, for reasons I shall elaborate, has to do with the denial of the importance of the mother.[4] In ways that are related, some mythologists have suggested that the death of the Sphinx symbolizes the end of matriarchy, perhaps notably the turn from an era when the queen-priestess was married to a new king each year, or more probably each long year that consisted of eight years[5] (Burkert, 1985; Graves, 1955). If we consider Oedipus to be a supplanter — that is, the hero who kills the husband of the queen-priestess representative of the Earth Mother at the end of the long year and marries the queen to provide her with a new, vital fertility — he was simply like all supplanters who kill the king-father and then marry the queen representative of the Earth Mother.

Lévi-Strauss (1955) relates the riddle and the entire myth of Oedipus to the conflict people had in giving up their belief that people arose from the ground — that is, autochthonously — rather than from two persons: a mother and a father. In a way, then, Lévi-Strauss is in agreement with Freud that the myth, if not the riddle, concerns the origin of babies, though in a different sense than Freud meant it.

The interpretation that the riddle and the death of the Sphinx concerns overcoming men's fear and awe of women, and the power of women, particularly the power of the mother and her hold on her sons, is, in part, in agreement with that of Lévi-Strauss. It does not simply concern the struggle, both in individual development and in the history of the development of cultures, of men to gain a sense of independence from their mothers and to individuate from them.[6] Like Lévi-Strauss, we seek the meaning of the riddle, not in the specific situation alone, but through examination of the corpus of the myths of the House of Cadmus and the mythical history of Thebes.

The early portions of the Cadmean myth appear to be very ancient and relate to the transfer of Near Eastern religions and traditions to Greece. Zeus, in the form of a bull, had abducted Europa from Phoenicia. Her father, Agenor, sent Cadmus and his brothers to find Europa and not return home without her. They searched the known world but could not find her. Eventually the Delphic Oracle told Cadmus to desist and instead follow a cow with an image of the moon on her flank and build a city where she lay down to rest. Cadmus found and purchased a cow with such markings in Phocis and drove her eastward, not permitting her to rest until she came to the future site of Thebes. He then set about sacrificing the cow to Athena and sent his companions to fetch water from a nearby spring. They did not know that the spring was dedicated to Ares and was guarded by a great serpent or dragon. The serpent slew most of Cadmus's men and in vengeance Cadmus crushed the monster's head with a rock. He then made the sacrifice to Athena who praised his feat and told him to sow the teeth of the serpent in the ground. He obeyed and immediately the sown men, or Spartoi, sprang fully armed out of the soil. Cadmus threw a stone among them. The Spartoi accused one another of the act, fought, and slew one another until only five remained. The five swore allegiance to Cadmus and became the ancestors of the Thebans. Ares, angered at the death of his serpent, had Cadmus sentenced to be his bondsman for a long year. Thus, the Thebans traditionally believed that their primal ancestors were autochthonous, born without mothers.

The tradition seems clearly to be related to the belief that serpents are spirits of the dead who guard the land on which they lived, and that infants are reincarnations of ancestors who exist as serpents for a time.[7] Serpents have been believed to be the spirits of the dead because they emerge from graves, but perhaps even more so because they shed their skins and are thought to be reborn. They are thus a symbol of rebirth as well as of the spirits of the dead. The belief that babies are reincarnations of ancestors has been widespread among primitive peoples.

Cadmus, like Tantalus, consorted with the Olympians. After his years of bondage and then having been initiated into the mysteries of Zeus, he married Harmonia, the daughter of Ares and Aphrodite. The wedding was attended by all of the Olympian gods who presented extraordinary gifts to the bride and groom. The gift of the golden necklace given Harmonia by Aphrodite and the problems it later caused do not concern us; but it is of interest that Harmonia was taught the rites of the Great Goddess by Jason's mother Electra, for it is another connection to the religions of Asia Minor. When Cadmus was old, he handed the reign of Thebes to his grandson Pentheus, and left with Harmonia to become the ruler of the Encheleans. Eventually both became serpents and as such lived happily and eternally on the Islands of the Blessed (Graves, 1955; Ovid, *Metamorphoses*).

The next Theban myth that involves the denial of motherhood concerns the birth of Dionysus, the twice-born god of liberation and ecstasy. He was the last god to enter Olympus and the only Olympian conceived of a mortal mother. Zeus fell in love with Cadmus's daughter Semele and appeared to her and seduced her in mortal form. When it was apparent that she was pregnant, Hera, who was always jealous of Zeus's affairs and antagonistic to his lovers, induced Semele to insist that Zeus reveal himself to her in his true form to make certain that she was not bearing the child of a monster. Zeus was angered by Semele's request and refused. According to some versions, he had to give way because, when he seduced her, he had promised to give her whatever she wished. In another version, Semele refused to have intercourse with him until he revealed himself. When she then complied, Zeus revealed his natural form, namely, thunder and lightning, that consumed Semele. Hermes, however, acted quickly and snatched the six-month-old fetus from Semele's womb and sewed it in Zeus's thigh where it remained until delivered three months later. Thus, Dionysus was called the twice-born, and like Athena was born of Zeus. The myths of the childhood of Dionysus differ and are confusing. According to some, Hera hated the baby and had the Titans tear it apart, but Demeter put Dionysus together again (as she had Pelops after Tantalus had served him to the gods). Herein lies another reason Dionysus was termed the "twice-born" or the "god of the double door." He may have been raised first by Semele's sister who dressed him as a girl to hide him from Hera and later by nymphs, which accounts for his feminine characteristics. As John Pinsent (1969) recognized, this myth, like that of the birth of Athena, "is a male myth expressing resentment and jealousy of women's role in childbirth" (p. 60).

The next episode of pertinence in Theban mythology provided the plot for Euripides's *The Bacchae* and concerns Semele's half-sister Agave and her son Pentheus whom Cadmus had made king of Thebes. Dionysus, the god of wine and ecstasy, had swept through Asia Minor and parts of Greece in triumph. He returned to Thebes during the reign of Pentheus, who hated his effeminacy and his Baccanals,[8] and sought to drive Dionysus from Thebes. According to some myths, his army was defeated by the Maenads, and according to others, he imprisoned Dionysus, but Dionysus was able to vanish from the prison. The women of Thebes flocked to Dionysus and joined the bacchic rites he held on Mount Cithaeron. Pentheus was unable to contain his curiosity, or perhaps his jealousy, and dressed in women's clothes he went to the mountain to witness the Bacchanal. He was caught spying from a tree, and the women tore him apart. His mother, Agave, who had joined the Bacchante, descended from the mountain bearing her son's head, which she had wrenched off thinking that she had killed a lion. The myth is another denial of motherhood, or, at least, the protective value of mothers.

The myths of the following generation or two seem to be confused. When Labdacus, Pentheus's nephew, succeeded him on the throne, he was still a child, and Nycteus served as his regent. Zeus was taken by the great beauty of Nycteus's daughter Antiope and impregnated her. Antiope feared her father's wrath and fled. After various adventures, she gave birth to twins in a thicket on Mount

Cithaeron and left them to die. They, as Oedipus would be, were saved by a shepherd who raised them. When they grew up, the twins, Amphion and Zethus, invaded Thebes and killed the regent who had replaced Nycteus and became the rulers of Thebes. According to some myths, they were the true founders of Thebes. Again, we have the tale of a Theban mother exposing her infants. It was after the deaths of Amphion and Zethus that Laius returned to rule Thebes.

Zeus clearly had been very occupied impregnating goddesses and mortals much to Hera's displeasure. Of course, he may simply have been a lecher who used his unsurpassed power to entice or rape; but there are alternative explanations of his reputed behavior. He may have offered a handy excuse for maidens who had children out of wedlock; various royal lines may have wished to fortify their positions and greatness by claiming descent from Zeus, and so on. However, it is likely that Zeus was representative of the ancestor who would be reborn as an infant in the days when the belief still existed that infants were reincarnations of ancestors. Zeus had, after all, first existed in the form of a serpent and, as has been noted, the dead were believed to continue to exist as serpents.

We are now back to Laius, Jocasta, and Oedipus and the tragic consequences of infanticide, particularly Jocasta's willingness to expose her child. Oedipus and Jocasta ruled for many years and had two sons and two daughters. Eventually, however, Thebes was again beset by a plague. Jocasta's brother, Creon, consulted the Delphic Oracle and returned with the prophecy that misfortunes would beset the city until the slayer of Laius was expelled from the city. Oedipus swore he would find the slayer, and soon learned through the long-lived, blind seer Teiresias and the two shepherds who had exchanged him that the curse on Laius and the dread prophecy that he would kill his father and wed his mother had been fulfilled. Jocasta took her own life and Oedipus blinded himself by piercing his eyes with the pin of a brooch from her robe. Oedipus wandered in exile guided and protected by his faithful daughter Antigone, and to a lesser extent by her sister Ismene. Oedipus received no help from his sons on whom he placed his curse. Oedipus's son Eteocles assumed the throne and his brother Polynices, feeling unjustly displaced, gathered a force to take the city. In line with the curse Oedipus had placed on them, the brothers killed each other when they met in single combat. Creon, or the city council, decreed that Polynices be left unburied because he had attacked the city. Antigone, however, believing that the bonds and obligations of kinship took precedence over the edict, carried out some burial rites. Detected, she was entombed alive by the order of Creon and was joined by her sister Ismene. According to another myth, Creon's son, who was betrothed to Antigone, also chose to die with her. Thus ended the line of the accursed Oedipus.

Whatever else the myth of Oedipus implies, and its interpretations are multiple, it underlines the penalties that ensue from filicide, patricide, and mother–son incest. However, when the Theban myths are viewed as a sequence with a common core, they convey efforts to deny the need for a mother, and concomitantly an undermining of the power of matriarchy and the sway of the cult of the Great Goddess that had permeated Asia Minor and gained importance in Cretan and Grecian cultures. Cadmus sacrificed the cow to Athena, the goddess born from Zeus without a mother, and his Spartoi arose motherless from the earth, though perhaps, as has been suggested, as reincarnations of ancestors from the teeth (semen?) of the indigenous serpent. Cadmus and Harmonia became serpents when they died, indicating the belief that serpents are ancestors awaiting rebirth, akin to the Australian aboriginal belief that fetuses are ancestor spirits that enter the wombs of young women who pass their totemic shrine. Dionysus, though conceived by Semele after she was impregnated by Zeus, was, like Athena, born from Zeus rather than from a mother (though in marked contrast to Athena, not from his head but his thigh, and became the god of liberation from reason — the id, so to speak, in contrast to Athena as ego). Agave helped tear her son Pentheus to pieces. Antiope, also impregnated by Zeus, exposed her twin sons, Amphion and Zethus, on Mount Cithaeron, as Jocasta later exposed Oedipus.

The Sphinx is a symbol of the chthonic deities, the underworld defenders of mother-right who antedated the Olympians in Greece — a carry-over from the time when the mother having been impregnated by an ancestor spirit was the child's only blood relative. She is a Ker, related to the Erinyes who pursued Orestes after he murdered his mother. She is the strangler, the possessive mother who dominates her sons and does not permit them an independent existence — the mother who the son fears will devour him and reincorporate him rather than permit him to live his own life. All humans are of course born of mothers and remain dependent on them for many years, identifying with them as well as desiring to possess them, and when liberated by the intervention of a father figure, they still ambivalently wish for a surcease from the responsibilities of independence through the embrace of an all-caring mother. It is she, the Sphinx, who blocks the youth's way to independent manhood, and thus is related to the Great Mother goddesses such as Cybele who were worshipped in Asia Minor. Cybele loved Attis, who may have been her child and may also have been her consort, and who castrated himself when he was unfaithful to her. Cybele's priests, the Galloi, similarly castrated themselves to remain dependent on her without being erotically attached to her.[9] The Erinyes did not disappear when Zeus and the Olympians assumed power in a patriarchal religion, but remained as a feared underworld, an unconscious and not so unconscious concern over the spirits of the dead in the various forms taken by the Keres. In the plays of Aeschylus and Sophocles they are, so to speak, appeased and bought off by being turned into the benevolent Eumenides, but they still haunted the people and seem to have played a prominent role in the Eleusian mysteries that may have persisted for a thousand years (Burkert, 1985, pp. 185–190). Nor was Cybele banished for she even regained prominence in Rome when an oracle predicted that her worship would prevent Hannibal from capturing Rome; and the great need of humans for a mother goddess is shown by the way in which Mary has gained greater importance than the son of God in various parts of the Western world. Zeus, too, persisted in some areas in chthonic form, Zeus Meilichios, even after he became the sky god, or the Thunderer who ruled Olympus.

Oedipus symbolized, as has been suggested by various scholars, the youth who overcame the dominance of the mother or the sway of matriarchy. As noted previously, abandoned by his parents and managing to survive despite having been exposed, he could stand on his own feet without fear of them. He could kill the man who sought to dominate him and beat him, not knowing the man was his father. He could confront the Sphinx as he had no reason to feel dependent on his mother and hold her in awe. He had come into his manhood independently and thus could solve her riddle. He could marry his mother for she had not been a mother to him, and he did not know her. His conquest of the Sphinx and his marriage to Jocasta were the ultimate expressions of the theme that runs through Theban mythology: the denial of the mother. Perhaps it would be more correct to say, the ultimate denial that the mother was the parent, somewhat akin to Lévi-Strauss's (1955, p. 18) opinion that the myth concerns the "inability of a culture which holds man is autochthonous to find a transition — to knowledge that humans are born from union of men and women." However, the evidence suggests that here "autochthonous" means "born of a woman who has been impregnated by an ancestor spirit."

Now, Oedipus was able to overcome the fear or awe of the power of women in contrast to his father, Laius, who found refuge in homosexuality and feared to have relations with Jocasta. Although Oedipus symbolically overcame the fear of sexual relations with his mother, it should be emphasized that he paid an extreme penalty for overcoming the barrier presented by the strangling, incorporating Sphinx. He blinded himself when he finally "saw" what he had done — an act that can be, and has been, taken as symbolic of self-castration — and he thus renounced his masculinity and kingship; he went into exile, which for the Greeks was an extreme punishment; his mother-wife killed herself; he could not be a good father to his sons but rather placed a curse on them that led to the ultimate sibling rivalry in which they killed one another; and, paradoxically, despite his revolt against men's dependence on mother figures, he spent his last years dependent on women, that is, his daughters. Men's need for sheltering, protective women persisted and has persisted.[10]

It becomes apparent that there are inconsistencies and confusions in the interpretation presented here of the riddle as well as in the understanding of the Oedipus myth. Indeed, there can be a variety of interpretations. In part, the various understandings are possible because myths, very much like dreams, are open to a multiplicity of interpretations because of the conglomeration of associated material that enters into them. The early Greek myths are especially dependent on the syncretism of the religious and cultural belief systems that fused in Greek religion. As can be noted in Burkert's (1985) *Greek Religion*, particularly its first three chapters, and to a somewhat lesser degree from Harrison's (1903) *Prologomena to the Study of Greek Religion*, Minoan, Assyrian, Phoenician, Egyptian, and early

Mycenaean beliefs were further confused by the Doric conquests that led to a "dark age" during which earlier beliefs were partly obliterated as well as modified but not extinguished. The Oedipus myth, as has been noted, certainly had very ancient roots as Laius was believed to be a contemporary of Pelops who supposedly was an early Mycenaean ruler, and the myth was surely modified and took on new meanings in the thousand or more years that intervened before Sophocles wrote his tragedy. Various influences have been cited, and still others probably have importance. How much does the cult of the Magna Mater enter, relating Oedipus to Attis, and more broadly Jocasta to the queen-priestess whose fertility controlled the fertility of the land and had to be maintained by the replacement of her consort at eight-year intervals? Was Laius leaving Thebes at the end of his infertile term to be killed by Oedipus, his supplanter, who became king because he married Jocasta who was the queen-priestess? Do the tales of the exposure of infants on Mount Cithaeron derive from the practice of the exposure–sacrifice of infants on mountain tops, and even to the cannibalism of infants known to have existed through the findings of recent excavations (Burkert, 1985, p. 27)? Do the exposures and returns of Oedipus, Amphion, and Zethus as well as Dionysus relate to the initiations that took the boys from their mothers (as by the Kouretes, and as currently practiced in New Guinea)? The concepts of ancestors becoming serpents and infants being reincarnations of ancestors have been emphasized above. The very important place of homosexual relations between youths and men in Greek societies, and perhaps particularly in Thebes,[11] does not seem of marked significance in the oedipal myth aside from the homosexuality of Laius that underlines men's fear of women. The importance of the Keres, and the image of a Ker as the Sphinx as well as the relationship of the Sphinx to the Erinyes, may have derived from Cretan, Cypriot, or even Egyptian beliefs, and clearly predated the Olympian gods who appear in the Oedipus myth.

To psychoanalysis it is of particular interest that when Freud first utilized the Oedipus legend to symbolize an unconscious set of impulses, wishes, or drives to which all men are subject, or, we might say, indicate the fate to which all men are bound, he commented on the importance of the father's role, citing how Uranus killed his sons and Kronos ate them; and fathers in general dominated and even tyrannized their sons thus contributing to the sons' hostility to their fathers (Freud, 1900, pp. 256–257). However, Freud later placed the major, if not the entire, emphasis on the son's desire to kill or castrate his father because of his libidinal desires to possess his mother sexually. The very important question arises from psychoanalytic practice, as it does from the myth, of how the cycle of patricidal and filicidal wishes started. Was it with the father's desires to be rid of a son because of his jealousy of the son as a rival who preempts too much of his wife's affection and attention? Does his wife's affection for the son reawaken an old sibling rivalry in the father? May it not be that the father projects onto his son the death wishes he had toward his own father when a child? If he had wished to kill his own father, may his son now wish to kill him? These are not questions readily resolved even in individual cases, but it is often apparent that the boy's fear that his father may kill or castrate him unless he rescinds his eroticized desires for his mother is not simply a projection of his own wishes, but, rather, the son has become aware of his father's jealousy. In any case, it is essential for the establishment of a harmonious family, and therefore for the stability of a society and its culture, that the cycle be broken so that a son can trust his father and seek to identify with him, and later be capable of welcoming and cherishing his own son. The wife-mother who is apt to be the focus of the rivalry plays a major role through her ability or inability to provide affection to both husband and son — a role that Jocasta relinquished at the birth of Oedipus.

The myth of Oedipus, like most primal myths, tells of heroic deeds and misdeeds carried out by ancient forbears and their consequences. Sometimes, they set standards that their descendants seek to emulate but perhaps more often warn of the dire consequences that will befall those who act similarly. In the myth, Oedipus killed his father and slept with his mother unknowingly. Laius acted out of fear, and Jocasta instead of protecting her infant agreed to expose the child. As Sophocles had the Chorus chant of Jocasta after she killed herself, "ills wrought not unwittingly, but of purpose — those griefs smart most which seem to be of our own choice." It was the purposeful act of Laius and Jocasta that enabled a son to kill his father and marry his mother guiltlessly. And the consequences, as did the misdeeds in the House of Atreus in the other series of great Greek tragedies, continued through subsequent generations.

Sophocles appears to have had still other purposes in writing *Oedipus the King*. Whatever else he had in mind, consciously or unconsciously, he emphasized the dangers of hubris and conveyed the fragility of greatness to those who might envy greatness and seek it for themselves. The tragedy as it has come down to us ends:

> Behold, this is Oedipus, who knew the famed riddle, and who was a man most mighty; on whose fortunes what citizen did not gaze with envy? Behold into what a stormy sea of dread trouble he hath come!
>
> Therefore, while our eyes wait to see the destined final day, we must call no one happy who is of mortal race, until he has crossed life's border free of pain.[12]

It is apparent, as has been emphasized, that the myth and perhaps the riddle can have variant meanings, but the interpretation I have offered here provides one with new insights into this important myth and its riddle, and thereby further enlightens us as to the vicissitudes of human nature and their intimate interrelations with the nature of the family and the behavior of a person's forbears.

NOTES

1. The Sphinx, according to some, was the child of Echidna and Typhon. "Sphinx" means "strangler," but some Greeks envision her less balefully as an oracle who was predicting that Oedipus would be a blind man in his old age. A famous amphora painting now in the Vatican Museum shows the Sphinx seated on a Doric pedestal being consulted by Oedipus. The paradoxical conceptualizations can be clarified. According to Jane Harrison (1912), an eminent authority on primitive Greek religions, and also according to Róheim (1934), the Sphinx was a type of Ker. The Keres originally were the spirits or anima of the dead who played a central role in pre-Olympian beliefs and continued in what may be termed an underground role in later times. They were initially envisioned as tiny female objects with wings emerging from the mouths of the dead. As the Erinyes they pursued the slayers of the dead, as they did Orestes after he killed his mother; and they seem to have been the protectors of mother-rights. However, as Greek culture matured, they changed into the benevolent Eumenides who protected Athens. The Sphinxes may also have been avenging Keres, but they became simply the protectors of the dead, which would explain the presence of the great Sphinx near the pyramids of Giza. It is noteworthy that the Cypriot sarcophagi in the Metropolitan Museum of Art in New York have at each corner small benevolent Sphinxes emerging from a lotus (a symbol of eternal life).
2. It does not make sense that the feet of an infant had to be fettered, which suggests that Oedipus was older when exposed. He was not the first ruler or future ruler of Thebes to be exposed or killed on Mount Cithaeron. Pentheus,

as well as the twins Amphion and Zethus, preceded him, as will be presented later. It seems possible that the tales of the exposure of boys reflect either the ancient practice of sacrificing or feeding the firstborn son to the gods (as Abraham was about to sacrifice Isaac and is reflected in the Jewish practice of redeeming the firstborn son from the priests, as well as Tantalus's feeding Pelops to the Olympians); or the ritual taking of boys from their mothers by the Kouretes to be initiated into the male cult and then kept from women for many years as practiced on Crete and in parts of Greece in very ancient times (see J. Harrison [1912, pp. 35-37] and also G. Herdt [1981, 1987] for similar rites in modern Papua New Guinea).

3. The two great myth sequences of ancient Greece — that of the descendants of Tantalus and that of the descendants of Cadmus — with which we are concerned reach their climaxes with infractions of men's two greatest taboos: Orestes kills his mother, and Oedipus marries his mother.

4. It is of interest that even though Oedipus's solution killed the Sphinx, not everyone agrees that it was correct. Freud stated in two places (1905, pp. 194–195, and 1925, p. 37) that the riddle of the Sphinx is the basic riddle of childhood — namely, "Where do babies come from?" — but he offers no explanation of his interpretation. Róheim (1934, p. 210) specifically denies the correctness of Oedipus's solution and in accord with his own preconceptions states that the riddle refers to the primal scene.

5. A long year is the time it takes for the solar year and the lunar year to coincide.

6. Gunther Grass's (1977) satirical novel *The Flounder* rests heavily on men's longings to regress to an era when they were totally satisfied both gastronomically and sexually by mother figures as during infancy.

7. Such beliefs have been prominent among the indigenes of Papua New Guinea and the aborigines of Australia in modern times. The place of the serpent in ancient Greece is extremely complicated. Zeus was originally a serpent — Zeus Meilichios — and was worshipped as such (Harrison, 1903, pp. 18-19), which may connect to the earlier awe and worship of the Erinyes who were also conceptualized as snakes. Cecrops, the daimon of Athens, was depicted on coins as a snakeman.

8. Despite the myth of Dionysus's Theban origins, he was more likely a foreign import into Greece, related to, or confused with, Zagreus, who also had rites associated with alcohol and who presumably came from Crete though some believe he came to Greece from the north.

9. The Galloi actually cut off their entire genitalia and assumed women's dress, a practice that apparently established the feminine or gender-ambiguous dress of monks that has continued into the present. (See E. Weigert, 1938).

10. Though in much of Greece the desire or need for "shelter" turned into a dependent homosexual relationship with an older man from whom a man gained "arete," a masculine spirit and courage. The need to gain masculinity through indoctrination and insemination by a man while still seeking dependency and protection seems to have resembled the practices in Papua New Guinea as presented by Lidz and Lidz (1986) and even more specifically by Herdt (1981).

11. In historic times the Spartans first met defeat at Leuctra in 371 B.C. at the hands of the famous Theban Band that was comprised of pairs of male lovers, each of whom would die heroically lest he appear a coward to his partner (Vangaard, 1972). There was, of course, nothing effeminate about these rela-

tionships, being, as they were, established to teach a boy the proper behavior of a noble man.

12. Some scholars and critics believe that Sophocles did not write these final lines, but that they were added in a revision of the play.

REFERENCES

BURKERT, W. (1985). *Greek Religion*. Cambridge, MA: Harvard University Press.

FREUD, S. (1900). The Interpretation of Dreams. *Standard Edition*, 4 & 5.

_____ (1905). Fragment of an Analysis of a Case of Hysteria. *Standard Edition*, 7.

GRASS, G. (1977). *The Flounder*. New York: Fawcett Crest.

GRAVES, R. (1955). *The Greek Myths*. Baltimore: Penguin.

HARRISON, J. (1903). *Prologomena to the Study of Greek Religion*. New York: Meridian, 1955.

_____ (1912). *Themis*. New York: Meridian, 1969.

HERDT, G. (1981). *The Guardians of the Flutes*. New York: McGraw-Hill.

_____ (1987). *The Sambia*. New York: Holt, Rinehart & Winston.

LÉVI-STRAUSS, C. (1955). The Structural Study of Myth. In T. A. Sebeok (Ed.), *Myth: A Symposium*. Bloomington: Indiana University Press, 1958.

LIDZ, T., & LIDZ, R. W. (1986). Turning Women Things into Men: Masculinization in Papua New Guinea. *Psychoanal. R.*, 73:117–135.

PINSENT, J. (1969). *Greek Mythology*. London: Paul Hamlyn.

RÓHEIM, G. (1934). *The Riddle of the Sphinx*. London: Hogarth.

SOPHOCLES. (1958). *Oedipus the King*. (R. C. Jebb, Trans.) In W. J. Oates & E. O'Neill, Jr. (Eds.), *The Complete Greek Dramas*. New York: Random House.

VANGAARD, T. (1972). *Phallos*. London: Jonathan Cape.

WEIGERT, E. (1938). The Cult and Mythology of the Magna Mater from the Standpoint of Psychoanalysis. *Psychiatry*, 1:347–378.

Department of Psychiatry
Yale University
25 Park St.
New Haven, CT 06519

THE BODY OF OEDIPUS*

Lowell Edmunds

The Greek tragedians' Oedipus is the first of many Oedipuses
whom European culture has discovered. This Oedipus is a beginning. But, from another point of view, also an end. The Greeks had
told the story of Oedipus for many centuries before he became a
protagonist in Greek tragedy. Oedipus was also, independently of
myth and tragedy, a figure in Greek religion — a cult hero who received worship in several places (Edmunds, 1981a). The Greek
tragedians gave a fixed, canonical form to the myth, and, thereafter,
it passed into literary history and handbooks of mythology. In our
own century, however, the myth has come alive again in many new
ways: in psychoanalytic theory, in theater, film, and music. In this
atmosphere, one senses the ancient power of the myth and wonders
about its origins, which, if Freud is right, are not only in our cultural
past but are still alive in each of us. This paper offers some thoughts
on the body of Oedipus as a psycho-mythological structure, as an
artifact of myth and, at the same time, a dynamic of the psyche.

The myth of Oedipus draws attention explicitly to two parts of
the hero's body: his feet and his eyes. At the time of his exposure, his
feet are pierced, and from this wound he gets his name, Oedipus,
"Swollen Foot." The riddle of the Sphinx, too, with its various numbers of feet, points to the hero's own feet. After the discovery of his
crimes, which comes about partly through the scars on his feet,
Oedipus blinds himself.

Both of the mutilations, however, that of the feet and that of the

---

*This article is a translation and revision of "Il Corpo di Edipo: Struttura Psico-
mitologica," in B. Gentili and R. Pretagostini (Eds.), *Edipo: Il Teatro Greco e la Cultura
Europea: Atti del Convegno Internazionale* (pp. 237–253). (November, 1982) Rome:
Ateneo, 1986). It is printed here by the kind permission of Professor Gentili.

eyes, are connected in the myth with the crimes of Oedipus. Through the murder of Laius, Oedipus replaced his father in his mother's bed. One of the mutilations was intended to prevent these crimes; the other was intended to punish them. It can be shown that these mutilations bear particular reference to the crime of incest; furthermore, that the eyes and the feet stand for the genitals of Oedipus. The myth presents this tripartite body by means of three relations: between feet and genitals, between eyes and genitals, and between eyes and feet.

These relations, unapparent in the narrative itself, come to light in the perspectives of comparative mythology and of psychoanalysis. In Greek myths, several other heroes, wounded either in their eyes or their feet, provide suggestive comparison with Oedipus. He indeed suffers both the wounds of which the others suffer only one, and, in this way, he is strangely privileged among Greek heroes. The myth seems to stress the symbolism of his wounds. The symbolism that I believe can be discovered in comparative mythology is corroborated in the second of the two perspectives just mentioned. Psychoanalytical theory suggests that the body of Oedipus is not only a mythological structure but also a psychological one. I should add here that I do not find such a structure in the character of the Sophoclean Oedipus nor do I believe that it is useful to examine the individual psychology of any Greek hero. This has been the mistake of much psychoanalytic research on Greek mythology. At the same time, nothing prevents the interpretation of the hero of a Greek myth as a general psychological type. Freud meant no more than that by the interpretation of *Oedipus the King* in terms of the Oedipus complex.

Before I turn to the analysis of the myth, some methodological reflections are in order. The word "structure" in the first paragraph of this paper indicates a well-known principle of methodology, the distinction between the diachronic, narrative aspect of myth, on the one hand, and its synchronic structure, on the other (Lévi-Strauss, 1955). As a preliminary indication of the distinction between structure and narrative in the Oedipus myth, I might point to the place in the myth of the mutilation of Oedipus's feet. Already in antiquity, it was observed that this mutilation was superfluous in the case of a newborn child (scholiast on Euripides, *Phoenician Women*, l. 26) that was exposed on a mountain and would soon die for that reason alone. Furthermore, the scars or other results of the wound are ignored by the characters in the myth until the moment of discovery. Teiresias, for example, does not mention them, even though he denounces Oedipus as the guilty one at the beginning of the Sophoclean tragedy. In the narrative, then, this mutilation is unnecessary, gratuitous. Its only function is to explain the name, Oedipus, "Swollen Foot." But nothing required that the myth explain the name, and, in fact, most Greek myths lack an etymological episode of this sort. The suspicion arises that the mutilation of the feet belongs to an order of signification independent of the narrative. Serving in the story only to explain the name of the hero, the mutilation must have some ulterior purpose. In this paper, the mutilated feet of Oedipus and other parts of his body are studied as signifiers in a synchronic dimension of the myth.

I turn, then, to the analysis of the myth in this dimension, that is, to the three relations between the parts of the hero's body, beginning with that between eyes and genitals. George Devereux (1973) showed that in *Oedipus the King*, by Sophocles's own design, Oedipus's explanations for his self-blinding are inadequate. The real cause is, as the Chorus believes, madness. If madness is the cause and if rational explanations fail, the self-blinding must be understood symbolically. In other words, Sophocles's dramatic technique leaves intact a superorganic or extra-textual significance of blinding. This significance appears in a pattern found in several other Greek myths: A sexual crime is punished by blinding (Buxton, 1980). Blinding is deemed an appropriate punishment because of the connection of eyes with love and sex. In particular, the eye is connected with the male genitals (Deonna, 1965, pp. 68–70). The representations on Greek vases of phalluses with eyes are well-known. The variants of the myth of the hero Phoenix are built on the symbolic relation of eyes to genitals. In one variant, preserved in the *Iliad* (Book 9, ll. 453–456), Phoenix is somehow rendered sterile by the Erinyes, those spirits of punishment. They are invoked by his father, after he has slept with his father's concubine — a near-incest. In another variant, the more common one, he is not sterilized but blinded (Aristophanes, *Acharnians*, l. 421; Apollodorus, *The Library*, Book 3, Ch. 13, Sect. 8). Blinding and sterilization are thus mythically equivalent punishments for the same sexual crime, and this mythical equivalence is possible because of the connection of the eyes with the genitals, a connection of which Freud was aware but which he never incorporated into his interpretation of the Oedipus myth (Edmunds, 1985a, pp. 96–97).

Another example is the hunter Orion. He raped Merope, the daughter of Oinopion, and, in revenge, Oinopion blinded him. From Hephaestus, the blind Orion received a young smith, Kedalion, as a guide, and strode through the sea toward the east, where he recovered his sight by looking into the rays of the rising sun (Hesiod, frag. 148). A clue to the significance of Kedalion is provided by the gloss of the lexicographer Hesychius (probably 5th century A.D.) on *kedalon*, namely, *aidoion*, "phallus." In other words, Kedalion, "Little Phallus," is the recompense for blindness and leads Orion to a cure. In the Oedipus myth, then, self-blinding can be taken to represent self-castration (Caldwell, 1974; Neumann, 1970, p. 163), condign self-punishment for incest. The symbolism of self-blinding rests on the fundamental relation of eyes and genitals. Though sometimes denied (May, 1961, p. 48), this relation is almost a truism. Angelica, a character in a novel by David Lodge (1984), states in a lecture at the annual meeting of the Modern Language Association: "We are none of us, I suppose, deceived by the self-blinding of Oedipus as to the true nature of the wound he is impelled to inflict upon himself, or likely to overlook the symbolic equivalence between eyeballs and testicles" (p. 322). The question might arise: Why did Oedipus not just castrate himself? Why was this symbolism necessary? The answer lies in the decorum of the Greek hero myths. Neither the Oedipus myth nor any other could admit a castration. The myths of the gods, however, were less restrained, and the castration of Kronos will provide a useful comparison later in this paper.

The significance of the blindness of Oedipus is reinforced by the blindness of the prophet Teiresias, whose importance in the myth has been reconfirmed by the discovery of a papyrus fragment of the poet Stesichorus (6th c. B.C.) (Parsons, 1977, especially p. 20). Caldwell (1974) has shown that, whereas the blindness of Oedipus and Teiresias is asymmetrical at the level of narrative and of theme (pp. 202, 214–215) since the two are distinguished with respect to knowledge and acceptance of limitations, the cause of the blindness is the same, since "the blindness of Teiresias can be interpreted as the result of oedipal sexual curiosity and incestuous wishes" (p. 208; for another interpretation, see Brisson, 1976, pp. 52–53). The various myths of Teiresias provide, in addition to blindness, at least two symbolic castrations of other sorts. Therefore, in what I have called the structural dimension of the myth, the character of Teiresias could be said to over-determine, as a kind of repetition not strictly necessary to the logic of the narrative, that of Oedipus with respect to the relation between eyes and genitals. The Sphinx episode will provide another example of an over-determination of this sort.

The second relation I wish to consider is that between eyes and feet. According to a German proverb, *Ein guter Fuss ist ein gutes Auge* (A good foot is a good eye), but in Greek mythology we could say that an injured foot is an injured eye (Lambrinoudakes, 1971, pp. 276–279). The mythical equivalence of such defects is clear in the case of Lycurgus (Brelich, 1958, pp. 247–248). In the *Iliad*, he was blinded by Zeus (Book 6, ll. 139; Diodorus of Sicily, Book 3, Ch. 65) after he drove Dionysus into the sea. But in Hyginus, Servius, and elsewhere, Lycurgus wounded his own feet or legs in attempting to cut down the vines of Dionysus (Servius on Vergil, *Aeneid*, Book 3, l. 14; Hyginus, *Fabulae*, no. 132; First Vatican Mythographer, no. 122). Another example is Anchises. While he is blind in one version of his myth, he is lame in another (Sophocles, frag. 344). In Roman mythology, one can point to Horatius Cocles. His name indicates that he was one-eyed (cf. "Cyclops"); according to Roman tradition, he was also lame (Dionysius of Halicarnassus, Book 5, Chs 23–25; Plutarch, *Publicola*, Ch. 16, Sect. 5; *Precepts of Statecraft, Moralia*, 820E; Brelich, 1958, p. 248, n. 65). In the myths of Lycurgus and Anchises, the variation between injuries to the eyes and to the feet indicates the functional equivalence of these motifs in the narrative. This equivalence must rest on the symbolic equivalence of these parts of the body. In the case of Horatius Cocles, one hero is afflicted in both eyes and feet by a reduplication of the motif.

The same is true of Oedipus (Hay, 1978, pp. 125–126). Furthermore, in variants of the Oedipus myth, the hero suffers both mutilations at the same period in his life. In the lost *Oedipus* of Euripides, the hero was blinded by the soldiers of his father, Laius, thus when he was still a child or a youth (scholiast on Euripides, *Phoenician Women*, l. 61; Euripides, frag. 541). In another variant, he was blinded by his foster-father, Polybus, to prevent the fulfillment of the prophecy (scholiast on Euripides, *Phoenician Women*, l. 26). Whereas in the Sophoclean version, the self-blinding of Oedipus was condign self-punishment for incest, the earlier blinding at the hands of Polybus is prophylactic against incest. The attachment of the blinding motif to the youth of Oedipus is further evidence of the mythical equivalence of injuries to the feet and the eyes. In the text of Sophocles's *Oedipus*, the connection is revealed by the metaphorical use of *arthra*, "joints," for eyes (1. 1270). Earlier in the tragedy, Sophocles used the same word for Oedipus's ankles (1. 718). Again, references in tragedy to the brooches/fibulas (*perōnai*) of Jocasta indicate a connection between the feet and the eyes of Oedipus. In Sophocles, he blinds himself with these implements (1. 1269). In Euripides's *Phoenissae*, Jocasta uses them to pierce the ankles of the infant Oedipus (1. 805).

The third relation of the parts of Oedipus's body is that between feet and genitals. The relation between these parts is a commonplace of folklore and psychoanalysis (Aigremont, 1909; Róheim, 1945; Till, 1971), and is well attested in Greek literature (Aristophanes, *Lysistrata*, 1. 419; Eubulus, frag. 108; Epicrates, frag. 10; Euripides, *Medea*, 1. 679 and the scholiast on this line). It is reflected in the ancient Greek belief that injury to the feet could cause swelling of the groin (Aristophanes, *Wasps*, ll. 275a–277a; *Lysistrata*, ll. 987–988; *Frogs*, 1. 1280). Although the Oedipus myth presents no explicit relation, it has been suggested that the reading "Oiduphallos" of a word on a Linear B tablet indicates that Oedipus, "Swollen Foot," is a euphemism (Ventris and Chadwick, 1973, p. 173). The likelihood is increased when we consider the narrative function of the mutilation of Oedipus's feet. I have already suggested that the mutilation is superfluous. But, not to mention its relation to the staff Oedipus carries (Segal, 1981, pp. 215ff), perhaps it has a tacit function that has been overlooked. This possibility emerges from a comparison of the Oedipus myth with other Greek and Roman stories of exposed children. In a collection of 121 of these stories (Binder, 1964), in which the royal child is usually exposed to prevent his succession to the throne, Oedipus is the only one who suffers a mutilation. One can suggest that this over-determination of the exposure motif by mutilation matches the over-determination of the prophecy motif. It is prophesied not only that Oedipus will kill his father, the king, but also that he will marry his mother. The mutilation of the feet would then be a thwarting of the prophesied incest, and the feet as symbols of the male organ are the appropriate locus. The self-blinding of

Oedipus is thus a reduplication of the earlier mutilation. The mythical equivalence of the two mutilations would also explain why in some variants Oedipus is blinded in his youth. If his feet could be mutilated, then so could his eyes.

The relation of feet and genitals is also implicit in the Sphinx episode, and one could even venture the hypothesis that this episode, otherwise marginal, has the infra-narrative or structural function of affirming this relation. Before this hypothesis can be tested, the narrative marginality of the Sphinx, who has sometimes been regarded as the core of the myth (for a critique, see Edmunds, 1981b) and who is the favorite of the vase painters (Moret, 1984), must be demonstrated. First, the Sphinx simply appears around the time of Laius's death, and her appearance bears no relation to the rest of the myth. Second, Oedipus challenges the Sphinx without any motive. He receives the hand of the widowed queen because he solved the riddle, but he did not solve the riddle in order to win a bride (*Oedipus the King*, ll. 383–384; *Oedipus at Colonus*, ll. 539–541; cf., however, Apollodorus, *The Library*, Book 3, Ch. 5, Sect. 8). The Sphinx episode, then, like the Teiresias episode discussed above, must have some infra-narrative function, as I have hypothesized.

The Sphinx's *modus operandi* is to pose a riddle to young Thebans or passers-by on the condition: answer correctly or die. In its simplest form, the riddle goes: "What has one voice and yet becomes four-footed and two-footed and three-footed?" (for the text see Lloyd-Jones, 1978, pp. 60–61). Though an Indo-European origin of this riddle has been proposed (Porzig, 1953), it has been recorded in many places — in Sumatra (Damsté, 1917), the Philippine Islands (Hart, 1964), and sub-Saharan Africa (Fraser, 1914). It undoubtedly had an existence independent of the Oedipus myth. How did this riddle come to be attached to the Sphinx? Presumably because of the connection, which is not made explicit in the narrative, between the hero's name, "Swollen-Foot," and the form of the riddle, which describes its subject in terms of numbers of feet.

How then do the genitals of Oedipus form part of the Sphinx episode? Following Lévi-Strauss (1973), one can suggest that the riddle-solving is an image of incest and that the marriage to Jocasta, who is not explicitly connected with the Sphinx, is thus prefigured. In *Anthropologie structurale deux*, he compares the myth of Oedipus with an Algonquin tale in order to show that the latter can be under-

stood as, not the cognate, not the adaptation, but the logical transformation of the other. Although the Sphinx is apparently absent
from the Algonquin tale, the owl plays a role, and in this bird Lévi-
Strauss discovers the Sphinx. The owl, he says, is the American
Sphinx (1973, p. 33). His demonstration of the connection between
the two narratives is as follows. The role of the owl in the Algonquin
tale is to denounce the hero's incestuous marriage. In other Algonquin lore, owls pose neck-riddles (*Halsrätseln*). Thus the Algonquin
owl poses riddles and denounces incest. Riddles, however, are extremely rare among the North American Indians. Besides the Algonquin riddles, there are only those posed by the ceremonial clowns
of the Zuñi. These clowns are believed to be the offspring of incestuous unions. Riddles thus "present a double Oedipal character: by
way of incest, on the one hand; on the other, by way of the owl"
(Lévi-Strauss, 1973). Lévi-Strauss goes on to propose a relation of
homology between incest and riddle: "Like the solved riddle, incest
brings together terms destined to remain separate: the son is united
to the mother, the brother to the sister *just as the answer* [to the riddle]
*does in succeeding, contrary to all expectations, in reuniting itself with its ques-
tion*" (1973, p. 34; emphasis in original). One can add that the affini-
ty of the Oedipus folktale for riddles (Edmunds, 1985, p. 35) corrob-
orates Lévi-Strauss's suggestion. (Compare also the *Historia Apollonii
Regis Tyri*, in which a king poses a neck-riddle to his daughter's
suitors. The subject of the riddle is the king's incestuous relationship
with his daughter.) The relation of the Sphinx and her riddle to
Jocasta, then—a relation completely unavowed by the narrative—
must appear much closer, and one must agree with Lévi-Strauss
(1973, p. 34) that the marriage to Jocasta does not follow arbitrarily
from the victory over the Sphinx (cf. Lesky, 1929, cols. 1717–1718).
Lévi-Strauss's conclusion is corroborated by a psychoanalytic interpretation of Jocasta's role according to which she is a Great Mother
to whom Oedipus is subjected and from whom he attempts to free
himself (Manieri, 1986).

   I shall conclude my discussion of the relations of feet and eyes
and of feet and genitals with some remarks on the feet of Oedipus as
he is portrayed in Sophocles's *Oedipus the King*. It is a curious fact that
his deformed or scarred feet emerge in his consciousness only toward
the end of the play, when he cross-examines the messenger from

Corinth (ll. 1031-1037), who had received him as an infant from the
Theban shepherd who will soon appear and confirm Oedipus's identity and guilt. Thereafter, Oedipus curses the one who released him
from his shackles and allowed him to live (ll. 1349-1351). Earlier in
the play, however, Teiresias makes no mention of Oedipus's feet when
he denounces him as the one who has defiled the city (ll. 300-462).
And when Jocasta describes the "yoking" of the feet of her infant son
(ll. 717-718), not yet identified as Oedipus, he fails to grasp the clue.
Classical scholars have concluded that Oedipus did not know the
cause of the scars on his feet (Brown, 1966, pp. 21-23) or that his
feet were not mutilated at all (Maxwell-Stuart, 1975). And yet
"Sophoclean characters in other plays beside this one suffer from
dramatically convenient transitory amnesia" (Dawe, 1982, p. 22),
and thus Oedipus's mental lapse is probably best explained. The
dramatic convenience of the lapse is not, however, simply a matter of
retarding the denouement. The audience has already been reminded
of the connection between the Oedipus's name, "Swell-foot," and his
solving of the Sphinx's riddle. At line 397, as he boasts of his victory
over the Sphinx and heaps scorn on Teiresias, he unconsciously puns
on his own name: it was *ho mēden eidōs Oidipous*, with no claim to
prophetic or other knowledge, who stopped her. In the vicinity of the
participle *eidōs*, from the verb "to know," the first element in the
name Oedipus sounds like the first person of the verb *oida*, "I know."
Thus he is "the know-nothing-I-know-the-foot." He did indeed know
the feet in the riddle of the Sphinx, but he does not know his own feet
and does not become aware of them as part of his identity until the
penultimate phase of his discovery that he is himself the criminal
whom he is seeking. He becomes conscious of his feet, then, as he
becomes conscious of the crimes of parricide and incest, a discovery
that is simultaneous with the discovery of who he is. The messenger
from Corinth states: "From this misfortune [i.e., the mutilation] you
were named who you are," enunciating in one line the complex:
name-mutilation-identity. Oedipus *is* his feet, and, since his feet are
symbolically the equivalent of his eyes and of his genitals, he *is* the
tripartite body I have described.

The analysis of the myth I have now given would of course require
further substantiation and argumentation, but much corroboration

is already available in a remarkable monograph by Jules Brody (1985), which shows, on the basis of an analysis of the fundamental metaphor of binding in *Oedipus the King*, that

> the "plot" of Sophocles' play may legitimately be viewed as a sequence of amplifications of the matricial message that is rooted in the *double-entendre* contained in its title: how "swell-foot" became "know-foot," or, more pointedly still, how the foot-loose Oedipus, king errant, *homo viator* and archetypal transgressor, gets to "know" the story behind his swollen feet. (p. 20)

Perhaps enough has been said to suggest that the body of Oedipus is a remarkably complete instantiation of a structure of symbolic relations given in Greek hero myth. These symbolic relations undoubtedly have different functions in different myths. I have not assumed any archetypal or central meaning. In the Oedipus myth, the symbolism indicates castration, and, as I have said, this myth seems, with its double mutilation, to wish to leave no doubt. Furthermore, the symbolic castrations are linked with incest, and mother–son incest is another rarity in Greek hero myths. Besides Oedipus, there is only Menephron, known from a single passing reference in Ovid (*Metamorphoses*, Book 7, l. 386; cf. Hyginus, *Fabulae*, no. 253) and Perdiccas (Riese, 1906, no. 808; Fulgentius, *Mythologiae*, Book 3, Ch. 2). Boupolos, the butt of the iambic poet Hipponax, is sometimes mentioned as an example, but his case is problematic (Citti, 1984).

The question thus arises of the connection between incest and symbolic castration in the Oedipus myth. At the level of narrative, there is of course no explicit connection between the mutilation of the feet and incest. The connection between self-blinding and incest is somewhat clearer. But we have already had to look beneath the level of the narrative in order to discern the castration in the first place. Is there also some infra-narrative connection between incest and castration? In order to answer this question, I pursue a suggestion made by Angelo Brelich in *Gli Eroi Greci*, a book to which much that I have already said is indebted. Pointing to the examples of incest among the gods in Greek myths, Brelich (1958) asks, "the first human couples . . . or other heroic couples — couldn't they have an incestuous relationship in a sense analogous to or perhaps derived from that of divine models?" (p. 288). This notion of a divine model or analogue may be useful for understanding castration in the Oedi-

pus myth. Could we not look to myths of the gods, and, in particular, to the most famous castration, that of Uranus by Kronos?
Kronos uses the agricultural implement, the sickle, to perform the
castration, and the verb *emēse* "he reaped," describes his action in the
text of Hesiod (*Theogony*, 1. 181). Kronos, indeed, has been regarded
as an agricultural god. But would castration as reaping, as harvest-
ing have any bearing on the Oedipus myth? In particular, on the
motif of incest, with which the symbolic castrations appeared to be
connected?

I would offer the following reflections on incest in Greek myth
and belief, which are a summary of research already published by
myself and others (Edmunds, 1981a). In myths of the gods, incest is,
of course, not only blameless but even benign in its marvelous fecundity. Similarly, in ancient Greek belief, it is possible to discover a
homology of incest and autochthony, birth from the earth. Incest
appears as the human counterpart of the primal and ever-renewed
fecundity of the earth, the source of all life. In the very text of
Sophocles's *Oedipus the King*, we can see traces of the homology. In
several places, Oedipus speaks of his sexual relations with his mother
in agricultural terms (Pucci, 1979, pp. 130–131). Oedipus refers to
his wife as "seeded alike" (*homosporos*, 1. 260) by him and by Laius.
The seer Teiresias uses the same adjective of Oedipus, though in an
active sense: "murderer of his father and fellow-seeder [with his
father of his mother]" (1. 460; for the seed metaphor, cf. ll. 1246,
1405). After the discovery of the crimes, the Chorus asks: "How
could the furrows that your father ploughed endure you?" (ll. 1211–
1213). Oedipus seeks Jocasta in the palace, "the double furrow [i.e.,
womb] of him and his children" (1. 1257). Addressing his daughters
in the final scene of the play, he says that he has been revealed as
"their father from the same place where I was ploughed [i.e., begot-
ten]" (1. 1497). When he describes their future as "barren" (*khersos*, 1.
1502), he uses a word that is applied elsewhere in Greek literature
only to land, never to persons.

This agricultural imagery is not, furthermore, the invention of
Sophocles. In Aeschylus's *Seven Against Thebes*, the same imagery of
incest is used. The imagery was, then, traditional in the Oedipus
myth. It belonged to the myth, not to any single poem, and, for that
matter, was not the exclusive property of the Oedipus myth. The
universal poetic homology of sexual and agricultural reproduction

(Eliade, 1963, pp. 259–260, 354–356) has only been given a particular application to the homology of incest and autochthony.

To return for a moment to *Seven Against Thebes*, in this tragedy
the protagonist, Eteocles, one of the two sons of Oedipus and Jocasta, patriotically invokes the myth of the Spartoi, the "Sown Men,"
from whom the original families of Thebes were descended. The
offspring of an incestuous union tends to identify with these autochthonous Spartoi, and his and his brother's mutual slaughter before
the gates of Thebes is a re-enactment of the fratricidal strife of those
original Spartoi (Zeitlin, 1984, pp. 29–36). This tragedy could be
said to show that the result of Oedipus's incestuous marriage is a
return to the violent instability of the pre-political, undifferentiated
conditions of the autochthonous age.

The infra-narrative connection, then, between incest and castration becomes clearer. If incest and autochthony are alternate
modes of reproduction, then it is quite appropriate that the incestuous figure should also be castrated, that is, reaped, harvested. The
autochthon, the man-plant is castrated-reaped, and thus seeds
mother-earth. If this explanation is correct, we could better understand why, in one ancient tradition, Oedipus is buried in a precinct
sacred to Demeter, the goddess of grain (Edmunds, 1981a), and why
the folklore cognates or analogues of the Oedipus myth sometimes
have a chthonic episode (Edmunds, 1985b, p. 38). This agricultural
aspect of Oedipus harmonizes with the role of sacred king that has
been ascribed to him (Róheim, 1930; Edmunds, 1985a, pp. 98–100;
cf. Longo, 1984).

We could also perhaps better understand the theme of intelligence in Sophocles's *Oedipus the King*. In that tragedy, the intelligence
of Oedipus is manifested in his solving the riddle of the Sphinx.
Sophocles makes much of the tragic irony of Oedipus's pride in his
mental powers. But it is not at all clear, from a mythological point of
view, why the incestuous one, the parricide, should be characterized
by high intelligence, assuming that this intelligence is traditional in
the myth and not the invention of Sophocles. The body of Oedipus,
with its symbolic emphasis on the genitals of Oedipus, may provide
an answer. In Greek, the word *mēdea* is ambivalent. It can mean
either "thoughts, schemes," or "genitals" (Nagy, 1974, pp. 265–278).
We can sense why "Swollen Foot," whose sexual potency left not even
his own mother untouched, should also have been a figure of the

highest intelligence. One must also consider the connection of *mētis*, "cunning intelligence," with physical defects in Greek mythology (Giangiulio, 1981, pp. 11-23).

Let us return once more, however, to the myth of Kronos. Hesiod relates that the blood from Uranus's several genitals dripped upon the earth and produced the Erinyes, who are also called the Eumenides, the Semnai, the Furies, and so forth. They provide a direct link with the Oedipus myth. The Erinyes, born from the earth as the result of a castration, are associated with Oedipus in almost every one of his appearances in Greek poetry. This fact is not surprising, given the Erinyes' special concern with punishing crimes committed within the family. Furthermore, the Erinyes' favorite modes of punishment included blinding, mutilation, and castration (Aeschylus, *Eumenides*, ll. 186-190, though ll. 187-188 might mean only sterilization, not castration). Oedipus was the perfect object of their vengeance, but his crimes were never fully expiated. In historical times, a family that believed itself to be descended from the Theban kings founded a cult to propitiate the Erinyes of Oedipus (Herodotus, *Histories*, Book 4, Ch. 149). The Erinyes were never satisfied. At the same time, Oedipus himself acted like the Erinyes. He was not only the object but also the subject of their powers. The parallel function of Oedipus and the Erinyes in *Oedipus at Colonus* has often been noticed. In that tragedy, Oedipus curses his own sons and thus causes their death. In relation to them, he is an Erinys.

The Erinyes are, then, further support for the comparison of Oedipus and Kronos, though we would now have to say that Oedipus plays the roles of both Kronos and Uranus. In any case, from this comparison we have been able to discover a chthonic or agricultural dimension in the figure of Oedipus, and, in this dimension, a central ambiguity. In Oedipus are concentrated the forces of both generation and blight. In the mythical narrative and in tragedy, these forces must appear in terms of sex and of the family. They must thus appear as crimes and punishments. But tragedy preserves the primitive ambiguity. The chthonic Oedipus has not been completely lost. In *Oedipus at Colonus*, the scapegoat-king (Vernant, 1977-1978), driven from Thebes, has wandered to Colonus. In this place, he dies in a miraculous fashion. Sophocles writes: "The passing of the man was not with lamentation, or in sickness and suffering, but above mortal's wonderful" (ll. 1663-1665). Oedipus has apparently disappeared into the earth. But the body of Oedipus would not require a normal burial.

REFERENCES

Fragments are cited in the following editions. Comic poets: T. Kock, *Comicorum Atticorum Fragmenta* (Leipzig, 1880–1888). Tragic poets: A. Nauck, *Tragicorum Graecorum Fragmenta*, 2nd ed. (Leipzig, 1889). Hesiod: R. Merkelbach and M. L. West, *Fragmenta Hesiodea* (Oxford, 1976). There are no translations of these works. Two books reached me just as I was sending the final draft of this paper to the editor of *The Psychoanalytic Review*: the collection of papers from the conference on Oedipus held in Urbino in 1982 (see note at beginning of this paper) and Peter L. Rudnytsky, *Freud and Oedipus* (New York: Columbia University Press, 1987). I regret that I was unable to make adequate use of these books in this paper.

AIGREMONT, D. (Baron Siegmar von Schultze-Galléra). (1909) *Fuss- und Schuh-Symbolik und -Erotik*. Leipzig.

BINDER, G. (1964) Die Aussetzung des Königskindes. *Beiträge zur klassischen Philologie*, 10: Meisenheim am Glan: A. Hain.

BRELICH, A. (1958) *Gli Eroi Greci*. Rome: Anteneo.

BRISSON, L. (1976) *Le mythe de Tirésias: Essai d'analyse structurale*. Leiden: Brill.

BRODY, J. (1985) *"Fate" in* Oedipus Tyrannus: *A Textual Approach*. Buffalo, NY: Arethusa Monographs 11.

BROWN, A. D. FITTON (1966) Four Notes on Sophocles. *Proceedings of the Cambridge Philological Society*, 12:18–23.

BUECHLER, F., RIESE, A. (1906) *Anthologia Latina* (Vol. 1; Part 2; 2nd ed). Leipzig: Teubner.

BUXTON, R. G. A. (1980) Blindness and Limits: Sophokles and the Logic of Myth. *J. Hellenic Studies*, 100:22–37.

CALDWELL, R. S. (1974) The Blindness of Oedipus. *Int. R. Psychoanal.*, 1:207–218.

CITTI, V. (1984) Edipo e Bupalo. In R. Uglione (ed.), *Atti delle Giornate di Studio su Edipo* (pp. 85–92). Turin: Associazione Italiana di Cultura Classica, delegazione di Torino.

DAMSTÉ, P. H. (1917) Oedipus Indicus. *Mnem.* New Series, 45:231–232.

DAWE, R. D. (1982) *Sophocles: Oedipus Rex*. Cambridge: Cambridge University Press.

DEONNA, W. (1965) *Le symbolisme de l'oeil*. Paris: Boccard.

DEVEREUX, G. (1973) The Self-Blinding of Oidipous in Sophokles: Oidipous Tyrannos. *J. Hellenic Studies*, 93:36–49.

EDMUNDS, L. (1980) The Oedipus Myth and African Sacred Kingship. *Comparative Civilizations Bulletin*, 8:1–12.

———— (1981a) The Cults and the Legend of Oedipus. *Harvard Studies in Classical Philology*, 85:221–238.

———— (1981b) *The Sphinx in the Oedipus Legend*. Beiträge zur klassischen Philologie, 127. Hain: Königstein. /Ts. (Partially repr. in L. Edmunds and A. Dundes [Eds.], *Oedipus: A Folklore Casebook* [1983; pp. 147–173]. New York: Garland.)

———— (1985a) Freud and the Father: Oedipus Complex and Oedipus Myth. *Psychoanal. & Contemp. Thought*, 8:87–102.

_____ (1985b) *Oedipus: The Ancient Legend and Its Later Analogues*. Baltimore: Johns Hopkins University Press.

ELIADE, M. (1963) *Patterns in Comparative Religion* (R. Sheed trans.). New York: New American Library.

FRASER, D. (1914) *Winning a Primitive People*. Westport, CT: Negro Universities Press, 1970.

GIANGIULIO, M. (1981) Deformità eroiche e tradizione di fondazione. *Annali della Scuola Normale di Pisa* III, 9:1–24.

HART, D. V. (1964) *Riddles in Filipino Folklore: An Anthropological Analysis*. Syracuse: Syracuse University Press.

HAY, J. (1978) *Oedipus Tyrannus: Lame Knowledge and the Homosporic Womb*. Washington, DC: University Press of America.

LAMBRINOUDAKES, B. K. (1971) ΜΗΡΟΤΡΑΦΗΣ. Athens: N. & M. Aoanasopoulou.

LESKY, A. (1929) Sphinx. In *RE* (2nd series, 6th half vol., cols. 1703–1726).

LÉVI-STRAUSS, C. (1955) The Structural Study of Myth. In *Structural Anthropology* (pp. 202–228). Garden City, NY: Doubleday/Anchor.

_____ (1973) *Anthropologie structurale deux*. Paris: Plon.

LLOYD-JONES, H. (1978) Ten Notes on Aeschylus, *Agamemnon* (pp. 45–61). In R. D. Dawe, D. Diggle, & P. E. Easterling (Eds.), *Dionysiaca*. Cambridge: Editors.

LODGE, D. (1984) *Small World*. London: Martin Secker & Warburg.

LONGO, O. (1984) Regalità, polis, incesto nell'Edipo tragico. In R. Uglione (Ed.), *Atti delle Giornate di Studio su Edipo* (pp. 69–83). Turin: Associazione Italiana di Cultura Classica, delegazione di Torino.

MANIERI, F. (1986) Edipo: un sogno. In B. Gentili & R. Pretagostini (Eds.), *Edipo: Il Teatro Greco e la Cultura Europea: Atti del Convegono Internazionale* (pp. 237–253). Rome: Ateneo.

MAXWELL-STUART, P. G. (1975) Interpretations of the Name Oedipus. *Maia*, 27:37–43.

MAY, R. (1961) The Meaning of the Oedipus Myth. *R. Existential Psychol. & Psychiatry*, 1:44–52.

NAGY, G. (1974) *Comparative Studies in Greek and Indic Meter*. Cambridge, MA: Harvard University Press.

NEUMANN, E. (1970) *Origins and History of Consciousness*. Bollingen Series XLII. Princeton: Princeton University Press.

PARSONS, P. J. (1977) The Lille "Stesichorus." *Zeitschrift für Papyrologie und Epigraphik*, 26:7–36.

PORZIG, W. (1953) Das Rätsel der Sphinx. In R. Schmitt (Ed.), *Indogermanische Dichtersprache* (pp. 172–176). Wege der Forschung CLXV, Darmstadt: Wissenschaftliche Buchgellschaft.

PUCCI, P. (1979) On the "Eye" and the "Phallos" and Other Permutabilities in *Oedipus Rex*. In G. W. Bowersock, et al. (Eds.) *Arktouros* (pp. 130–131). New York: De Gruyter.

RÓHEIM, G. (1930) *Animism, Magic and the Divine King*. New York: Knopf.

_____ (1945) *The Eternal Ones of the Dream*. New York: International Universities Press.

SEGAL, C. P. (1981) *Tragedy and Civilization: An Interpretation of Sophocles*. Cambridge, MA: Harvard University Press.

TILL, W. (1971) *Schuh- und Fussförmige Anhänger und Amulette*. Diss. Munich: Ludwig-Maximilians-Universität.

VENTRIS, M., & CHADWICK, J. (1973) *Documents in Mycenaean Greek* (2nd ed.). Cambridge: Cambridge University Press.

VERNANT, J.-P. (1977–1978) Ambiguity and Reversal: On the Enigmatic Structure of *Oedipus Rex*. (Page duBois, Trans.). *New Lit. Hist.*, 9:475–501.

ZEITLIN, F. (1984) *Under the Sign of the Shield*. Rome: Ateneo.

The Johns Hopkins University
121 Gilman Hall
Baltimore, MD 21218

THE TROUBLED HOUSE OF OEDIPUS
AND CHRÉTIEN'S *NÉO-TRISTAN*:
RE-WRITING THE MYTHOLOGIES OF DESIRE

Daniel Rubey

OEDIPUS, TRISTAN, AND ARTHUR

Myths have power for us because they seem to be fragments of another age and another reality, of inaccessible prehistoric origins, the time of primal fathers and totems. Myths seem to offer encoded truths that can be retrieved by penetrating the obscure or scandalous surface of the text. They promise illuminations authorized by antiquity and tradition. But at the same time, any actual myth is only a version, an interpretation of a pre-existing myth, a recreation of an inaccessible original. Originals seem timeless, beyond history; but interpretations have a historical dimension that is relatively accessible, that is subjective and ideological.

The Oedipus myth was used in this way by Freud in developing his theory of the Oedipus complex and in arguing for its universality (Freud, 1900, pp. 261–264; 1926, pp. 211–214).[1] Freud drew on the timeless, mythic quality of the Oedipus story to assert its universality, but he actually used a particular version of the myth, Sophocles's *Oedipus Rex*. In that dramatic version, as Cynthia Chase (1979) has argued, Oedipus's discovery of the truth about his own origins parallels the process of self-discovery around which Freud constructed the new science of psychoanalysis. Freud's version of the Oedipus myth, the Oedipus complex, has been re-written by his followers and revisers for their own purposes, just as their re-writings will be revised in the continuing process of intertextuality.

The continuing usefulness of the Oedipus myth and its continuing availability for reinterpretation suggests that there are some significant constants running through all versions. First, the Oedipus legend functions as a map of connections between the individual and the social, as the scene where those orientations intersect, perhaps as the zone of interaction between them. In this context, it is important that Oedipus is a king as well as a man, because kingship links his personal fate with the fate of Thebes. His actions bring plague to the city, a sign of dislocation in the natural order. The crimes of Oedipus, parricide and incest, are crimes against the social order, against the fundamental taboos upon which civilization is based. His sons initiate a fratricidal war over the throne, thus threatening to destroy the city, a rupture in the natural and social orders that is the subject of Aeschylus's *Seven against Thebes* and the background of Sophocles's *Antigone*.

Second, the Oedipus myth carries a related subtext about both the necessity of repressing desire as the price of preserving the social order and the fear that desire cannot be repressed, that its consequences must necessarily be handed down from generation to generation. The chain of guilt and punishment stretches back into autochthonic prehistory and forward into the unimaginable future. Oedipus plays out the destiny Laius set in motion when he violated the prohibition against engendering an heir. According to some versions, the curse on Laius resulted from his rape of the son of Pelops; in others, the tragedy begins with Apollo's curse on the house of Labdacus, the father of Laius. Oedipus's sons, Eteocles and Polynices, carry that destiny into the next generation when they break their fraternal compact to share the throne of Thebes (see Balmary, 1982, ch. 1; Edmunds, 1985, pp. 8–9, 16–17; Lukacher, 1986, pp. 240–241).

This social dimension of the Oedipus myth, a significant absence in Freud's version, has been variously restored by the neo-Freudians, by Jacques Lacan (1936, 1953) who sees language as the missing social dimension, and by Gilles Deleuze and Félix Guattari (1972) in their work on capitalism and schizophrenia. But in Western European literature, this awareness of the social dimension of the Oedipus myth can be traced at least to the twelfth century, the moment when a vernacular written narrative literature began to establish itself.

The term *romance* was first used in a generic sense by Chrétien de Troyes and comes from the Old French word *romans*, meaning simply the vernacular French language. These new narratives combined tales of adventure with the courtly love poetry of southern France to form a new literature of sexual desire, a written literature based on oral sources but explicitly concerned with interpretation and textuality. Chrétien distinguishes his first romance, *Eric et Enide*, from its oral sources by the skillfulness and beauty of its *conjointure*, a term which, in this context, means both narrative structure and the interpretations and commentary built into the work. Romances are infused with a new reflexivity, a new sense of themselves as texts to be read and interpreted; they are the antecedents of the novel, the most characteristic and original contribution of European literature to the canon of literary genres.

The primary myth of this new form of written literature is the story of King Arthur and his Round Table, a set of legends reconstructed or remembered from oral sources and elaborated in written texts for three centuries. At the center of this myth is an adulterous relationship that finally destroys the Edenic dream of feudal order that the Round Table represents, the love of Lancelot, Arthur's finest knight, and Guinevere, Arthur's queen.

The incestuous content of this triangle is disguised, but re-emerges in the story that Arthur slept with his half-sister, Morgan Le Fay, and engendered the son, Mordred, who eventually revolts against Arthur, seizes Guinevere, and causes Arthur's death in the final apocalyptic battle on Salisbury Plain. But just as the source of the initial guilt or fall recedes into past generations in the Oedipus myth, so, too, Arthur himself was begotten by his father, Uther Pendragon, through deceit and magic on the wife of one of his vassals, a fundamental violation of the feudal system of vassalage relationships.

This incestuous content of the lovers' triangle is more overt in what seems to have been the first of the Arthurian romances, the story of Tristan and Isolt, in which Tristan is King Mark's nephew and Isolt his wife. Both of these adulterous triangles, Arthur/Guinevere/Lancelot and Mark/Isolt/Tristan, can be read as parallel versions of the Laius/Jocasta/Oedipus triangle, Freud's triangle of the nuclear family. This structural similarity suggests that in the western European novel tradition that began with the French *roman*, adultery serves as a screen for parricide and incest, the Arthurian myth for the Oedipus myth.

The fundamental importance of adultery as a constitutive theme for romance and the treatment of love in Western literature in general was the theme of Denis de Rougemont's classic work, *L'amour et l'Occident* (1939).[2] De Rougemont's thesis has been applied to the novel by Tony Tanner in his *Adultery and the Novel* (1979). Tanner argues that "it is the unstable triangularity of adultery, rather than the static symmetry of marriage, that is the generative form of Western literature as we know it" (p. 12).

Chase (1979) has contended (pp. 55–56) that Freud's solution of the sexual riddle of why sexuality is so uniquely enigmatic through his discovery of repression and the unconscious becomes the principle of his reading of the oedipal riddle, the peculiar power of *Oedipus Rex*. But this specific relationship between sexuality and textuality in both Freud's and Sophocles's versions of the Oedipus myth also seems deeply inscribed in Western narrative literature itself from its twelfth-century beginnings.

Chrétien's *Cligés*, written around 1176, is a crucial text for understanding the nature of desire and the Oedipus myth as it is inscribed in the new written narratives of the twelfth-century French romance. It is in this text, the most original of Chrétien's works, that the interlinked strands of the Oedipus, Tristan, and Arthur legends come together most overtly, and come together in ways that refer to the contemporary social, political, and dynastic struggles of the period.

This conjunction is possible in part because the lines between myth, literature, and historiography were much less clearly drawn during the Middle Ages than they were later. Arthur was believed to be a historical figure connected by lineage to current rulers. The use of comparisons between contemporary figures and characters from classical myths had considerable explanatory power because such comparisons were analogous to scriptural typology, the most powerful explanatory model available to the age.

Given this tendency to explain and understand through analogy and type, when Richard of Devises, a twelfth-century chronicler, refers to the house of Henry II of England as "the troubled house of Oedipus," he is offering a political and historical analysis that uses the Oedipus myth as both an explanatory and a cautionary model. The meaning of this analysis will be clearer if we look first at Chrétien's *Cligés*.

Cligés is the second of Chrétien's romances, but the first to make systematic use of the courtly love motifs developed in troubadour lyrics. Since *Cligés* is Chrétien's least known work as well as his most original, a brief summary is appropriate.

Alexander, the eldest son of the Emperor of Greece and Constantinople, travels to Britain to enter King Arthur's service and become a knight. Arthur's court is now the most famous in the world, Europe having displaced Greece as the center of civilization. Alexander is well received because of his courtly manners and makes many friends. He sails to Brittany with Arthur and his court, while England is left in the care of Count Angres of Windsor. During the passage, Alexander falls in love with Soredamors, one of Guinevere's ladies. Soredamors loves him as well, but they are afraid to speak to one another because neither knows the other's feelings.

Back in England, Count Angres rebels and raises an army against Arthur's return. Alexander is knighted and joins in the war against the traitor. He and his men disguise themselves in the captured armor of Angres's men and succeed in deceiving the traitor and capturing him, ending the rebellion. Angres is put to death, but his men are spared. Alexander does not ask for Soredamors as a reward because he does not want to take her against her will. Guinevere perceives their love for each other and intercedes for them. Alexander and Soredamors are married; Cligés is born to them.

Meanwhile, back in Greece, the Emperor dies. Everyone there believes Alexander is dead because of a false story that he died in a shipwreck told by a messenger in the service of Alis, Alexander's younger brother. Alis is crowned emperor; Alexander hears of his brother's usurpation of the throne and returns to Constantinople with a company of armed Britons. The Greek nobles refuse to support Alis against Alexander because a civil war would tear the kingdom apart. Alis is forced to agree to retain the throne in name only, giving the real power to Alexander and promising that he will not marry and that Cligés will succeed to the throne after his death.

But Alis renounces the agreement after Alexander's death and decides to marry, despite his oath. He chooses for his bride the daughter of the Emperor of Germany, Fenice, whose name resembles the name of the legendary phoenix [Fenice/Fenix]. Cligés ac-

companies Alis to Cologne for the marriage and fights to defend his
uncle's claim to Fenice against the Duke of Saxony, to whom she had
been betrothed. Cligés and Fenice fall in love. Alis and Fenice are
married, but Fenice vows she will never be the agent of Cligés's
displacement from the throne by bearing Alis an heir. Fenice's nurse
prepares a magic potion that deceives Alis into thinking that he has
made love to Fenice, when he has only embraced her in his dreams.
The potion is given to him by Cligés.

Following wishes his father expressed before his death, Cligés
goes to Arthur's court in Britain to win fame. Disguising his identity,
he participates in a three-day tournament at Oxford and wins all the
honors. He reveals his identity and is accepted into the court with
rejoicing. Cligés stays with Arthur until his love for Fenice causes
him to return to Constantinople.

Fenice refuses to run away to Britain with him, saying that
would be too much like the behavior of Isolt. Instead, the lovers plan
for Fenice to feign death with the help of another magic potion from
her nurse.

While the court mourns for their empress, a group of doctors
from Salerno suspect the trick and try to force Fenice to admit she is
still alive by torturing her. They beat her with thongs and pour
boiling lead through her palms, but Fenice does not speak. As they
are about to place her on a grate and roast her over a fire, her maids
break in and throw the doctors out of the tower window, killing
them. Fenice is placed in an ornate sepulchre; Cligés removes her
secretly and takes her to hidden underground chambers in a tower
built by his serf Jehan, where she recovers with the help of her
nurse.

The lovers are happy together in the secret tower. But Fenice
needs fresh air and light, and the lovers are discovered sleeping in
the tower's enclosed garden by one of Alis's men. Cligés and Fenice
flee to Arthur's court; Arthur prepares an army to support Cligés's
claim to the throne. But before the army can leave England, Jehan
arrives with the news that Alis has died of grief and rage at not being
able to capture the lovers. Cligés and Fenice return to Constantinople, where they are married and crowned. Chrétien says that Cligés
never kept Fenice confined, but that since that time, every empress
in Constantinople has been confined in her quarters for fear she
would deceive her husband as Fenice deceived Alis.

Cligés has long been understood as an anti-*Tristan* or *Néo-Tristan*, to use Jean Frappier's term (1968, p. 106), a *Tristan* that ends as a comedy rather than a tragedy. Both works begin with the love stories of the hero's parents. Tristan's parents, Rivalin and Blanchefleur, fall in love but are unable to marry. They die apart, Rivalin on the battlefield and Blanchefleur of grief. Tristan's name is taken from *triste*, for sorrow. Tristan recapitulates the tragic history of his parents in his love affair with Isolt.

Cligés's parents, Alexander and Soredamors, are able to marry, due to Guinevere's intercession, but they are denied the throne by the machinations of Alis, Alexander's younger brother. The lovers achieve a temporary success in resolving the conflicting demands of desire and society, but their success is unstable, blocked by the false report of Alexander's death, and then later by his actual death from disease.

The story of Cligés and Fenice is a re-writing of Cligés's parents' destiny on the dynastic level. Their joint marriage and coronation completely reconciles the individual and the social order, desire and responsibility. *Cligés* acknowledges a tragic past, but the romance creates a new present in which the oedipal rebellion is licensed by the society. The fantasy project that drives *Cligés* as a text is the reconciliation of oedipal desire and the harmony of the social fabric, the project deemed impossible in the Tristan story, and in De Rougemont's *L'amour et l'Occident* (1939) and Freud's *Civilization and Its Discontents* (1930). As such, it attacks the basic compromises on which society is founded; it is the revolutionary project at its most elemental.

The strategy of Chrétien's re-writing of the Oedipus myth depends on a two-part displacement drawn from mythological sources. The first part displaces the oedipal guilt onto Cligés's uncle, the bad-father figure, through feudal legalisms that reflect contemporary interest in secular law. This displacement draws its mythic authority from the story of the Siege of Thebes, the war between the sons of Oedipus.

The second, darker, perhaps more primal, part of the strategy displaces the punishment (castration, death) for the oedipal revolt onto the woman, Fenice, using two related death and rebirth mythologies: the classical phoenix, and the crucifixion and resurrection of Christ. Both strategies are written on the body of Fenice, inscribed as a machine for the production of heirs in the feudal/legal system, as the already-castrated female body in the death and re-birth fantasy. Both strategies demonstrate clearly that the sexual, social, and textual are inextricably intertwined in romance, and that sexuality is necessarily a social system.

GUILT OF THE FATHER, WAR OF THE BROTHERS

The displacement of guilt to the bad-father figure, Alis, the first level of Chrétien's strategy, is already anticipated in the Oedipus story itself, in the prehistory of Laius and Labdacus, father and grandfather. In *Cligés*, Alis breaks his legal contract with Alexander through his marriage to Fenice and his attempt to engender heirs, thereby denying Cligés's inheritance of the throne. It is important for the realization of this fantasy project that Cligés be guiltless, and Chrétien therefore avoids having him rebel against Alis. Such a war of vassal against lord, nephew against uncle (son against father), would imperil the social order rather than reintegrate it.

Instead, Chrétien has King Arthur intervene as a superior authority figure, as the feudal personification of Lacan's Name-of-the-Father. Arthur's willingness to support Cligés against Alis recasts the struggle between vassal and lord into a struggle between kings, the rebellion of son against father into a struggle between good father and bad. In this new context, Arthur becomes the supporter of justice in the feudal system and succession in the parental one.

Alis's decision to marry has already violated the feudal order and canceled Cligés's obligations to him. His renunciation of his oath mirrors a large breakdown in the system of feudal obligations, a breakdown related to the growth of centralized power and the progression toward absolute monarchy.

Once Arthur's support is established in principle, it becomes unnecessary in practice, and the conflict is solved within the terms of the oedipal conflict itself. Jehan arrives at Arthur's court with the message that Alis has gone mad in his anger at being unable to capture the lovers, and has died of rage. Jehan's message re-writes the earlier false message of Alexander's death in the first part of the romance, closing the rupture opened by that earlier lie. Cligés is received joyfully in Constantinople; he is married to Fenice, and they are both crowned.

Alis's treachery against Cligés has already been anticipated by his plot to take the throne from his brother Alexander. In that first conflict, Chrétien establishes a direct connection between his story of the struggle for the throne of Constantinople and the Oedipus myth. Chrétien's model for the threatened war between Alexander and Alis is the war over the throne of Thebes fought between the sons of Oedipus, Eteocles and Polynices, the fratricidal war which endangered the social order.

When Alexander returns from Arthur's court with a company of men and threatens to take the throne by force, Alis's barons refuse to support him. Chrétien says, "But none of them supported him in the war; they all say that he should remember the war Polynices undertook against Eteocles, his brother-german, and how they died at each other's hands. 'So it may happen with you, if you go to war and destroy the land'" (Chrétien, 1957, ll. 2496–2505; my translation).

The Middle Ages knew the story of Oedipus primarily through the *Thebaid* of Statius (*c.* 40–96 A.D.), the source of the first extant romance, the Anglo-Norman *Le Roman de Thebes* (*c.* 1150). In the *Roman*, the story of Oedipus, Laius, and Jocasta occupies only 500 lines in a work of over 10,000. The discovery of the incest is dealt with in a few lines, and the work gets on with its main concern, the war between Eteocles and Polynices. The poem ends, after the death of the brothers and most of their supporters and the destruction of the city, with a reference back to Oedipus and the admonition to do nothing against nature to merit such punishment.

Unlike the *Thebaid*, which is largely concerned with guilt, *Le Roman de Thebes* primarily reflects medieval fears of disorderly succession, fears appropriate enough in this anarchic period between the death of Henry I in 1135 and the accession of Henry II in 1154, when England was torn by the wars between Stephen and Matilda, and when Louis VII in France had not yet produced a male heir. Once Oedipus kills his father and takes Jocasta and the throne, the social order is destroyed and anarchy threatens.

The war between the brothers is simply another stage in the working out of destiny, a repetition of their father's parricide and incest. The fratricidal war symbolizes an anarchic society in which hierarchical principles have been abandoned and every man strives for his own good. The agreement of the brothers to alternate the throne between them is doomed to failure because, for medieval (and classical) audiences, contractual agreements (laws) are not yet a convincing substitute for patriarchal hierarchy.

Freud never mentioned this fratricidal aftermath of the oedipal crime. Instead, he rewrote his own version of the fate of the brothers in his own Lamarckian "myth" of parricide in the patriarchal horde in *Totem and Taboo* (1913, pp. 156–157). (For an argument that Lamarckianism was central to Freud's thought, see Horden [1985, p. 18].) In Freud's version, the murder of the father is followed by the brothers' renunciation of incest in order to avoid killing each other over possession of the mother and sisters. For Freud, the killing of the primal father opens the door to a contractually based civilization of law. This anthropological fantasy is Freud's fairy tale, his own *Néo-Oedipus*, the new myth that Freud elaborated in the abandoned essays recently published by Ilse Grubrich-Simitis (1987).

The contradiction between Freud's citing of Sophocles's *Oedipus Rex* as an affirmation of the universality of his theory of the Oedipus complex, on the one hand, and his re-writing the classical aftermath of the murder of the father, on the other, reveals the importance of what is at stake. Freud's myth of the evolution of human society from murder to law seems to be an analogy for the successful psychoanalytic process itself, an analogy that denies Freud's darker thoughts on both human nature and on the possibilities of therapeutic cure.

Like Chrétien's re-writing of the Tristan legend, Freud's re-writing of the Oedipus myth holds out the wished-for possibility that displacement of the father need not have tragic consequences. In the aftermath of the father's murder in the primal horde, according to Freud's myth, the brothers were able to break the cycle of murder and incest. Law, the product of the ego, was substituted for patriarchal despotism as a successful structure for ordering society. The myth seems to represent Freud's hope for the possibility of human progress, a progress to be aided by the new science he had created. The fragility of that hope is underscored by the publication date of *Totem and Taboo* the year before the outbreak of World War I.

Like Freud's new myth, Chrétien's textual re-writing of the Tristan/Oedipus myth is rooted in contemporary aesthetic and social issues. A clue about the nature of this relationship between text and social context comes, unexpectedly, in the narrative space seemingly most removed from any reflection of current realities—the secret garden in which Cligés hides Fenice after her simulated death.

Without a fundamental restructuring of society that reconciles desire and law, desire can be realized only in fantasy locations outside the social world, in lovers' worlds hidden from the eye of the Father. Such worlds, specifically marked as fantastic even within the fiction of the romance, are integral to romance as a genre. They have about them the aura of the past, the unknown, the spirit world, the world of the dead.

The Cave of Lovers in *Tristan* and the secret garden in *Cligés* are both timeless worlds outside the central narrative space, static palaces of art decorated with sculpture, gold, and jewels. They are realms of pure pleasure, where the lovers pass time by making love and telling stories. But these Edens of wish fulfillment are unstable, temporary interludes only, because they are cut off from society, from the supporting nexus of social relationships and intercourse which constitute human life.

Just as they are outside of time, these hidden worlds seem outside of language as well. The authors can only describe them at a distance, in the same way that they describe the sexual act itself. No dialogue is reported, no details given. These *loci amoeni* seem to exist in the pre-linguistic, pre-social world of the Lacanian Imaginary, rather than in the socially inscribed world of the Symbolic.

In both romances, the lovers are discovered by agents of the Father and forced to return to the social world and their socially inscribed destinies. But the difference in the histories of how these retreats of the Imaginary were constructed gives some clues to the differences between the destinies themselves. The Cave of Lovers in Gottfried von Strassburg's *Tristan* was carved into a wild mountainside by giants in pagan prehistory. The realm of the Imaginary remains a world of oral legend, a world that can be briefly glimpsed through art (or dream), but a world outside the Symbolic, with no access to the social.

In *Cligés*, on the other hand, the tower to which Cligés takes Fenice, with its subterranean chambers and enclosed garden, has been constructed in time by Jehan, Cligés's serf, an artist bound to Cligés within the feudal system of obligations. When Cligés decides to ask Jehan to build a hidden place for Fenice, Jehan's position as artist and serf seem equally important. Cligés says of him:

> There is a master craftsman [mestre] whom I can ask to do this, who inlays and sculpts marvelous things. There is no land where he is not known for the works he has made and carved and engraved. Jehan is his name, and he is my serf. There is no craft, no matter how diverse,

in which he could not surpass all others if he was intent upon it; next to him, all others are novices, like a child with a nurse. The artisans of Antioch and Rome have learned everything they know by imitating him; and, there is no man more loyal. (1957, ll. 5314–5328)

There is a link between Jehan and Chrétien himself in their role as artists. By placing the construction of the tower in the narrative present rather than the legendary past, Chrétien draws an analogy between the tower as a palace of art and his own poem, his *Néo-Tristan*, which is also a creation of the new, re-written present rather than the invariable past of oral tradition. Just as Jehan is free to design his tower according to his own wishes because he is the master craftsman, so Chrétien, the master craftsman of the new genre and the French language, designs his work according to his own insights and concerns.

Cligés is a new text, a new inscription not bound by the received tragic orientation of the older Tristan story. Exact reproduction is crucial in oral tradition (and in mythology in general) if contact with the authoritative past is to be maintained. Oral storytellers can elaborate, but they cannot change outcomes, since to do so would violate the pattern of audience anticipation and satisfaction upon which the oral aesthetic depends. The creation of a vernacular literature in the twelfth century is achieved at the moment when scribes, entrusted with *copying* in order to preserve divine writing unchanged, become *writers*.

So the hyperbole in Cligés's description of Jehan's abilities serves to call attention to artistic creation itself and to the status of *Cligés* as a created text. But this elaboration of Jehan's excellence as an artist also serves to intensify the sense of dislocation and rupture when Cligés enlists his help 100 lines later by referring to his status as a serf and offering to free him:

"Jehan, do you know what I wish to say? You are my serf, I am your master, for I can give away or sell your body and your goods, like anything else which is mine. But if I could entrust myself to you in something I am planning, I will make you free for the rest of your days, and the heirs which you may have." And Jehan, who greatly desires freedom, responds immediately: "Sire," he said, "there is nothing you can imagine that I would not do in order to see myself a free man, and my wife and children free." (1957, ll. 5427–5441)

These lines pose the danger of an anachronistic overreading for modern readers. But these startling aporia, these exposures of the seams of medieval class relations, are characteristic of Chrétien's work, and the issues raised in this passage recapitulate the central concerns of *Cligés*. Like Fenice, Jehan's mind and heart are free to create and to desire, but his body is the possession of another. The sign of freedom would be the ability to pass on his status as a freeman to his own heirs, just as Alexander wanted to pass the throne to Cligés, his heir.

So if the shift from oral tradition to written text, copying to rewriting, is one dimension of the new possibilities encoded in Chrétien's *Néo-Tristan*, the evolving social system of twelfth-century Champagne which lies behind Cligés's offer to make Jehan a free man is another. Romance has usually been thought of as an aristocratic genre reflecting the interests and world view of the feudal ruling class, a genre patronized in particular by aristocratic women from the highest levels of French and Anglo-Norman society, women like Eleanor of Acquitaine and Marie de Champagne. Erich Auerbach's (1953) treatment of romance in *Mimesis* as the genre of an aristocracy sealing itself off from bourgeois interlopers by developing courtly codes of behavior has been widely influential. But, in fact, both of these hypotheses need revision. There is little or no evidence that women like Eleanor or Marie actually read or patronized romance, and the last half of the twelfth century in Champagne was a period when knights were entering the aristocracy for the first time. Before the twelfth century, knights were paid mercenaries who held fiefs from their feudal lords in a vassalage relationship, but who did not have hereditary rights to the land and could neither keep it after leaving the lord's service nor pass it on to their heirs. By the end of the twelfth century in Champagne, knights had legal status as aristocrats and could bequeath their fiefs (Evergates, 1975, pp. 93–98; 109–115, 130, 145–151). This change in legal status and in the right to bequeath fiefs is the social subtext of the inheritance issue in *Cligés*.

There is a parallel in *Cligés* between the social position of Jehan as a serf who cannot dispose of his own body, Soredamors as a ward of Arthur to be married to whomever he chooses, and Fenice as the unwilling bride of Alis. All three are powerless to determine their own fate within the traditional limits of feudal society; all three are given a degree of autonomy within the structure of Chrétien's fiction.

This linkage between women, as members of a structurally subordinate sex within medieval society, and men from the lower levels of the class hierarchy, is constitutive of romance as a genre. The genesis of romance as a genre is not due to the experiences of any single social group like the aristocracy, as has been held traditionally, but rather to the experiences of several groups that were all moving up in the social hierarchy: knights, members of the newly established bourgeoisie, the bureaucrats and clerks attached to the courts of kings and great feudal lords, and women.

Knights serve as a model for all of these groups because knights, as a class, were the most socially successful and fit most easily into traditional social classifications. The aspirations of all these groups are supported by what Georges Duby (1968) has called the ideology of *chevalerie*, an ideology that valued individual merit and behavior, as opposed to lineage and wealth, the basis of *nobilitas*, the more traditional ideology of the upper level of the aristocracy.

Romances are still several centuries away from having non-aristocratic heroes, and the fact that the characters who best demonstrate the qualities of *chevalerie* are usually the sons of kings speaks for the essentially conservative nature of romance and its assumption that the social order is basically just. But on the other hand, romance heroes usually move at some point in the narrative from a position as disguised or unknown outsiders to positions at the center of society through their own efforts in the stylized arenas of tournament, war, and love. Alexander's trip to Arthur's court is one example, Cligés's disguise at the Three Day Tournament is another.

This pattern of movement from obscurity to fame is basic to romance and suggests that social mobility, theoretically impossible in feudal society but actually occurring in the twelfth century, was one of the basic fantasies encoded in romance narratives. The recognition of this social change and the encouragement of these fantasies is one of the elements responsible for the differences between *Tristan* and *Cligés*. The world of the *Tristan* is static and tragic, drawing its authority from the past; *Cligés* embraces a changing social order.

In *Tristan*, Mark is blameless, caught in a system that allows him no options, a victim of the love potion just like Tristan and Isolt themselves. In *Cligés*, Alis is characteristically treacherous, a plotter and oath-breaker, and his guilt is used to exonerate Cligés and Fenice and clear the way for a resolution of desire and the social order, the Imaginary and the Symbolic.

THE LAW OF THE FATHER RETURNS

The importance of social mobility as a subtext helps explain the centrality of women in medieval romance, as opposed to their relative unimportance in epic or *chanson de geste*. Women function in romance both as a sign for the lower structural position in social and power hierarchies and as the means to social mobility. Hypergamy was the most common way for poor knights to increase their wealth and social position, and the production of heirs and the ability to bequeath property to them were signs of aristocratic status.

This change in the position of women in the social/semiotic system of feudal society opened up a space for the investigation of internal states, for the creation of a new vocabulary in romance for emotions and feelings. If women have a voice in the selection of their husbands, love and personal characteristics become newly relevant. A new vocabulary for relationships between mind and body is necessary, a vocabulary that does more than simply reject the body in favor of the mind. Since women's bodies are now the site for reconciling the conflicting demands of desire and social responsibility, this new romance vocabulary is necessarily sexual, political, and textual.

Just as *Cligés* as a work is a re-writing of *Tristan*, so Fenice sees herself in terms of her fictional prototype, Isolt, and re-writes her own life in order to avoid Isolt's duality of heart (desire) and body (the social/political sphere). The body of Isolt/Fenice is a part of the social/political sphere because within the feudal system of social relationships, a woman's body is seen primarily as a machine for the production of noble heirs. Those heirs are the legitimate children inscribed within the legal system as eligible to inherit property, thereby establishing the property and kinship relationships that serve as the basis of political alliances.

When Fenice realizes her love for Cligés, she refers directly to the Tristan story and repudiates Isolt's behavior: "I could not accept the life that Isolt led. Her love was base [*trop vilena*] because her heart belonged entirely to one, and her body was possessed by two [*Que ses cuers fu a un entiers,* / *Et ses cors fu a deus rentiers]"* (1957, ll. 3110–3114). The choice of rhyme is illuminating, because *entiers* also has the sense of virginal and chaste, and *rentiers* has the sense both of one who is sequestered and one who pays rent. Thus, from the point of view of women, sexual relations are seen as both imprisonment and property relations.

Fenice interprets Isolt's story in terms of a heart and body dualism in which the tragedy results from Isolt's inability to reconcile the desires of her heart with the demands made on her body by the social system, an inability to make inner perceptions and feelings coherent with external behavior. The distinction between *cuers* and *cors* is a distinction between the fantasy body, the desiring heart on the one hand, and the body as machine, as possession. The *cuers* is the desiring subject, the exchanger of signs; the *cors* is the desired object, the sign. Fenice rejects the fragmentation of experience that would be caused by sharing her body between two men, a fragmentation threatened in literal terms in the episode with the doctors. Her deception of her husband with the magic potion is a temporary strategy for retaining her integrity of heart and body, desire and behavior.

In the same way, the coronation of Cligés and Fenice which follows their marriage reunites the society by reuniting moral and legal authority with the actual possession of power. The love theme and the social/political theme in *Cligés* are inextricably intertwined. Just as Alis's refusal to relinquish the throne to Alexander when he returns to Constantinople creates a threat of civil war, so his marriage to Fenice is an attempt to deny Cligés his rightful inheritance. When Fenice says that she will never be the cause of Cligés's disinheritance by bearing Alis a child (1957, ll. 3133–3136; 3148–3153), she establishes the connection between love and social role, between her body as subject and as sign.

Given this semiotic complex, Fenice's association through her name with the immortal phoenix (Fenix) marks her role as a producer of heirs. This equation of heirs with immortality was a common theme in the twelfth century, even though it seemingly contradicts Christian doctrine. John of Salisbury, a twelfth-century English humanist and philosopher, saw the hope of rulers for earthly immortality through heirs as one of their strongest desires. Therefore, social control of the rights of inheritance seemed one of the strongest ways to control the power of princes. In this passage from the *Policraticus,* a work completed in 1159, John of Salisbury (1927) ascribes the origin of inheritance to pagan, pre-Christian times; but inheritance was just as much of an issue for Christian rulers in the twelfth century:

> For I know that the law was speaking to a carnal people, who having as yet a heart of stone and being uncircumcised of mind if not of the flesh, were still for the most part ignorant of eternal life, and set chief store by having the good things of the earth. . . .
>
> And so to the carnally minded a carnal promise was given, and a long duration of time was promised to those who had not yet conceived the hope of eternal blessedness; and the prospect of a temporal kingdom with succession from father to son was held out to men who as yet did not seek an eternal one. . . .
>
> But, since there is nought which men more desire than to have their sons succeed them in their possessions, even as men foreseeing that death is an incident of their mortal state seek to prolong their own existence in the heirs of their body, therefore this promise is given to princes as the greatest incentive to the practice of justice. (pp. 48, 50)

But on the deeper level of the oedipal fantasy, the desire represented by Fenice/Phoenix is not simply a wish to gain a substitute immortality through heirs; it is a desire for personal immortality, a desire to inherit but not bequeath, a desire to stop time in one's own moment. The first part of *Cligés* ends with the birth of Cligés and the deaths of Alexander and Soredamors. The second part does not replicate this pattern by ending with the birth of children to Cligés and Fenice; it stops instead at the pinnacle of their success: the "happily ever after" ending of fairy tales and romance.

The notion that the desire for the mother in the oedipal fantasy is, at least in part, a desire for immortality was central to the work of Otto Rank after he broke with Freudian orthodoxy. Rank suggested in *Modern Education* (1964, p. 306) that the oedipal fantasy represents a wish to beget oneself on the mother and be reborn from her in a timeless circle of birth and rebirth. Harold Bloom (1973) says in *The Anxiety of Influence*:

> Freud's poem, in the view of this book, is not severe enough, unlike the severe poems written by the creative lives of the strong poets. To equate emotional maturation with the discovery of acceptable substitutes may be pragmatic wisdom, particularly in the realm of Eros, but this is not the wisdom of the strong poets. The surrendered dream is not merely a phantasmagoria of endless gratification, but is the greatest of all human illusions, the vision of immortality. (p. 9)

For Rank, and perhaps for Bloom as well, the oedipal dream of possessing the mother seems separable from the fear of castration. Rank replaces fear of castration with fear of separation from the mother as the primary source of anxiety; Bloom turns blindness into insight, misreading into creativity. For both, fear can be overcome by the creative artistic will.

For Chrétien, however, even in his *Néo-Tristan*, the poisoned wound in the loins that destroys Tristan is not so easily avoided. The Law-of-the-Father re-enters the garden in Jehan's tower when Bertran, Alis's man, climbs over the wall and discovers the naked lovers. Cligés has his sword with him and manages to cut off Bertran's leg, giving the castrating wound rather than receiving it. But the lovers are forced to flee their new Eden, re-enacting the expulsion of Adam and Eve.

This persistence of castration anxiety at the center of the fantasy suggests another meaning for the identification of Fenice with the legendary phoenix, beyond her illusory death and rebirth. In his essay "The Acquisition and Control of Fire" (1932), Freud suggested a symbolic equivalence between the phoenix and the phallus. Having established an equivalence between Prometheus's liver (the organ consumed by the vulture and regrown everyday as punishment for the theft of fire) and the phallus, Freud goes on to say:

> A short step further brings us to the phoenix, the bird which, as often as it is consumed by fire, emerges rejuvenated once more, and which probably bore the significance of a penis revivified after its collapse rather than, and earlier than, that of the sun setting in the glow of evening and afterwards rising once again. (p. 191)

This identification of a woman with the phallus seems a strange reversal of expectations, and, in fact, medieval poems and bestiaries refer to the phoenix as masculine when they identify its sex. But Lacan's understanding of the phallus as a signifier rather than an organ helps to explain how Fenice can be the phoenix, the phallic signifier. In the essay from *Écrits* translated as "The direction of the treatment and the principles of its power" (Lacan, 1977), Lacan reports a dream recounted to his impotent patient by the man's mistress. In the dream, the woman tells the patient, she has a phallus, which she can feel under her clothes, but this does not prevent her from having a vagina as well, nor from wanting this phallus to enter it. On hearing the dream recounted, Lacan says, the patient's virility is immediately restored.

On the simplest level, Lacan suggests, the discovery that the woman has a phallus removes the patient's fear of castration. If the dreamer has a phallus, she will not have to take it from the patient, and his fear of his castrating mother, repeated in his relation with his mistress, is allayed. On the other hand, Lacan warns, we must not be misled by "this assurance that the subject receives from the fact that the dreamer has a phallus, that she will not have to take it from him — except to point out, wisely, that such an assurance is too strong not to be fragile." For Lacan, the assurance carries weight precisely because it impresses itself in a sign, and because it makes the sign appear where it cannot be in biological terms, because it is a "denial of nature" (pp. 265–269).

In a similar way, "courtly love," as it has been called since Gaston Paris coined the term in an article on Chrétien's *Lancelot* in 1883, is seen by Chrétien himself as a denial (or inversion) of nature. Courtly love is a fantasy system in which the normal roles or positions of men and women in the medieval hierarchy are reversed. The Middle Ages did not invent romantic love, but the concept was reformulated in troubadour poetry on the model of the strongest non-kinship relationship in the society, the relationship between lord and vassal, and, in particular, on the hoped for generosity of the lord and the reciprocal devotion of the vassal.

In a reversal of the accepted medieval male/female hierarchy, the lover declares himself a vassal and addresses the lady as his lord. The occitane term *midons*, used to address the lady, is a combination of the feminine possession *mia* and the masculine *dominus* (lord). Knights occasionally had their shields engraved with their hands placed between the clasped hands of their ladies, the symbolic gesture of submission used in the homage ceremony. Thus, there seems to be a linkage between the sexual relationship of lover and beloved, and the property relationship of vassal and lord, embedded in the courtly love fantasy system, a linkage that implies reversal of "natural" (i.e., received or conventional) hierarchies.

Chrétien describes the love affair of Cligés and Fenice in terms of a similar disruption of natural hierarchies in a digression on the art of love occasioned by the lovers' fears about voicing their love.

Chrétien sees Fenice's fear as natural, since she is a young girl, while Cligés's fear is unnatural. "It seems to me," Chrétien says,

> as if I should see dogs flee before a hare, and a crab hunt a beaver, a lamb a wolf, a pigeon an eagle, as if a peasant fled from his spade which gives him life and work, and a falcon fled from a duck, a gyrfalcon from a heron, a pike from a minnow, as if a stag should hunt a lion, and all things would be reversed." (1957, ll. 3802–3812)

The association of Fenice with the phoenix/phallus is another such reversal, perhaps the most basic one. The power of the signifier in the fantasy depends, as Lacan suggests, on its "impossibility," its reversal of nature. It is this impossible reversal that suggests the possibility of change in the social system, the desire that determines the formation of romance as a genre.

What Lacan describes is a dream retold within the context of a particular relationship. But something like this fantasy seems, in twelfth-century France, to have taken on a much more widespread character due to changes in the social, legal, and economic environment. The reversal of sexual hierarchy that constitutes the courtly love fantasy system seems to have become widespread because it articulates, on the level of fantasy, changes in the social and economic systems that cannot be voiced within the more conservative speech of medieval political theory.

Romance, as a genre, is the new discourse that voices changes like the rise of the knights to aristocratic status, the newly acquired right of women to inherit property (thereby making them avenues of social mobility for propertyless knights), and the aspirations of other structurally similar groups within the society. *Cligés*, as a specific text, uses the Arthurian and Oedipal myths to give authority to Chrétien's articulation of these social changes, drawing the cloak of antiquity around his re-writing of the Tristan legend.

But social change is not achieved without a price, even in fantasy. A change that favors the son over the father (Cligés over Alis) necessarily invokes castration anxiety within the oedipal fantasy structure, an anxiety that the guilt of the father is not enough to allay. *Cligés* temporarily solves the fear of castration connected with oedipal desire by displacing the punishment onto the woman. The displacement of guilt onto the father-figure is already anticipated in some versions of the Oedipus story, but the displacement of punishment onto the woman, through the torture and symbolic death and rebirth of Fenice, seems to represent something more than a simple repetition of Jocasta's suicide.

The torture of Fenice is sacrificial and redemptive, a medieval contribution to the oedipal fantasy system written on the body of Fenice, a contribution with far-reaching implications for the subsequent development of Western narrative. Romance as a genre establishes the problems of desire as the preeminent topic for Western fiction, and it is tempting to see prefigured in the torture of Fenice the fates of Clarissa Harlowe, Anna Karenina, and Emma Bovary, among others, all female martyrs to male desire.

Fenice, conscious, but lying in a death-like coma brought on by Thessala's drug, is tortured by the doctors from Salerno in a scene that seems drawn from a saint's life and is referred to in the text as martyrdom (1957, l. 5941). In order to make Fenice admit she is only feigning death, the doctors strip her, beat her with leather thongs until her flesh is torn, pour boiling lead through her palms, and finally prepare to place her on a grill and roast her over a fire before they are stopped by her ladies.

The fire, suggesting the fire in which the legendary phoenix dies and is reborn, threatens to turn the simulated death into a real one. Cligés joins the mourners in earnest, not knowing whether Fenice will be alive or dead when he is able to rescue her from the tomb. Medieval bestiaries often associate the phoenix with the death and resurrection of Christ, and this sequence resonates with allusions to Christ's flagellation, crucifixion, burial, and resurrection. By taking Cligés's place and undergoing the torture and symbolic death that makes their life together possible, Fenice becomes a sacrificial Christ figure, sparing Cligés the symbolic castrating wounds suffered by Chrétien's other heroes (Erec, Yvain, and Lancelot).

This merger of mythological streams, Greek and Middle Eastern, Oedipus and Christ, tragedy and romance, makes it possible to imagine a world in which change is possible. The tragic legacy of Oedipus is passed on to his sons, but Christ's sacrifice breaks the chain of guilt and punishment, making possible a new restructuring of society, a new beginning. The phoenix links the mystery of sexuality with the mysteries of birth and death, with guilt and redemption; it is a fitting name for the heroine in this new text of desire.

And yet, as Lacan (1977) suggests in another context, the reversal of sexual roles and the assignment of the phallus to Fenice upon which this fantasy solution rests is "too strong not to be fragile." The idyll in Jehan's garden, a figure of the Garden of Eden, is unstable because it is based on a "denial of nature." When Bertran, as the agent of the Father, discovers the two lovers asleep in each other's arms in the garden, they are naked, like Adam and Eve. Fenice awakens first, and cries out to Cligés that they are dead (*nos somes mort* [1957, 1. 6382]). Cligés wakes, and Chrétien tells us that he has brought his sword into the garden with him and laid it down beside him. Cligés takes the sword and cuts off Bertran's leg as he flees over the wall; but Bertran escapes, and the lovers are forced to flee, exiled from paradise.

This moment — the discovery of the naked lovers, the assertion that Cligés has the sword, the symbolic castration of Bertran, and the exile from the garden — seems a mythic recapitulation of a crucial moment in the psychic life of the child. This determining moment is the moment when, in Freudian terms, the child discovers that the mother is "castrated," that the mother "does not have it," as Lacan puts it in his essay on "The Signification of the Phallus" (1977, p. 289). The moment of discovery in the garden reveals that it is Cligés, not Fenice, who "has" the phallus (the sword), even though the fantasy depends on sexual reversal, on Fenice being the phoenix, the phallic mother. This discovery exiles the pair from the garden, into the world of the Father.

Of this moment, Lacan says, "Here is signed the conjunction [*conjonction*] of desire, in that the phallic signifier is its mark, with the threat or nostalgia of lacking it," that is, with the threat of castration for the male subject and nostalgia (or *Penisneid*) for the female subject (p. 289). This remark recalls Lacan's much quoted statement several lines earlier: "The phallus is the privileged signifier of that mark in which the role of the logos is joined with [*se conjoindre a*] the advent of desire" (p. 287).

Jane Gallop (1985), in her illuminating discussion of this key passage, notes that *conjonction* is the nominative form of the verb *conjoindre*, which commonly means not only "conjoin," but also "marry." (Rose translates Lacan's clause as "where the share of the logos is *wedded to* the advent of desire.") Gallop goes on, "In the first quotation we are considering, a 'conjunction is *signed*': legally binding, a marriage contract between desire and the castration complex. Desire shall henceforth be wed to castration because the phallic signifier is the mark of desire" (p. 145).

But *conjoindre* also recalls Chrétien's *une molt bele conjointure*, the phrase he uses to distinguish his work from the inferior efforts of his predecessors. The word has always been understood as having to do with narrative structure, but it is also true that one of Chrétien's most original notions is the development of *marriage* as a solution to the problems of desire raised in his fictions, as the resolution that joins desire and law, desire and the castration complex, to borrow Lacan's insights. There is something striking in the use of the same word by these two masters of the inscription of desire in the French language, Chrétien and Lacan, a pairing perhaps made less surprising by Lacan's frequent passing references to medieval French literature.

Romance then becomes the genre in which desire is wedded to castration, the collection of texts in which the role of the logos is joined with the advent of desire, in which a discourse of desire (rather than satisfaction or demand) is created. As a genre, romance is limited by the two poles represented by *Tristan* and *Cligés* (the *Néo-Tristan*), by the text that delivers the full weight of the Law of the Father and realizes the castration threat, and the text that goes as far as possible toward displacing the threat and subverting the Law for the oedipal hero's benefit.

Romance, like mythology in general, looks to the past. But more than simply looking to the past, romance is primarily a genre of nostalgia, a genre that longs for the lost golden age of the Arthurian past. That golden age is the era when the symbolic Father, the dead Father insofar as he signifies the Law of the castration complex, was still alive, still able to make modifications of the kind that save Cligés and Fenice.[3] The longing, or nostalgia, that romance represents, then, is a longing to return to the mother's womb, to Eden, joined with the realization that such a return is impossible. As Gallop (1985) puts it:

> If we understand the nostalgia resulting from the discovery of the mother's castration in this way, then the discovery that the mother does not have the phallus means that the subject can never return to the womb. Somehow the fact that the mother is not phallic means that the mother as mother is lost forever, that the mother as womb, home-

land, source, and grounding for the subject is irretrievably past. The
subject is hence in a foreign land, alienated. (p. 148)

For Lacan, there is no fundamental difference between Freud's
version of the Oedipus myth (which he calls "the latest born myth in
history") and the story of "the forbidden apple," the story of Adam
and Eve in the Garden of Eden, except that the Oedipus myth is
"distinctly less oppressive (*crétinisant*)." Both are versions of the myth
of original sin; what is real, according to Lacan (1977, pp. 317–318),
is the castration complex.

Exiled from the garden, Cligés and Fenice are thrown back into
history in the still mythic Arthurian time, when the Father has not
yet died at the hands of his son(s) on Salisbury Plain, the time of
romance when Arthur can still intervene in the name of Law, when
happy endings are still possible. But Chrétien does not end his romance there; he returns, instead, to his own time, to twelfth-century
France. Through a cryptic reference, almost a riddle, to modern
emperors and empresses and the dynastic struggles of his own day,
Chrétien returns us to the "troubled house of Oedipus" of Richard of
Devises, and to the overt meaning of the Oedipus myth for twelfth-
century writers.

At the end of the romance, after Cligés and Fenice return to
Constantinople in triumph, Chrétien tells us that Cligés makes his
lover (*s'amie*) his wife (*sa dame*), but that she has no cause for com-
plaint because he still loves her as a lover, and she him. He never
doubted her, Chrétien says, she never blamed him for anything.
Their union represents the impossible equivalence of desire and
demand, impossible (for Lacan) because desire is unsatisfiable, because desire is what remains after any particular articulation of
need, any specific demand, has been satisfied.

As a sign of this perfect union, Chrétien tells us that Cligés
never kept Fenice confined, as so many women who lived after that
time have been. But ever since, he adds, the emperors in Constantinople have kept their wives confined because they are afraid their
wives will deceive them, as Fenice deceived Alis (1957, ll. 6633–
6663). These final lines return the audience to the twelfth century,
out of the mythic past when a married couple could still be lovers,
when desire and law could be joined. In the present, there is only
Alis and Fenice, only marriages joined for property and for dynastic

motives. This is the world of Law, not justice, the castrated world of the Symbolic.

Chrétien is referring directly to the Byzantine emperors, but it is difficult not to see this coda as a covert reference to Henry II, who imprisoned his wife, Eleanor of Acquitaine, in 1174, two years before the writing of *Cligés*, for what turned out to be the rest of his life. Eleanor was imprisoned for her support of the rebellion against Henry by their son, the Young King as he was called, a rebellion supported by the Louis VII, the king of France, and the powerful Philip of Flanders. Henry's struggles with his sons were replicated in the sons' struggles with each other, particularly those of Richard and John.

All of this had an oedipal resonance that was not lost on medieval chroniclers, who used the Oedipus myth as a way of understanding the Angevin dynasty. Richard of Devises, a Winchester monk writing in the last decade of the twelfth century, begins his life of Richard I with this statement: "And so that this little book may have a beginning of some importance, I have started a little earlier than we agreed, and the boundary of my work is 'the troubled house of Oedipus' ['*Edipode confusa domus*']" (Richard of Devises, 1927, p. 3). The phrase has been taken from the *Thebaid* of Statius (1:17), and the casual way it is used suggests that the association was a common one.

Since Henry II died in 1189 in the midst of a war with Richard, it would seem that Richard is intended as Oedipus, and Henry as Laius. But, in fact, Devises identifies Richard and John as Eteocles and Polynices, making Henry himself Oedipus. This interpretation sees the struggles of Richard and John over the thrones of England and Acquitaine as an outcome of Henry's oedipal transgression, just as the war for the throne of Thebes followed from the sacrilege of Oedipus. Devises moves the oedipal rebellion back a generation in order to absolve Richard, establishing that his rebellion against his father's wish to bequeath Acquitaine to John is simply an inevitable outcome of Henry's own transgressions.

If Henry II is Oedipus, then Eleanor, 12 years older than Henry, and Louis VII of France are Jocasta and Laius. Henry married Eleanor secretly after Louis divorced her, secretly because he was Louis's vassal for his lands in France as was Eleanor, and Louis would not have approved a marriage that gave Henry so much French territory. The grounds for the divorce of Louis and Eleanor was consanguinity; the real reason was lack of heirs. But Henry and Eleanor were no less closely related than Louis and Eleanor, and their marriage made something of a mockery of the divorce, as well as violating the feudal ties of both Henry and Eleanor to Louis.

William of Newburgh (1136–c. 1200), author of a chronicle on the reign of Stephen, attributes the conflict between Henry and his sons to his marriage with Eleanor and its violation of their obligations to Louis (Brandt, 1973, pp. 151–152). That this violation of the vassal–lord relationship was seen by medieval writers as a kind of incest is indicated by a story fabricated by Gerald of Wales in his *De Principis Instructione*. According to Gerald, Henry was warned by his father, Geoffrey, to have nothing to do with Eleanor both because she was the wife of his lord, Louis, and because *Geoffrey himself* had committed adultery with her, thereby making any relationship between Henry and Eleanor incestuous (Appleby, 1962, p. 26). It is difficult to imagine a clearer demonstration of the conscious connections for twelfth-century writers between the Oedipus myth, incest, violation of feudal ties, and contemporary political history.

So finally, then, Chrétien's *Cligés* is a text that uses the mythologies of the House of Oedipus and the days of King Arthur to create a new narrative discourse about desire and society, a discourse set within the social issues and changes of twelfth-century France and rooted in the deepest levels of human fantasy. This linkage between the oedipal fantasy system and social theory is coherent because incest is also a social crime, a violation of the bonds that hold society together.

Lévi-Strauss (1968) has argued that incest is the most fundamental crime against society because society has always been founded upon the exchange of women by men. The refusal to exchange women between family groups is a refusal to establish the ties of communication and mutual interest that hold the larger society together (see also Mitchell, 1975, pp. 370–376). From a patriarchal point of view, the view of the Middle Ages, marriage as a system serves to protect and certify patriarchal lineage. The central concern in *Cligés* with lineage and inheritance reveals a basic anxiety within the patriarchal *nobilitas* ideology, an ideology subverted by both courtly love and the *chevalerie* of the romances.

But the break with patriarchal authority is costly and only temporary, even in a text that goes as far as any work in the genre toward licensing the oedipal rebellion. Payment for the transgression is shifted to the woman, the fantasy of the phallic mother being clearly unstable even within the work, and Chrétien ends with a coda that places the work in the mythic past and returns abruptly to present realities. The future of romance in the thirteenth-century vulgate cycles is a future of sexual renunciation in the grail romances, not a reconciliation of desire and social structure.

But for twelfth-century France, *Cligés* does articulate, perhaps more clearly than any other romance, the combination of sexual and social issues at the heart of the genre and, most strikingly, a fantasy solution that allows the realization of those desires. In the *conjointure* of desire and marriage that characterizes *Cligés*, Chrétien inscribed a new language of desire that influenced European fiction well into the nineteenth century.

NOTES

1. For a survey of non-psychoanalytic versions of the Oedipus story, see Edmunds (1985). For an early attempt to summarize psychoanalytic use of the Oedipus myth as a paradigm for the complex, see Mullahy (1948).
2. *L'amour et l'Occident* was translated by Montgomery Belgion and published in both English and American editions in 1940. The American edition was titled *Love in the Western World*; the English edition was titled, interestingly in the context of this paper, *Passion and Society*.
3. On the dead Father, see Lacan's (1977) essay "On the possible treatment of psychosis" (p. 199).

REFERENCES

APPLEBY, J. T. (1962) *Henry II: The Vanquished King*. London: G. Bell & Sons.
AUERBACH, E. (1953) The Knight Sets Forth. In *Mimesis: The Representation of Reality in Western Literature* (Willard R. Trask, Trans.). Princeton, NJ: Princeton University Press.
BALMARY, M. (1982) *Psychoanalyzing Psychoanalysis: Freud and the Hidden Fault of the Father* (Ned Lukacher, Trans.). Baltimore: Johns Hopkins University Press.
BLOOM, H. (1973) *The Anxiety of Influence*. New York: Oxford University Press.
BRANDT, W. J. (1973) *The Shape of Medieval History: Studies in Modes of Perception*. New York: Schocken.
CHASE, C. (1979) Oedipal Textuality: Reading Freud's Reading of *Oedipus*. *Diacritics*, 9(1):54–68.
CHRÉTIEN DE TROYES (1957) *Cligés* (Alexandre Micha, Ed.). Paris: Honore Champion.
DELEUZE, G., & GUATTARI, F. (1972) *Anti-Oedipus: Capitalism and Schizophrenia* (Robert Hurley, Mark Seem, & Helen R. Lane, Trans.). New York: Viking, 1977.

Duby, G. (1968) The Diffusion of Cultural Patterns in Feudal Society. *Past & Present*, 39(April):3–10.

Edmunds, L. (1985) *Oedipus: The Ancient Legend and Its Later Analogs*. Baltimore: Johns Hopkins University Press.

Evergates, T. (1975) *Feudal Society in the Bailliage of Troyes under the Counts of Champagne, 1152–1284*. Baltimore: Johns Hopkins University Press.

Frappier, J. (1968) *Chrétien de Troyes*. Paris: Hatier.

Freud, S. (1900) The Interpretation of Dreams. *Standard Edition*, 4 & 5.

_____ (1913) Totem and Taboo. *Standard Edition*, 13:1–161.

_____ (1926) The Question of Lay Analysis. *Standard Edition*, 20:177–250.

_____ (1930) Civilization and Its Discontents. *Standard Edition*, 21:59–145.

_____ (1932) The Acquisition and Control of Fire. *Standard Edition*, 22:191.

Gallop, J. (1985) *Reading Lacan*. Ithaca, NY: Cornell University Press.

Grubrich-Simitis, I. (1987) *A Phylogenetic Fantasy*. Cambridge, MA: Harvard University Press.

Horden, P. (1985) Thoughts of Freud. In Peregrine Horden (Ed.), *Freud and the Humanities* (pp. 1–25). New York: St. Martin's Press.

John of Salisbury (1927) *The Statesman's Book of John of Salisbury, Being the Fourth, Fifth and Sixth Books, and Selections from the Seventh and Eighth Books, of the "Policraticus"* (John Dickinson, Ed.). New York: Alfred A. Knopf.

Lacan, J. (1936) Au delà du principe de réalité. *Evolution psychiatrique*, 3:67–86.

_____ (1953) Fonction et champ de la parole et du langage en psychanalyse (Rapport de Rome). *La Psychanalyse* (1956), 1:81–166.

_____ (1977) *Écrits: A Selection* (Alan Sheridan, Trans.). New York: Norton.

Lévi-Strauss, C. (1968) *Structural Anthropology*. (Claire Jacobson & Brooke Grundfest Schoepf, Trans.). London: Penguin.

Lukacher, N. (1986) *Primal Scenes: Literature, Philosophy, Psychoanalysis*. Ithaca, NY: Cornell University Press.

Mitchell, J. (1975) *Psychoanalysis and Feminism*. New York: Vintage.

Mullahy, P. (1948) *Oedipus: Myth and Complex*. New York: Hermitage.

Rank, O. (1964) *The Myth of the Birth of the Hero and Other Writings* (Philip Freund, Ed.). New York: Vintage.

Richard of Devises (1927) *The Chronicle of Richard of Devises of the Time of Richard the First* (John T. Appleby, Ed.). London: Thomas Nelson & Sons.

Rougemont, D. (1939) *L'amour et l'Occident*. Paris: Plon.

Tanner, T. (1979) *Adultery and the Novel: Contract and Transgression*. Baltimore: Johns Hopkins University Press.

Lehman College Library
City University of New York
Bedford Park Boulevard West
Bronx, NY 10468

LATE MEDIEVAL REPRESENTATIONS
OF SAINT MARY MAGDALENE

Edmund Leach

Many different types of scholar write about myth; they include psychoanalysts, students of comparative religion, anthropologists, but they seldom agree about the meaning of the term. Indeed, even in my own anthropological neck of the academic woods, I and my most celebrated colleague, Claude Lévi-Strauss, to whom I am very greatly indebted, use the word in entirely different senses. So I must start by explaining what I am talking about.

For me, a myth is any story about the past that is used in a religious, moral, or political context to justify an irrational belief about the present. A typical example is when a poster on a church notice board proclaims: "Jesus Lives." The various texts of the Christian Bible are all parts of a mythology that purports to justify belief in that assertion.

In vernacular discourse, the adjective "mythical" is the equivalent of "untrue" but in my argument the opposite is the case. For the believer, a myth is not just true but dogmatically true. In the present case, I shall concern myself only with religious contexts, mostly Christian.

As we have learned from Lévi-Strauss, individual myths cannot usefully be considered in isolation. They must be viewed as elements in a corpus that adds up to a cosmological system. This is a very crucial point. Myths are usually told one by one as if they were records of historical fact. Two stories, with characters of different names, that appear to be "patterned" in the same way (or perhaps in systematically opposite ways) are, from this "historical" point of view, different stories. But when viewed as part of a corpus, they may be considered as transformations of one and the same story. They add up; the message that they convey may be the same message in a different form. The biblical and non-biblical stories about "the repentent sinner" Mary Magdalene, with which this essay is primarily concerned, are all permutations of seemingly quite different stories about the "sinless" Virgin Mary.

The vast range of stories in the Hebrew Bible plus the Talmudic glosses thereon form a single mythology. The same is true of the Christian Bible and its Apocryphal additions. Furthermore, for the Christian, the Old Testament and the New Testament are interdependent. In either case, Jewish or Christian, the devout believer derives from his or her corpus of sacred books and sacred pictures a set of messages about the relationship between "this world" of mortal, morally corrupt, men and "the other world" of immortal, morally perfect, supernatural beings. But while the stories are partially shared, the differences of sectarian doctrine show that the messages are highly ambiguous. This is a characteristic of all mythological systems. There is no uniquely valid procedure for interpretation. One tries to avoid interpretation by pure hunch but some degree of guessing is unavoidable.

Nearly all religions presuppose the existence of other worldly, supernatural beings who are the counterpart of this worldly, of natural men. The limited potency of men is then viewed as a quality that is ultimately derived from the omnipotence of gods. In this cosmological framework, the central function of religious practice and religious storytelling (including the painting of religious pictures and the acting of religious drama) is to provide a bridge between this world and the other along which there can be a flow of potency from gods to men.

Judaism and Christianity belong to that very widespread class of religious systems which solve this problem of bridge-building by creating a category of semi-divine beings (god-men, divine kings, prophets, shamans, saints, heroes, priests) who have, as it were, a foot in both camps, and thereby act as intermediaries between gods and men. But, like Islam and Buddhism and unlike Hinduism, these two "major" religions have the peculiar characteristic that, in their now orthodox forms, they have failed to come to terms with the fact that half the human race is female! The idea of God is, to use Andrew Lang's phrase, a magnified non-natural man, not any kind of non-natural woman.

There is no obvious reason why deity should be viewed as either male or female; if it is one it is also the other. In the ancient world, as in modern India, the active potency of God was usually perceived as female or at any rate as half female: Isis, Ishtar, Aphrodite, Athena, Parvati, Durga, Kali. The earliest cult images discovered by archeologists have usually been interpreted as depicting "mother goddesses." But in Judaism, Christianity, and Islam, God is unambiguously male, or so it would at first appear.

Judaism however allows for "heroic" (but in various ways "abnormal") females — Miriam, Deborah, Jael, Judith, Rachab, Ruth, Naomi, Esther, and so forth — while Christianity, especially in its pre-Lutheran forms, comes very close to turning the Virgin Mary into a deity and credits a vast variety of local female saints with miraculous powers that are similar to those of the Holy Virgin.

There are good grounds for supposing that during the formative years of Christianity, prior to the middle of the second century A.D., doctrinal orthodoxy with regard to the sex of the deity was even less clear cut. Murray (1975, ch. 4) goes into all the intricate details. The pertinent chapter is entitled "The Church, Bride and Mother." The key theme is that the female goddess (who is the Virgin Mary and Mary Magdalene rolled into one — both the sinful First Eve and the sinless Second Eve) was often treated as a symbol of the Church as a whole. On that basis the Holy Mother of God must always be subordinate to her Son.

We now possess many of the original documents of the so-called "gnostic heresy." The Gnostics, it seems, were the source of these ideas of the central place of woman in Christian belief. They appear to have thought of the ultimate high god as a feminine entity, divine Wisdom (Sophia). Some Gnostic prayers are addressed not only to God the Father but also to God the Mother. The Holy Spirit is unambiguously represented as female, a combination of both the mother and the consort of God the Father. In such cases, God the Mother appears to be the more powerful half of the hermaphrodite deity. This is also the case in contemporary Saivite Hinduism.

From a psychoanalytic viewpoint this may seem surprising. Two of the papers collected in Jones (1923) argue, on quite rational grounds, that the Holy Ghost, who impregnated the Holy Virgin, must have been male. But the Gnostics and the other Syriac Christian fathers were symbolists rather than literalists.

Apart from this uncertainty about the gender of the ultimate deity, the Gnostic Jesus Christ, in his human form, appears to be credited with normal sexual relationships. His lover is Mary Magdalene who is also his special confidant, a circumstance that generates great jealousy among the other principal disciples, especially Simon-Peter.

And why not? The earliest Christians were not celibate monks; it would have been surprising if they had not credited the god-man Jesus with a normal human sexual life. But in any case, until Christianity became the official religion of the Roman Empire early in the fourth century A.D., there had been a large number of rival Christian sects all of which claimed to be orthodox. In the course of the political upheavals that accompanied the shift from a paganism, in which the Emperor was rated as divine, to a Christianity, in which the Emperor himself was the principal patron, every effort was made by those who had access to the Emperor's person to denounce their rivals as heretics and to destroy the documents that supported their rivals' cause.

In this endeavor they were only partially successful. It has long been known that Clement of Alexandria, who flourished around 180 A.D., claimed to be an orthodox Christian but that he showed sympathy for the Gnostic view that God is feminine as well as masculine. Consequently he argued that women can participate as equals with men in priestly activity. But Clement's contemporary, Tertullian, held the opposite opinion that, since Jesus Christ was male, all males are superior to all females and that no woman could serve as a priest. Tertullian's view prevailed and until very recently indeed it has hardly been challenged. But, on this issue, Christianity might easily have developed very differently.

That we now know as much as we do about Gnostic heresies is largely because of the discovery in 1945 in Upper Egypt of the Nag Hammadi texts (Robinson, 1977; Pagels, 1980). These texts constitute a "library" in Coptic (i.e., texts written in the Egyptian language, but using Greek script) of translations from Syriac originals. The Nag Hammadi documents themselves mostly date from the fourth century A.D. but at least some of the Syriac originals appear to date back two centuries earlier. The authors thought of themselves as Christian, but it was a markedly different sort of Christianity from any of the kinds with which we are now familiar. The peculiarity with which I am here concerned is the role given to Mary Magdalene.

In the canonical Christian Gospels, as we now have them, Mary Magdalene is something of an anomaly. She appears to be a minor character yet in all four gospels she is made the first witness of the empty tomb and the first human being to see the risen Christ, whom she at first mistakes for a gardener. This story is complemented by the fact that Mary the Virgin, the mother of Christ, does not appear at all after she has witnessed the Crucifixion (John 19:25) though she is mentioned in Acts 1:14 as one of the original body of 120 disciples. The text provides no explanation of why Mary Magdalene should be honored by this kind of precedence.

Earlier references confuse her with several other women called Mary. She is on one occasion described as "whom Jesus loved," an expression also applied to St. John the Apostle. Insofar as Mary Magdalene has any personal identity she is a woman from whom "seven demons had been cast out" and a repentent "sinful woman." Hagiography has subsequently made her into a type of repentant whore but it needs to be remembered that, until very recently indeed, the career of an upper class courtesan was one of the very few that provided a single woman with a life of dignified and affluent independence.

But in the Gnostic Gospel of Philip, which is a very "mystical" document, we have formulae that seem more appropriate to modern Indian Saivite theology than to any surviving form of Christianity. For example:

> For the perfect conceive through a kiss and give birth. Because of this we also kiss one another. We receive conception from the grace which is among us. There were three who walked with the Lord at all times. Mary his mother and her sister and Magdelene whom they called his consort (*koinonos*). For Mary was his sister and his mother and his consort [saying 31–32]. (Robinson, 1977)

Modern Hinduism takes many forms. Sometimes the male phallic deity Shiva is merged with his counterpart, the Goddess, but more often we encounter a cluster of separate male and female deities. As a general rule, Shiva is essentially inactive and male; his power derives from his yogic exercises in which he abstains from completed intercourse with his consorts, who have many names, but are usually distinguished as having three functions: Parvati, the irresistable seductive and creative force ("the lover"); Durga, the divine protectress ("the mother"); and Kali, the spirit of death ("the black one," "the destroyer"). All three "goddesses" are however only aspects of a single entity "the Goddess" (*devi*), or *Sakti*. Sakti is the active force of deity and is always viewed as primarily female whether creative, protective, or destructive (Chatterjee, 1953).

The parallel with the Gnostic theory of the three Marys who were simultaneously Christ's mother, sister, and consort and who "walked with the Lord at all times" is not exact but it is very close.

As explained already, once the gnostic doctrine of the equality of the sexes (both divine and human) came to be rated as a heresy, the status of Mary Magdalene became downgraded from privileged mistress to penitent whore and in the gospels (as we now have them) there are only residual traces of the idea that she might once have had some special personal relationship with Jesus. But she remains the first witness of the Resurrection, the central fact of Christian theology, a privilege for which some early theologians (e.g., Origen) considered that a penitent whore was wholly unsuitable. The same theologians also found it impossible to believe that the Holy Mother of God should not have been a witness of the Resurrection.

The Eastern church got out of this difficulty by juggling with the Gospel texts so as to make it appear that one of the other Marys at the empty tomb was in fact Jesus's mother and the mother of Jesus's siblings or half-siblings. Some Syriac texts went further by deliberately running the Virgin and her antitype the Magdalene into one (Murray, 1975, p. 145). But the Roman church became so deeply committed to the doctrine of the perpetual virginity of the Mother of God that Western theologians had difficulties with this solution. Instead, they invented various apocryphal stories to the effect that the risen Christ appeared first of all to his mother even though the Gospels say nothing of this event.

But in later centuries good Christians, especially the artists, remained puzzled. Admittedly, the hagiographers and martyrologists managed to invent a large number of female, hermit-saints whose mythology is based on that of the (revised) story of Mary Magdalene. For example, St. Margaret (alias St. Marina alias St. Mary alias St. Pelagia) is, in one version, one of the 14 "Auxiliary Saints" or "Holy Helpers." She suffered martyrdom in horrible circumstances for refusing to marry Olybrius the prefect of Antioch;

but in another version she starts out as an immensely wealthy actress, dancer, prostitute in Antioch and ends up as a hermit in the desert masquerading as a man.

Some of these hermit repentant sinners aroused the interest of great artists in later centuries. For example, there is a figure by Donatello in the Baptistry at Florence in which Mary Magdalene is dressed only in her own hair, grown miraculously to preserve her modesty and cover her wasted limbs (Warner, 1976, p. 40). But, despite the disapproval of the Holy Fathers, the Gnostic story that the Magdalene was Christ's "consort" seems to have survived in shadowy form.

There is an early sixteenth-century window in King's College Chapel, Cambridge, which depicts the meeting of Mary Magdalene with the risen Christ disguised as a gardener (John 20:14). There are several close precedents in the Flemish art of the period. Plates 1 and 2 show one of these sixteenth-century Flemish pictures; it comes from Tombu (1927). The Magdalene is suitably dressed as a king's mistress but there is certainly nothing in her appearance suggesting the penitent whore.

There is another sixteenth-century picture in King's College Chapel which once served as an altarpiece. The artist was Siciolante Girolamo Sermoneta who worked in Rome. The picture (not illustrated here) depicts the Deposition from the Cross. There are three prominent figures in the foreground. On the left, the nearly naked body of the dead Christ lies at the foot of the cross. On the right stands a somberly dressed Mary, the Virgin Mother, but in the center kneeling in front of the body in an attitude of adoration and sexual longing is a woman dressed in golden silk. Undoubtedly it represents Mary Magdalene, and it is she who attracts the attention of the observer. Heretics like myself find it a powerful and disturbing picture; the more conventional Protestants with whom I have discussed the matter seem to regard the whole thing as mildly pornographic without fully understanding what it is that they find objectionable.

The literature on the general theme of the legends of Mary Magdalene is extensive and has very recently been the subject of scholarly review. Mycroft (1985) is especially valuable for my purposes though he is rather weak on the German materials cited by Van den Wildenberg-de Kroon (1979).

There is no agreement among scholars as to how the relevant gospel texts should be interpreted. Is there just one Mary Magdalene or three different Marys who share her attributes? When it comes to her post-Ascension career everything is up for grabs. Her story becomes muddled up with that of the hermit Saint Mary of Egypt. Quite a separate set of stories take her to the Carmague and to Santiago de Compostela and yet another set bring her relics to Vezelay (for details, see Warner, [1976], especially ch. 15).

I will not attempt to explore all these avenues of legend. But fortunately a Flemish artist, usually known as the Master of the Legend of Mary Magdalene, painted a triptych around 1518 containing eight scenes from the legend that serve to show just which parts of the story were viewed as interconnected and significant at that date. Quite early in its history, the triptych was broken up into several separate panels, which were scattered, but the plates presented here show a reconstituted version of the complete original painting.

I shall assume that for present purposes the triptych includes the whole of the Mary Magdalene myth (even though I know that it does not!). I will start with a description of the various panels as illustrated.

1. Plate 1 shows the triptych with the hinged wing panels folded inward. The scene shown is that of the Magdalene meeting the risen Christ dressed as a gardener with a spade (John 20:14–15). There are a number of other figures in each panel that I shall consider presently. In the King's College Chapel version of the same scene, Christ and the Magdalene are the only individuals shown. The treatment is almost identical except that the Christ's hat is hanging down his back and is not on his head. The Magdalene's costume is very brightly colored. It should be noted that the Magdalene offers the Christ the "sweet spices" with which, according to the Gospel texts, she had intended to anoint his dead body. It is odd that she should have expected to be able to do this if the tomb was sealed. But the "sweet spices" in question (Exodus 30:34) seem to have doubled as aphrodisiacs.

The other figures are explained by Tombu (1927). In the left-hand panel, the standing figure on the left, facing the observer and separated from the Christ figure on the right of the panel by a gauntly phallic tree, is St. Louis, the beatified King of France. He

RECONSTITUTION DES VOLETS EXTÉRIEURS

Plate 1.
Reconstruction of the triptych with the wings closed.

holds a staff of regal office in each hand. The male donor appears below kneeling directly in front of the tree with his hands together in an attitude of feudal submission.

The design of the right-hand panel is similar. Mary Magdalene leans yearningly toward the Christ who forbids her to touch him. The figure standing behind the Magdalene is St. Margaret (alias St. Pelagia) whose ambiguous legend has been mentioned already. The female donor kneels in the center with her hands in the position of submission. Behind her kneels her daughter, dressed as a nun.

But if we compare this "closed" triptych with the "open" version of the whole picture (Plate 2), we realize that the two hinged wing panels are painted on both sides. The left-hand panel, which has Christ as a gardener with the male donor below on one side, is backed by Mary Magdalene in splendid costume riding a horse and presumably hunting. In a small-scale scene above, the Magdalene,

RECONSTITUTION DU TRIPTYQUE DE LA LÉGENDE DE MARIE-MADELEINE

Plate 2. Reconstruction of the triptych with the wings open.

still in splendid costume, listens to Jesus preaching. The right-hand panel, which on one side has the adoring Mary Magdalene responding to the "gardener's" words "do not touch me" (John 20:17), with the female donor below, is backed by a picture of the Magdalene preaching and a small picture of the naked hermit Magdalene being carried up to heaven by angels.

So the artist seems to be aware that the relation between the gardener Christ and the frustrated Magdalene is somehow the same as that between the two donors, man and wife, and also between the figures depicted on the front and the back of each panel. The donors are themselves depicted as "repentant sinners"! But there may be a thank offering element. One of the Magdalene's functions was to help with difficult pregnancies. There is a "Freudian" pun in the English language itself: The first meaning of the word *husband* is "to till the ground."

2. As indicated above, the main picture on the inside of the left-hand wing panel of the triptych shows the Magdalene out hunting. This shows that the artist accepted an apocryphal version of the story by which the Magdalene, before her repentance, was a well-born woman who acted the courtesan. Other scenes from this story (but not in this example) show the Magdalene dancing with a well-dressed male partner and sitting on a bench with a man in an attitude of courtship. In all cases, her costume is flamboyant.

2a. In the present case the small picture at the top which shows the Magdalene listening to Jesus preaching repeats elements of

3. the main picture on the right-hand hinged panel where the Magdalene's pulpit is the same as that of Jesus. In this part of the picture, she is still very respectably dressed with no signs of the penitent whore theme. Notice that the audience to her sermon seems to be all women and children. The story is apocryphal.

3a. However, in the small panel at the top of the picture the Magdalene is shown in her hermit role as depicted by Donatello. She is naked but her modesty is preserved by a wealth of magically grown hair. She is being carried up to heaven by angels. This story is also apocryphal, but in Italian medieval and Renaissance art the penitence of the Magdalene was very frequently shown by this device.

4. The main scenes in the center panel are biblical. On the left is the occasion of the Magdalene anointing the feet of Christ at the supper at the house of Simon the Leper. The artist has combined

elements from Matthew 26:6f., Mark 14:3f., Luke 7:36f., and John
12:1f. but is especially concerned with the version in John where it is
emphasized that Lazarus, who had been raised from the dead, was
present. Probably Lazarus is the figure sitting directly opposite Jesus. John also asserts that Judas Iscariot "which should betray him"
was Simon's son. Judas is probably the individual with the expensive
looking hat depicted as in conversation with Jesus (John 12:4–8).

5. On the right hand of the main panel the Magdalene attends
the scene in which Jesus raises her brother Lazarus from the dead.
Lazarus has just come from the tomb with his wrists bound (John
11:44). Jesus stands center but somewhat to the rear. One of the
spectators in the foreground holds a nosegay; so we are reminded
that the disbelieving Martha has said that the corpse of Lazarus
"stinketh" (John 11:39). The later resurrection of Christ on the third
day repeats as closely as practical the resurrection of Lazarus on the
fourth day.

5a. At the top of this picture, above the heads of the audience to
the resurrection of Lazarus, is a complex scene that contains a string
of references to another Magdalene story that I shall summarize:

> [Fourteen] 14 years after the Passion the Magdalene arrived miracu-
> lously in Marseille where she converted the local Prince and his wife
> by her preaching. Through her blessing the Prince's wife became
> pregnant. The Prince expressed a wish to meet St. Peter. The wife
> "obstinately" insisted on coming with him. After a day and a night
> there was a great storm and the Princess gave birth but then died. The
> sailors wanted to throw her corpse and the child into the sea. The
> pilgrim prince was however helped by the Magdalene who magically
> produced a rocky island with a cave in which the dead woman and her
> child were entombed. On return from his pilgrimage the Prince revis-
> ited the island and found his child alive. It had been protected by the
> Magdalene. Later the dead mother of the child was restored to life.

At the top of the picture we see (1) the Magdalene blessing the
departing pilgrims; (2) the shipwreck; (3) the rocky island with the
child throwing stones into the sea.

What is it about this whole set of pictures that makes them hang
together?

In an earlier essay (Leach, 1983), I argued that the various
Marys of the Gospel story share more than just a name with the
Miriam of the Book of Exodus. I pointed out that in the Italy of the

sixteenth century it was taken for granted that when Michelangelo, in his Pietà (now in St. Peter's in Rome), made the dead Christ the same age as his mourning mother and gave them both the same features, he was echoing Dante's "Vergine Madre, figlia del tuo Figlio" (Virgin Mother, daughter of your Son), an imagery that is frequently reproduced in Renaissance paintings of the Coronation of the Virgin. The Gnostic Marys whom I mentioned earlier make the same point: the mother, the sister, the consort are all one and the same. They are like Isis in relation to Osiris-Horus in Egyptian mythology. In that earlier essay my rhetorical answer to my rhetorical question: "Why did Moses have a sister?" was "Because mythologic requires that his mother should be no older than himself."

But I made a rather different point with regard to the Magdalene. I argued that her presence at the empty tomb which made her the first witness to the fact of the Resurrection (along with the absence of the Virgin from this same scene) implies that, in a symbolic sense, she is the "mother" of the second birth. The child delivered from the Virgin's womb is God made into Man. The "untouchable" grown adult delivered from the tomb is Man made into God. It is mytho-logical that the woman who observes this reverse transformation should have exactly the opposite characteristics from the Virgin mother. Instead of purity and modesty, we have impurity and flamboyant immodesty. Instead of a mother, we have a sister (of Lazarus) or (as the Gnostics proclaimed) a consort of Christ himself.

But then we have a problem with which the Gospels do not deal. How do we get these highly symbolic characters off the stage?

According to legend, Mary the Virgin did not experience ordinary death; she fell asleep and was subsequently "assumed" into Heaven where she became the crowned queen and bride of Christ. Her transformation was thus from modest obscurity to the highest grandeur. So, logically, the Magdalene has to go the other way.

During her human lifetime, she had enjoyed (if we follow the artists rather than the Gospels!) a social life of great splendor. Thus, while she too has to be assumed into Heaven, it is as a destitute sexless hermit not as a princess. The Virgin is sinless; the Magdalene is the prototype of the (repentant) sinner. For this purpose, her story, as I have already indicated, was merged with that of St. Mary of Egypt, who, according to legend, lived the life of a harlot in Alexandria for 17 years and then, having managed to visit Jerusalem, spent the next 47 years as a hermit in the wilderness beyond Jordan. The Magdalene, unlike Mary of Egypt, was eventually carried up to heaven by angels after the model of Elijah (see Warner, 1976, 233–234).

Further stories about the later career of Mary Magdalene have her mixed up with James and John, "the sons of Zebedee" (once referred to as "Boanerges, the sons of Thunder") who have more than a passing resemblance to the pagan (Spartan) Dioskuroi, "the Heavenly Twins", the sons of Zeus.

One set of stories involves the Magdalene with Santiago (St. James) of Compostela, the patron saint of Spain, whose legend combines elements taken from both of the biblical Sts. James: (1) James the Apostle, the "twin" of the Apostle John, and (2) James "the Lord's brother" who appears briefly in Acts as head of the Church in Jerusalem. In another set of stories, the Magdalene accompanies John the Apostle to Ephesus. It seems significant that, in the Gospel story, John is explicitly made the substitute for Jesus himself (John 19:25). The evidence for most of this will be found in Saxer (1959).

The details of these subsidiary stories are not my immediate concern, but they do support my original point that individual myths never have sharp boundaries and also that there is no uniquely "correct" way of interpreting myth. The Magdalene is just one figure in a sea of related characters some of whom seem to belong as much to paganism or Hinduism or Judaism as to Christianity.

But that too need not surprise us. Freud discovered in Sophocles's stories of the relations between Oedipus, Jocasta, and Laius a pattern of incestuous longing and sexual frustration that he found relevant for the problems of his middle-class patients in early twentieth-century Vienna. Perhaps psychoanalysts might discover comparable universalities if they paid closer attention to the multiple sexual ambiguities of the mythical characters with whom this essay has been concerned.

REFERENCES

CHATTERJEE, S. C. (1953) Hindu Religious Thought. In K. W. Morgan (Ed.), *The Religion of the Hindus*. New York: Ronald Press.
JONES, E. (1923) *Essays in Applied Psycho-Analysis*. London: International Psycho-Analytic Press.
LEACH, E. (1983) Why did Moses have a sister? In Edmund Leach & D. Alan

Aycock (Eds.), *Structuralist Interpretations of Biblical Myth*. Cambridge: Cambridge University Press.

MURRAY, R. (1975) *Symbols of Church and Kingdom: A Study in Early Syriac Tradition*. Cambridge: Cambridge University Press.

MYCROFT, D. A. (Ed.). (1985) *A Critical Edition of the Legend of Mary Magdalene from Caxton's Golden Legende of 1483*. Salzburg: Institut für anglistik und amerikanistik, Universität Salzburg.

PAGELS, E. (1980) *The Gnostic Gospels*. London: Weidenfeld & Nicholson.

ROBINSON, J. M. (Ed.). (1977) *The Nag Hammadi Library*. Leiden: E. J. Brill.

SAXER, V. (1959) *Le Culte de Marie Madeleine en Occident des Origines à la Fin du Moyen Age* (2 Vols.). Paris: Auxerre.

TOMBU, J. (1927) Un triptyque du maitre de la Légende de Marie-Madeleine. *Gazette des Beaux Arts* (Paris), May, Issue 777:299–310.

WARNER, M. (1976) *Alone of All Her Sex: The Myth and the Cult of the Virgin Mary*. London: Weidenfeld & Nicolson.

WILDENBERG-DE KROON, C.E.C.M. (1979) *Das Weltleben und die Bekehrung der Maria Magdalena im Deutschen Religiosen und in der bildenden Kunst der Mittelalters*. Amsterdam: Rodopi.

Plates 1 and 2 reproduced with permission from Tombu, J. (1927).

The Birk
11 West Green
Barrington, Cambridge CB2 5RZ
England

THE ARTISTIC IMAGE AND THE INWARD GAZE: TOWARD A MERGING OF PERSPECTIVES*

Ellen Handler Spitz

The artist is the one who arrests the spectacle in which most men take part without really seeing it and who makes it visible. . . .
— M. Merleau-Ponty, 1948

There are moments, even in a wordy culture like ours, when images start from no preformed program to become primary texts. Treated as illustrations of what is already scripted, they withhold their secrets.
— L. Steinberg, 1984a

How shall I say
what wood that was! I never saw so drear,
so rank, so arduous a wilderness!
its very memory gives a shape to fear.

— Dante, *Inferno*

Inspired in part by attempts of Merleau-Ponty (1948) to grapple with the way in which art reveals truth, in this article I shall follow and extend John Ciardi's (1954) translation of Dante's lines by suggesting that works of art, through their images, give shape to inner experience. Furthermore, I shall claim that visual images, including the hallucinatory (in the present context, those called up by a literary text), serve, by combining maximum intensity with economy and latent ambiguity, a powerful and unique organizing function for psychoanalytic work.

For over three decades, Rudolf Arnheim (1966, 1969, 1974, 1986), the eminent psychologist of art, has developed his thesis that

*Versions of this paper were read at the Fall Meeting of the American Psychoanalytic Association, New York, December, 1986 and at the May, 1987 meeting of the Israel Psychoanalytic Society in Tel Aviv. The author wishes to express sincere appreciation to Dr. Stanley Leavy for his kind and thoughtful commentary.

visual perception plays a dominant role in the cognitive exploration of reality. I seek, by adopting a phenomenological perspective, to extend this thesis from cognition to affect and from the outer reality, with which Arnheim is principally concerned, to the deep and recondite wells of inner reality into which the psychoanalyst is drawn. If, with Arnheim, we agree that artistic creativity consists in structuring the bewildering chaos of external stimuli, then we must acknowledge that it draws on and likewise reveals the ordering of inner turbulance, of fantasy, and dream.

Therefore, despite the current vogue of taking psychoanalysis to task for making short shrift of history (see articles by Cavell, 1987; Davidson, 1987; Gilman, 1987; and Rand and Torok, 1987), I resist that tide here by stressing the experiential aspects of artistic imagery. In a reversal of the usual direction, which has been to "explain" art by appeals to universal psychoanalytic concepts, I shall claim that artistic images are primary and irreducible; that they are fundamental structurings and orderings to which the psychoanalyst can turn and return in his quest for knowledge of the human psyche. Although no clinical material is cited here, I trust that readers will be stimulated to remedy this omission by remembering and conjuring examples from their own past and current practice.

A suggestion has been made (see Michels 1983, 1985, 1988) that psychoanalysis be divided into two large bodies of theory: theories about technique and treatment, which involve relatively fixed principles, laws, rules of procedure (a claim that would, no doubt, be disputed by some); and a second category of theory which, unlike the first, consists of a loose network of interpretative models upon which the therapist can draw. Such models would include the familiar notions of drive and structure, of self and object, and the various developmental schemata, which analysts draw upon more or less freely in their interpretative efforts. Into this second body of theory would fall, for instance, the notion of the Oedipus complex, with its wealth of metaphorical proliferations. (For a recent reassessment of this construct that adumbrates a viewpoint similar to that which I am elaborating here, see Leavy [1985].)

According to this division of theory, which I shall stipulate for the present, only the first body, the rules for clinical practice, is prescribed, while the second body of theory is relatively open for addition and modification. Here, the analyst, in her interpretative work, is freer to experiment, to imagine, and to draw upon a wide range of personal, cultural, as well as clinical experiences as sources of inspiration. With this division firmly in place, it is clearly into the second body of theory that interdisciplinary work in the arts must fit and thereby find its psychoanalytic home. The clinical psychoanalyst who lives with and cherishes the arts and who is educated in one or more of them has thus the possibility of employing an ever-expanding interpretative repertoire and thereby contributing to her own theoretical preserve in the second sense. Works of art may come to serve, as they more than occasionally did for Freud, as primary sources of understanding about the human psyche. From time to time, for example, it may suddenly occur to a therapist that he has in treatment a Prometheus or a Cassandra, or, as Leavy (1985) suggests, "an Aeneas on the couch," or that, like Orestes, a particular patient is tormented relentlessly by the Erinyes.

I

Although the following essay manifestly addresses problems inherent in the application of psychoanalysis to Italian Renaissance art (in particular, that of the trecento and early quattrocento in Florence and Siena), its purview extends beyond the limits of this period, for the issues raised by such a project have a broader bearing. Thus, I shall take the art of this place and time as a paradigm for my proposal that images in and of themselves may serve, in reverse of the usual direction (psychoanalysis applied to art) as primary sources of enrichment for the analytic enterprise.

Pathography as a psychoanalytic approach to the realm of art (Spitz, 1985) is a model that depends upon detailed knowledge of an artist's personal life history, particularly the early childhood, in order to develop convincing hypotheses about the relations between that life and a body of creative work, about the influences upon artistic choice of unresolved trauma, persistent intrapsychic conflict, and unconscious fantasy. When one thinks, however, of Florentine and Sienese artists of the trecento and even of the quattrocento, it is fair to say that, with few exceptions, there is scant biographical information and less that is undisputed. Furthermore, what is known has to do not only with the exigencies of artistic convention but with the prodigious powers of patron and purse. It is now a commonplace that artistic decisions are culturally embedded—that is, decisions both as to form and content are not the result of individual artists' sensibilities alone but rather a tangled compromise between inexorable and warring factors: political, fiscal, clerical, as well as private. How difficult then to speak without nullifying qualifications about these artists' intentions and/or their developmental histories, to interpret works of early Renaissance painting as expressions of deep inner realities!

Artists in the period of the Florentine trecento were accorded status principally as craftsmen. They were not, with rare exceptions, considered, as in the nineteenth century, uniquely gifted, hypersensitive, exotically deranged, misunderstood. Artists of the early Renaissance, importantly, did not sign their works. Attributions, for this reason, are an ongoing source of dispute. Only within the past few years, for example, has the equestrian portrait of "Guidoriccio," that redoubtable fellow with his undulating lozenged draperies, riding along on the wall of the Palazzo Pubblico, the time-honored emblem of the city of Siena and taken for years as a genuine Simone Martini, come under suspicion of inauthenticity (see Raynor, 1984; Mallory, in press). Furthermore, it is well-documented that the price paid for materials was greatly in excess of that rendered for an artist's input or labor. Technical proficiency, craftsmanship, was valued far above innovation or originality (see Cennini [c. 1400], 1960).

Consider, along these lines, the constraints imposed on all Christian artists by the didactic imperatives of an illiterate audience. (For an interesting discussion of the effects of illiteracy on iconography, see Bryson [1983].) Conjure up the historiated predellas of numerous Annunciations and Crucifixions, all designed to be "read" as narrative strips by a churchgoing public, all requiring characters (saints, martyrs, confessors, the Holy Family) who could be recognized at a glance. Think of some favorite examples of this narrative obligation: Duccio's intricately detailed and elaborated *Maestà* panels in Siena; Giotto's deeply moving story cycles on the walls of the Scrovegni Chapel in Padua; or, over a century later, Piero's monumental *Legend of the True Cross* in Arezzo. It is not that such obligations left no room for the projection of the artists' fantasies. (A similar case might be made with regard to Attic black- and red-figure vase paintings or to Egyptian tomb paintings.) But, in such cases, we must take special care not to factor out the givens but, wherever possible, to detect and analyze the contributions of convention to the resultant imagery. An analogy with the psychoanalytic situation is apt: One could trace a fascinating history of sensitive psychoanalytic authors since (and including) Freud who have attempted to examine the effects of the givens of treatment on the form and content of productions and constructions in analysis — both those of the analyst as well as those of the patient.

Further problems appear when we consider these story cycles. For we no longer see them as they were once beheld by original artist and audience. We have only remnants, damaged and partial arti-facts, faded and eroded by time. Take Ambrogio Lorenzetti's *Allegories of Good and Bad Government*, again on the walls of the Palazzo Pubblico in Siena. Is it only chance that *Good Government* has survived virtually intact, whereas the portrayal of the sinister effects of *Bad Government* is in ruins, virtually destroyed? The very boundaries of many works are in question. When we see a panel that has been cut, mutilated (a donor's portrait removed, for example, possibly by a feuding enemy) or when the deterioration of a sixteenth-century wall painting reveals traces of a fourteenth-century fresco beneath it, how do we judge the extent of what is missing?

In addition, there is the problem of restoration with its awe-some complexities and wide variations in quality, appropriateness, and legitimacy. (For a fine recent discussion of these issues, see Saito [1985].) When does the restorer cross that tenuous line between recreating the original work and obliterating it? Substituting a new work in its place? How much guessing is too much guessing? By what authority and on what grounds are decisions made as to when and whether and how to restore a given work? How much of a piece should be reworked and how much of it left as is? Or, if one begins to restore the work, will it become necessary as a consequence to tamper with parts that at present seem intact? One notes already the poignant parallels with psychoanalytic process, with the difficult diagnostic and therapeutic choices of the analyst: what to touch and what not to touch. Or should the work be left in its present state? As a ruin. Ruins have their own aesthetic. (See Peter Fuller's [1980] fasci-nating psychoanalytic study of the history of the mutilated *Venus de Milo*.) Art historian Erwin Panofsky also cautions us:

When abandoning ourselves to the impression of the weathered sculptures of Chartres, we cannot help enjoying their lovely mellowness
and patina as an aesthetic value; but this value, which implies both
the pleasure in a particular play of light and color and the more
sentimental delight in "age" and "genuineness," has nothing to do with
the objective, or artistic, value with which the sculptures were invested by their makers. (1955, p. 15)

What we see is not what the artist saw. Consider the problem of
altered contexts. We do not experience works as they were once intended to be experienced because so often they have been moved:
from choir screen to nave wall, from church to gallery, from town to
city. Standing in the Academia before Michelangelo's *David*, all one's
perceptions are changed entirely if one suddenly remembers that this
colossal statue was originally intended to be placed high upon the roof
of the Duomo, much like the acroteria of ancient Athens. Or, imagine
sitting down quietly in the Cloister of Santa Maria Novella and
realizing that this is actually the very church Boccaccio chose for his
opening narrative in the *Decameron*. One begins to conjure up the
characters—Pampinea, Fiammetta, Dioneo, Filostrato, and the
others—when suddenly one realizes, looking about at the bewildering
assortment of architectural and sculptural features, that much of all
this post-dated 1350 and would have been entirely unknown to Boccaccio. Mentally, visually, now one tries to substract and substitute, to
imagine not only the church minus what was not there in the trecento
but—harder yet—to guess what in fact was in its place so that at least
one semblance of Boccaccio's original experience can be constructed,
some viable image of the church that he carefully chose to weave into
the first bright threads of his literary tapestry.

   In the light of such complexities, the task of the pathographer—
to reconstruct the artist's deepest intentions, to find a way back to
something approximating even the outer, not to mention the inner,
conditions of his art—seems Herculean. Those brave souls who have
attempted pathographies of Renaissance artists (see Liebert, 1983)
have chosen their subjects with great care, wisely selecting artists of
the High Renaissance who bequeathed a vast corpus of literary as
well as graphic and monumental work. But even the best of such
psychoanalytic authors has not escaped the sparks of interdisciplinary fireworks (Steinberg, 1984b). Each has been chided for not

taking sufficient account of the limited and tangled context for his interpretative endeavors.

What to do? Is there another tack that will avoid these shoals and whirlpools? Applied psychoanalysis need not be limited to pathography. Works of art can in part be severed from their makers and their milieus. They can be bracketed, framed, de- and re-contextualized. (See Kuhns's [1983] theory of enactments.) Freud (1914) attempted something of this sort in his "Moses" paper, and likewise analyzed selected works by Sophocles and Shakespeare without significant reference to these authors.

One problem is that, when we apply this approach to the trecento, we run up against a subset of the same obstacles that confront the pathographer. Chief among them is the issue of the boundaries of the work of art itself. We have already considered how very difficult it is to know precisely what a given work of art was like in its original state. However, suppose we set such worries aside. Let us consider, for example, just one panel of Duccio's enormous *Maestà* altarpiece in isolation (Figure 1). A spirited little *Temptation*, it does have, perhaps, much to say quite on its own, and its presence far from its native Siena provides an opportunity for viewing and interpreting it out of (at least its geographic) context.

The small wooden panel, which invites the spectator to approach closely, portrays a nasty but sinuously seductive little Devil who falls just short of dominating the scene by virtue of the sultry silhouette he forms against its golden sky. A somewhat effete but elegant Christ pointedly warns him to "get thee behind me, Satan," and we cannot fail to notice the two courtly angels who hover in the wings with graceful hands extended (just in case Christ should decide to take the dare and jump; see *Matthew*, 4:1–11). Nonetheless, our eyes are drawn magnetically to the Devil himself. Our gaze is riveted upon him — attracted by the shape of his mysterious dark silhouette, by the furtive, diabolical quality of his figure. Whereas every other form in the composition is illuminated, his is obscure. Thus, the image compels us, lures us, Faust-like, to desire knowledge of him. With consummate artistry and psychological acumen, Duccio co-opts the viewer, even across the centuries. As his image works its ineluctable effect on us, it embodies, it instantiates, it reproduces the very essence of temptation.

Figure 1. Duccio. The Temptation of Christ. Panel from the Maestà.
The Frick Collection, New York.

Another interesting example is Giotto's *Flight into Egypt* (one of
the panels from the Arena Chapel in Padua) with its epic quality and
sense of urgency: the Madonna tensely astride her patient donkey,
the baby held facing toward her and clinging to her mantel, gives
visible shape to what Freud (1914) would centuries later come to call
the notion of the "anaclitic"; Joseph's worried countenance betraying
his foreboding masked by serenity, and one small, gracious angel
overhead beckoning them on, gesturing to them, guides them
through the bleak and rocky landscape — a projection into imagery, a
making visible, of what Kleinians might see as the good, protective
parental introject. Another panel (also from Padua), is the *Entomb-
ment of Christ* with its great tragic diagonal of rock, tender in its
expression of human sorrow, its bevy of wildly grieving angels overhead, their delicate hands and faces, even wings, contorted by their
anguish, an exquisite evocation of the fragmentation produced by
tragic loss.

Consider, lastly, that most psychologically gripping and complex image of all, *The Betrayal* (Figure 2), Giotto's commanding vision
of the very essence of treachery: the blasphemous kiss of Judas. (For

a contemporary non-psychoanalytic formalist analysis of this painting see Bryson [1983].) With lips pursed, staring boldly under heavy-
lidded eyes into the face of his chosen master, the traitor envelops
Christ with a weighty yellow mantel in one magnificent, sweeping
gesture that condenses aggression, lust, identification, protection,
and shameless concealment.

How fascinating to realize while contemplating this image that,
nearby and during approximately the same decade, another immortal artist was creating a parallel image of treachery against the master — in poetry rather than in paint. For Dante, as well as for Giotto,
and in the common culture of trecento Florence, this act was considered the most heinous of all human crimes: Dante punishes Judas at
the very nadir of his *Inferno*. On the terrible ice of Judecca, the
broken body of the arch-traitor is gnawed and eternally bitten by the
"rake-like" teeth of Satan in a ghastly orgy of retributive oral sadism — oral sadism that not only echoes but also reveals the deepest
source of horror in the kiss of Giotto's painting.

Figure 2. Giotto. The Betrayal. Fresco. Arena Chapel, Padua. (detail)

II

Is it worthwhile or even possible, however, to bracket such images and set aside all problems of their boundaries, contexts, and sparse accounts of the artists who created them? To mine them for their own deep psychological content? To analyze the dream without the associations of the dreamer? It seems clear, without rehearsing the pitfalls inherent in such an approach, that to do this is largely to take one's own responses as primary data for the interpretation.

Yet is this really as radical a move as it first appears? Is it not merely a shift of focus to that which has always been present but peripheral? In an analogy with the psychoanalytic situation, Leo Stone (1961) among others, has stressed that psychoanalytic interpretations necessarily involve the analyst's own mental activity, emotional life, biases, and "subjective transformations" of patients' material. Recent studies of Freud's own life (e.g., Balmary, 1979; Rudnytsky, 1987) have demonstrated the "subjectivity" of his various technical, theoretical, and narrative choices. Such revelations, constructively read, serve not to diminish the stature of the resultant *oeuvre*, but rather to remind us of the power of the unconscious, the ubiquity of transference, and of the vast, non-objective wellsprings of all human endeavor.

Imagine walking slowly through the streets and by the monuments of contemporary Florence, including the Palazzo Davanzati, where everyday life in Renaissance Florence springs suddenly into being as palpable and real. The private houses were built tall with narrow stairwells and endless steps so that it is possible, while climbing today, to experience with immediate urgency the impact of Dante's famous passage from the *Paradiso* (Canto 17) in which he describes the pain of exile: "how salty tastes another's bread, and how hard a path it is to go up and down another's stairs."

While treading the stones of Florence, iconoclastic thoughts may surface: that, as I have been suggesting, a focus on *the perceptual and affective experience in the present* is not entirely out of place for psychoanalytic explorers of the arts; that it might prove refreshing to forego doomed struggles against the truth that Florence is today a layered city with one century overlapping or juxtaposing another; that *what* really happened *when* is recoverable only in fragments; that, just as in our psychoanalytic models of the mind, there are screens and scrims. There are images freshly cleaned and gleaming with a radiance that approximates their original state (e.g., the Raphaels in the Palazzo Pitti) alongside others, dusty and dark, like those beautiful Giottos of the Bardi and Peruzzi chapels in Santa Croce, waiting to be illuminated, waiting for the patient hands of a conservator, or, in the psychoanalytic analogy, waiting to be remembered, revived, and worked through.

Rather than struggle only to untangle knotted and broken threads, rather than import prepackaged psychoanalytic theories into this kaleidoscope or, worst of all, aim awkward potshots at works of art as if they were painted targets in a bizarre psychoanalytic shooting gallery, perhaps a more receptive approach is preferable. Perhaps, like the finest clinicians who allow theory to recede so that patients' material can gradually emerge as inner reactions and responses to it are monitored, we must allow the works of art to appear, to emerge, to reveal themselves to us as they are in the present. Perhaps we must allow *them*, by means of their rich resources of imagery, to teach *us*; treat them as primary sources of knowledge about the human psyche; give them the opportunity to blend their perspectives with ours and thus enrich our storehouse of interpretative possibilities.

I do not mean to suggest we abandon all efforts at historical reconstruction, forego pathography, or eschew the task of teasing out narratives of drive, defense, and unconscious fantasy in works of art. Methodological difficulties should and will continue to constitute an ongoing challenge for interdisciplinary studies. However, to choose to bypass that arduous route, at least temporarily, *as we all do* from time to time, and to go directly to the works themselves for primary inspiration, is not without special value for the psychoanalyst. A spirit of adventure is imperative. Like the daring, innovative Florentines themselves, we must be risk-takers in the art of interpretation. The images themselves — their color, their irrepressible affect, their eruptions of fantasy, and their stubborn refusal to be forgotten — can, if permitted, deepen clinical sensitivity and serve to reintegrate the humanities with the scientific aspects of the psychoanalytic endeavor.

In the history of psychoanalytic theory, an apt analogy might be made to the development of our changing views on countertransference. After being identified, labeled, and meticulously described, countertransference was initially considered an arch-enemy of good technique, an impediment to the requisite "blank screen" of the ideal analyst, inimical to the analytic attitude, a demon to be exorcised by further analysis. Gradually, however, countertransference came to be seen not only as an inevitable aspect of the analytic situation but, within limits, as a potentially helpful and at times even indispensable tool for deepening the exploration of the psyche. Having at least partially recognized it, one works with it, rather than limiting one-self to a struggle against it — as I believe can and should be more openly and consistently the case in applied psychoanalysis. Such a shift of focus may open new interpretative possibilities by, for exam-ple, serving to prevent the misuse of existing theory as a defensive barrier between us and the works of art we cherish.

III

In the paintings of Duccio, Giotto, Simone Martini, Fra Angelico, and the masters of the Black Death, such as Bonaiuti and Traini, in the pages of Dante and Boccaccio, are images that sear the mind and remain smoking through the mists of memory. In them we can actually *see*, we can discover, we can inspect (by means of shape, color, and graphics, visual tropes and metaphor) a range of human agony that bears directly on modern psychoanalytic practice. And although such human agony must, in all its intensity and complexity, elude our final comprehension, yet, in our never-ending quest for understanding, for illuminating representation, we will be rewarded by gazing at these Florentine images.

  To stand, for example, before Masaccio's fresco of the *Expulsion* (Figure 3) in the Brancacci Chapel of the Church of the Carmine is to grasp with visceral force the primitive bodily manifestations of shame. Here is the moment when Adam and Eve are driven out of the Garden of Eden. Masaccio has painted two adult figures, a man and a woman, whose naked bodies appear so lumpish, so awkward and unidealized that we, participating in their shame, are almost impelled to turn away from them to avoid exposing them to the further pain of observation. Leaving behind what is familiar, Adam walks forward blindly, his head bowed, both hands up before his eyes, concealing them from the world and the world (which has suddenly become strange) from his eyes. Eve walks by his side. Her head, by contrast, is thrust back, her mouth half-open in a moan or

Figure 3. Masaccio. The Expulsion of Adam and Eve from the Garden. Fresco.
Brancacci Chapel of Santa Maria della Carmine, Florence.

howl. Her left arm and hand are occupied in hiding her breasts, while her right hand covers her now offensive genitals. The image is one of utter desolation; the misery it evokes is complete. And, clearly, it is shame that moves us here, not guilt, as in Michelangelo's rendering of the banished couple on the ceiling of the Sistine Chapel nearly a century later. Here, in Masaccio, we are made to feel the horror of the couple's changed sense of themselves, their altered relations to their own bodies. Not the trespass or the sin, but the dissevering of self.

If we turn momentarily from painting to Florentine poetry, to the pages of Dante's *Inferno*, we enter a world of nightmarish imagery that refines with fevered intensity a fantasy world akin to that of early childhood, where the body and its projected parts and products serve as symbolic carriers for meaning: imagery that peels the layers of complex ideas and reveals within them their instinctualized core.

In Canto 20, for example, we come upon that moving and terrifying portrait of the false diviners and prophets whose damnation erupts grotesquely with what Freud would later call the "primary process." The retribution of these sinners, who practiced forbidden magic in an attempt to peer into the future, entails the reversal of their faces on their necks. Standing beside Dante as we scan his *terza rima*, we gaze into the pit and can actually see them coming on backwards, piteously staring at their loins, doubly blind as tears burst from their eyes and run in rivulets down the cleft of their buttocks. Their bodies proclaim their sin: Their punishment is a reversal of their act. Dante himself (as poetic persona) weeps at their cruel subjection to the talion law, their abject humiliation. Likewise, we also cringe, we who, often in our pride, seek brazenly to order, predict, and control the future while secretly nursing wishes to undo our past.

Another of Dante's unforgettable portraits is that of Filippo Argenti, in Canto 8, an image that has captured the imagination of artists from the Tuscan trecento at least through the French Romantic period—with Delacroix's monumental painting of *The Bark of Dante* (1822). Filippo Argenti, Dante's personal and political enemy, appears here as an angry sinner in the circle of the wrathful: Rising momentarily from the foul mud of the River Styx, he turns his insatiable fury against himself, biting his own body in a transport of primitive, impotent rage. And, in a striking, parallel moment of self-revelation, Dante permits himself a display of overt vindictiveness, an unveiling of his own sadism, his own cruel pleasure in the torments he is witnessing. This display, had it been omitted, would have diminished the truth, the whole appalling truth of his masterpiece.

Most uncanny of all, perhaps, among the single images of the *Inferno* is the figure of Bertrand de Born, in Canto 28, a Provençal brigand, sower of discord between kinsmen. He is condemned for eternity to the ninth ditch (*bolgia*) of the eighth circle of Hell. Having rent sacred bonds asunder by turning son against father, he now suffers, by a hideous synecdoche, the sundering of his own body: Doomed forever, he "holds his severed head by its own hair/swinging it like a lantern in his hand."

As emblems, as signs, as beacons of penetrating light, such visions require no added context. The art itself supplies what it requires, bestowing upon us simultaneously signifier and signified. Psychoanalysts, seeking to probe the many meanings of the human condition, need only gaze: Such images will return that gaze, establishing a phenomenal space, a potential space (as Winnicott would have put it) in which inward and outward foci converge.

IV

In arguing the case for "visual thinking," Rudolf Arnheim (1986) persuasively illustrates the centrality of perception to cognition by showing that even concepts at high levels of abstraction, such as logical propositions, cannot be understood without recourse to visual imagery. One of his examples concerns the syllogism — that formula of inferential logic which enables the thinker to draw a valid conclusion from two valid premises. Thus, "If all a are contained in b, and if c is contained in a, then c must be contained in b." He demonstrates that a glance at the famous diagram of Euler (three sets of concentric circles) will reveal the range of enclosure obscured by attending to the words alone. Even if we balk at claiming that such a concept cannot be understood without recourse to a model that represents its relations in spatial terms, we are nonetheless struck by the clarity afforded by the visual image.

In the foregoing paper, I have suggested a similar role for artistic imagery *vis-à-vis* psychoanalytic understanding. Freud himself knew well the power of the image. In addition to his diagrams in

Chapter 7 of *The Interpretation of Dreams* (1900) as well as his bulgy little sketch of the relations between the topographic and structural models of the mind (Freud, 1933), he enlivened all his writings with similes and metaphors as well as with continuous references to works of art.

Against prevailing intellectual fashion, which exalts the word at the expense of the image, I have argued here for a reconsideration of the artistic image as a primary, originary ordering of inner and outer, conscious and unconscious, perceptual, cognitive, affective, and kinaesthetic experience — an ordering with matchless and revelatory resources for the psychoanalyst. Although such a claim raises certain epistemological questions that lie beyond the scope of this paper, the effort here has been to propose a supplement if not an alternative to the usual dialogue between art and psychoanalysis by considering the possibility of a merging of horizons whereby emphasis shifts from historical reconstructions and appeals to a corpus of supposedly transhistorical principles to a more relative stance that stresses the dialectic between beholder and image and that highlights the encounter itself in the full impact of its immediacy and presence.

Another, perhaps more unsettling view, is also pertinent. In a recent study of the ways in which we speak and write about images, W. J. T. Mitchell (1986) considers the ongoing dialectic between iconophilia and iconophobia and the ways in which verbal language has been enlisted on both sides of this recrudescent struggle between the worship of images on the one hand and the fear of images on the other. Taking a psychoanalytic point of view on his discussion, we note that the role of words in either case is anxiously competitive — a position instantiated by the Second Commandment (see *Exodus*, 20:4, where the pre-eminence of the prohibition against idols testifies to the strength of the fear against which it defends). Word and image (the symbolic and the imaginary) vie for hegemony over our experience, and words, as bearers of the law, must win out. Words, naming, interpretation, the inscribing of histories, the constructing of narratives, are all means of establishing control over the lability of the image which, though devalued as a powerless, mute, inferior kind of sign, may easily be seen as stimulating this contempt as a means of warding off the danger it evokes. In this deep psychological sense, a sense adumbrated by David Freedberg's (1985) work on the motives of iconoclasts, there can be no art without history. For the image without the word, without the label, without the security of a narrative context, collapses all distance between signifier and signified: Image becomes reality—a phenomenon both too radically other and too horrifyingly same. To keep, therefore, images (and the arts) in place, to arrest them, volumes of history and criticism and papers such as this one are written—all to preserve our unsteady mastery over their troublesome ability to fix and transfix our gaze.

REFERENCES

ARNHEIM, R. (1966) *Toward a Psychology of Art*. Berkeley: University of California Press.

——— (1969) *Visual Thinking*. Berkeley: University of California Press.

——— (1974) *Art and Visual Perception*. Berkeley: University of California Press.

——— (1986) *New Essays on the Psychology of Art*. Berkeley: University of California Press.

BALMARY, M. (1979) *Psychoanalyzing Psychoanalysis: Freud and the Hidden Fault of the Father* (N. Lukacher, Trans.). Baltimore: Johns Hopkins University Press.

BRYSON, N. (1983) *Vision and Painting: The Logic of the Gaze*. New Haven, CT: Yale University Press.

CAVELL, S. (1987) Freud and Philosophy: A Fragment. *Critical Inquiry*, 13:386–393.

CENNINI, C. (c. 1400) *The Craftsman's Handbook: Il Libro dell' Arte* (D.V. Thompson, Jr., Trans.). New York: Dover, 1960.

DANTE ALIGHIERI *The Inferno: The Paradiso* (J. Ciardi, Trans.). New York: Mentor, 1954.

DAVIDSON, A. I. (1987) How to Do the History of Psychoanalysis. *Critical Inquiry*, 13:252–277.

FREEDBERG, D. (1985) *Iconoclasts and Their Motives*. Maarssen, The Netherlands: Gary Schwartz.

FREUD, S. (1900) The Interpretation of Dreams. *Standard Edition*, 4 & 5.

——— (1914) The Moses of Michelangelo, *Standard Edition*, 13:210–238.

——— (1933) New Introductory Lectures on Psychoanalysis. *Standard Edition*, 22:3–182.

FULLER, P. (1980) *Art and Psychoanalysis*. London: Writers & Readers' Publishing Cooperative.

GILMAN, S. (1987) The Struggle of Psychiatry with Psychoanalysis: Who Won? *Critical Inquiry*, 13:293–313.

KUHNS, R. (1983) *Psychoanalytic Theory of Art*. New York: Columbia University Press.

LEAVY, S. (1985) Demythologizing Oedipus. *Psychoanal. Q.*, 54:444–454.

LIEBERT, R. (1983) *Michelangelo: A Psychoanalytic Study of His Life and Images*. New Haven, CT: Yale University Press.

MALLORY, M. (in press) Guidoriccio and Resistance to Critical Thinking. *The Syracuse Scholar*.

MERLEAU-PONTY, M. (1948) Cezanne's Doubt. *Sense and Non-Sense* (H. L. Dreyfus & P. A. Dreyfus, Trans.). Evanston, IL: Northwestern University Press, 1964.

MICHELS, R. (1983) The Scientific and Clinical Functions of Psychoanalytic Theory.

In A. Goldberg (ed.) *The Future of Psychoanalysis*. New York: International Universities Press.

_____ (1985, June) How Psychoanalysts Use Theory. Paper presented to the Westchester Psychoanalytic Society, New York.

_____ (1988) Psychoanalyst's Theories. Freud Memorial Lecture, University College London, June 25, 1988.

MITCHELL, W. J. T. (1986) *Iconology: Image, Text, Ideology*. Chicago: University of Chicago Press.

PANOFSKY, E. (1955) *Meaning in the Visual Arts*. New York: Doubleday/Anchor Books.

RAND, N., & TOROK, M. (1987) The Secret of Psychoanalysis: History Reads Theory. *Critical Inquiry*, 13:278–286.

RAYNOR, W. (1984) The Case Against Simone. *Connoisseur*, 214:60–61. (See also, Discussion in 215:161–162, 1985.)

RUDNYTSKY, P. L. (1987) *Freud and Oedipus*. New York: Columbia University Press.

SAITO, Y. (1985) Why Restore Works of Art? *J. Aesthetics & Art Crit.* 44:141–151.

SPITZ, E. H. (1985) *Art and Psyche: A Study in Psychoanalysis and Aesthetics*. New Haven, CT: Yale University Press.

STEINBERG, L. (1984a) *The Sexuality of Christ in Renaissance Art and in Modern Oblivion*. New York: Pantheon.

_____ (1984b, June 28) Shrinking Michelangelo. *The New York Review of Books*:41–45.

STONE, L. (1961) *The Psychoanalytic Situation*. New York: International Universities Press.

---

37 Iselin Terrace
Larchmont, NY 10538

DOUBLING, MYTHIC DIFFERENCE, AND THE SCAPEGOATING OF FEMALE POWER IN *MACBETH*

Dianne Hunter

Psychoanalytic literary criticism has often been attacked as ahistorical. But the new historicism in Renaissance studies, coupled with recent feminist analyses of gender as a social construction, provide a multifaceted context for illuminating literary texts as ideological responses to and creations of the social fabric from which they are woven. In its double status as both recurrent archetype and ideological construct, myth provides a particularly rich array of topics for discussing the social texture of literature.

Fusing psychoanalytic feminist with contextual criticism, this essay examines the analogies between psychological dynamics and political processes in Shakespeare's *Macbeth*. My argument is that *Macbeth* sacralizes the difference between succession by primogeniture and succession by assassination, though the play's rhetorical and structural doublings dissolve that very difference. This paradox allows us to see the play as a myth in the structuralist sense as a mediator of unwelcome cultural contradictions, in particular, the tension between political hierarchy and the facts of life — between the politics of maintaining an ordered system of differences and the biological fact that succession involves the dissolution of the very differences hierarchy seeks to uphold among persons, sexes, and generations. What makes *Macbeth* tragic is that its ideology of succession requires an oedipal scapegoat; and what makes the play a patriarchal myth is that its imagery associates the dissolution of differences that inheres in father–son succession with illegitimate violence, preoedipal fluidity, and sterile female power.

Through scapegoating female powers in the form of demonized

Psychoanalytic Review, 75(1), Spring 1988

witchcraft and through mythically denying or uprooting the female biological function of sustaining the family tree, *Macbeth* dramatizes the political tensions between women and men resulting from women's power over childbirth and early infancy, and, therefore, over succession and continuity. The mythogenetic contradiction mediated by *Macbeth* is that man depends on woman for birth but must get rid of her in order to be (re)born. This idea mystified and justified James I's claim to the English throne by assigning a new (male) lineage to British royalty. Yet the importance of this myth for patriarchy in general may explain the enduring popularity of *Macbeth* in male-dominated cultures.

I

Doublings and confusions of categories are thematically and structurally central to Shakespeare's *Macbeth*. The doublings represent kinship resemblances as well as psychological and artistic symmetries. Yet the play's symmetries often dissolve into confusion; and its doublings often collapse into identities. The witches say, "Double, double, toil and trouble" (4.1.36). In the confused opening reports of the defeat of the rebels Macdonwald and the Thane of Cawdor, we hear that Macbeth confronted Cawdor "with self-comparisons, / Point against point, rebellious arm 'gainst arm" (1.2.55–56). When Banquo and Macbeth entered the battle with the Norweyan lord, "they were / As cannons overcharg'd with double cracks, so they / Doubly redoubled strokes upon the foe" (1.2.37–39). The second witch says, "When the hurly-burly's done, / When the battle's lost and won" (1.1.3–4). The internal rhyme in her first phrase is counterpoised by the paradox that dissolves opposing categories in the second. All the witches say, "Fair is foul, and foul is fair" (1.1.11), a reversal in phrases and a paradox that dissolves the difference between balanced, echoing opposites. The play is riddled with similar paradoxes: Banquo is "Lesser than Macbeth, and greater. / Not so happy, yet much happier" (1.3.65–66). Of her son, Lady Macduff declares, "Father'd he is, and yet he's fatherless" (3.2.27).

Macbeth's first words in the play are "So fair and foul a day I have not seen" (1.3.38). This comment on the changing and contradictory weather is also a summary of the contrasting fates of Cawdor, the foul traitor who has been defeated, and Macbeth, the valiant defender of the realm who has triumphed only to be set on the path of duplicating Cawdor's fate as a traitor. "What he [Cawdor] hath lost," declares Duncan, "noble Macbeth hath won." "Go pronounce his present death, / And with his title greet Macbeth" (1.2.64–67). The ominous rhyme on Macbeth's name announces the way in which he will live to fulfill the role of Cawdor, of whom Malcolm remarks, "Nothing in his life / Became him like the leaving of it" (1.4.7–8), a description that turns out to fit Macbeth, who seems to inherit Cawdor's fate along with his title. Duncan seems to foreshadow his betrayal by Macbeth with the ironic, double-edged observation, "There's no art / To find the mind's construction in the face: / He [Cawdor] was a gentleman on whom I built / An absolute trust" (1.4.11–14), which is followed by the stage direction, "Enter Macbeth."

This doubling of characters has a psychic parallel in the division fostered within Macbeth and Lady Macbeth by their hypocrisy as seemingly loyal subjects who plot to assassinate the king. Such splitting is matched by pairings of characters who seem to be psychological splits of one another: Macdonwald and Cawdor, Macdonwald and Macbeth, Banquo and Macbeth, Malcolm and Donalbain, Macbeth and Macduff, the two Doctors (one English, the other Scottish), Macbeth and Lady Macbeth, Lady Macbeth and Lady Macduff, the young and old Siwards, Lennox and Rosse, Banquo and Fleance. The long line of kings in the final apparition replicate one another: "And thy hair, / Thou other gold-bound brow, is like the first. / A third is like the former. . . . / And yet the eight appears, who bears a glass / Which shows me many more" (4.1.113–120). These mirroring images reflect the sameness of family resemblances, since the antagonists in *Macbeth* belong to the same kinship group or gens. Lady Macbeth says she would have murdered the King herself, "Had he not resembled / My father as he slept" (2.2.12–13). Macbeth is Duncan's "cousin"; as violently succeeded king, he becomes a counterpart.

But kinship resemblances and artistic symmetries are not the whole story of the doubling in *Macbeth*. The drama is a perfect revenge play. Its structure of crime and punishment dramatizes the reflexivity of the revenge motive: Do unto others what they have done unto you; or, in psychoanalytic terms, undo unto others what has been done to you. Revenge is a magical form of undoing in which the original victim exchanges roles with the original aggressor, and repeats the original crime in order to undo it and gain mastery of its psychological and concrete effects. This repetition for mastery thus involves a paradoxical identification with the (original) aggressor (Fenichel, 1945; Willbern, 1978). After the murder Macbeth says, "I have done the deed" (2.2.13), and after guilt overtakes her, Lady Macbeth says, "What's done cannot be undone" (5.1.68); yet Macduff does undo Macbeth's usurpation by repeating, with a difference, his crime of regicide.

The difference is that between Macduff's act of collectively sanctioned public violence and Macbeth's individually motivated, private slaughter. However, as Freud (1913) remarks, "Punishment will not infrequently give those who carry it out an opportunity of committing the same outrage under the color of an act of expiation" (p. 72). This deep structural similarity between the actions of Macbeth and Macduff is expressed in the two-wave design of Shakespeare's plot. The first wave, triggered by Macbeth's first encounter with the witches, leads up to Duncan's assassination. The second wave, set off by Macbeth's second encounter with the witches, whom he seeks out for further prophecies, culminates in the vengeance that assassination exacts. And the symmetrical coupling of these two regicidal characters, Macbeth and Macduff, gets played out as a set of overlapping antitheses in the play's final scenes. Macbeth thinks he is charmed, but it turns out to be Macduff who is charmed. Macbeth has violated the security of the realm; Macduff restores it, at least temporarily. Macbeth's confrontation with his "self-comparison" Cawdor leads to madness, duplicity, and duplication of his fate; his confrontation with Macduff at the end of the play brings about a sacralized restoration of the political order, purged of the Macbeth disease.

Macduff and Malcolm arrive from England to undo the original crime of treason and regicide by repeating it in a collectively sanctioned, public ritual authorized by Shakespeare's mythic and dramatic transformation of Macbeth into a nightmare tyrant, the crowned monster of Scottish history. From where, we might ask, did such a mythic transformation and resolution come in Shakespeare's own time; and how have they retained their power within and beyond English-speaking societies today, wherever *Macbeth* is still performed? To begin to answer these questions, one might do well first to review some fundamental propositions concerning what myth is and how it works. At least since Lévi-Strauss, we have learned to think of myth as a story that gets retold because it embodies a sequence of images narrating an essential cultural conflict or recurrent set of cultural tensions. As literary anthropologist René Girard (1986) writes, "Myth involves a lack of differentiation" (p. 30), meaning that its narratives both disclose that fact and seek to cover it over. Girard thus characterizes myth as a process of dissolution and reinstitution of hierarchy, which he defines as sacred differences or binary oppositions maintained by structural boundaries. Moreover, since myth embodies both the disintegration and recomposition of differences, it may also be read as an account of its own genesis, retrospectively transfigured by the re-establishment of differences (Girard, 1979). Though Girard himself is an apologist for such hierarchical differences, his analysis of tragedy acknowledges the hidden violence latent in all hierarchy and the scapegoating that is the ritual process by which hierarchy is maintained. In thus allowing us to focus on the ways in which tragedy stages as a process of cultural transgression and resolution the re-emergence of what was hidden—or, in psychoanalytic terms, the return of the repressed—Girard's analysis of the role of myth in dissolving and maintaining differences opens the way for a deconstruction of Shakespeare's uses of the Macbeth myth.

Girard holds that mythic differentiations are achieved by sacralized violence, through collective expulsion; and that beneath the ordered distinctions that constitute culture, all differences between transgression and punishment simply disappear. In their sacrificial form, tragedies stage de-differentiations that issue in ritual violence, both echoing and rehearsing the crisis out of which culture originally emerged. In this view, tragedy undermines myth, or at least dissolves mythic differences even as they are being re-established. The cultural function of tragedy for Girard is to recreate the conditions under which reciprocal violence (the antithesis of culture) becomes collective violence (the essence of culture) and is cast out of society in a scapegoat ritual that echoes the origin of human social bonding. As Freud (1930) remarks, it is always possible to bind people together in love provided they are given a common enemy to hate (p. 114). Though Girard says scapegoating is fundamental to culture, he fails to specify that he means *patriarchal* culture, and that the de-differenti-

ation he fears as the essence of anti-culture is preoedipal and feminine. The imagery of *Macbeth* makes vivid an equation between
female power and anti-culture, which perhaps explains the play's
enduring popularity in patriarchal culture, from Shakespeare's time
to our own.

II

As every student of the play has learned, *Macbeth* was topical at the
time of its composition. It was written to celebrate the coming of the
Stuart dynasty to the English throne, and to please and flatter
Shakespeare's new royal master, King James VI of Scotland and I of
England, with whom Shakespeare's acting company had established
a "special relation" early on. Only ten days after his arrival in London, James had ordered a royal patent to be drawn up for Shakespeare's company, which soon came to be called "the King's men"
(Schoenbaum, 1977, p. 250). Although the transition from the Tudor to Stuart dynasty proved a smooth one, there had been anxiety
about Elizabeth's successor during her reign. As the son of the dread
assassin Mary, Queen of Scots, James VI might have been viewed
with some suspicion when he assumed Elizabeth's throne, yet Shakespeare seems to have been more an admirer of James than he had
been of Elizabeth, or at least to have been remarkably sensitive to his
new sovereign's tastes and interests. Scholars have surmized that
Shakespeare was present in Oxford during the summer of 1605,
when King James approved Gwinn's *Tres sibyllae*, with its references
to James's ancestry, and let it be known that he preferred short plays;
James had also written on divine monarchy, demonology, and witchcraft, and in the same summer of 1605 heard a debate on "whether
the imagination can produce real effects" (Evans, 1974, p. 1308). All
these themes are dramatized in *Macbeth*, which also gives special
attention to James's genealogical identification with the mythic Banquo, and is Shakespeare's shortest tragedy.

The Macbeth story Shakespeare revived to celebrate James's
ancestry and sacred right to the English throne had both historical
and legendary roots. The historical Macbeth reigned in Scotland
between 1040 and 1057, and seems to have been a vigorous, successful, and—for his era—even a pious ruler. That he killed his prede-
cessor, Duncan I, and was in turn killed by his successor, Duncan's

son Malcolm III, was simply in the nature of how monarchical power changed hands in tenth- and eleventh-century Scotland. As John Dover Wilson (1968) has pointed out, of the nine kings who reigned between 943 and 1040, all but two were killed, either in feud or directly by their successors. This state of affairs was the result not so much of the barbarism of the age, says Dover Wilson, as of the ancient Scottish custom of alternate or collateral succession, which preceded the law of primogeniture. According to this more ancient Scottish custom, on the decease of a king, his crown passed not to his direct descendant, but to the brother or cousin or even more remote collateral relative who seemed the strongest person within the royal family group. Though this system had evident utility in a period when strength at the helm was a precondition of survival for any institution, it encouraged the strongest man in the royal family group to end the ruling king's reign in advance of its natural termination, at a moment convenient to himself.

Sometimes, however, it worked the other way. For example, Malcolm II broke custom by killing off members of the alternate branch of his family in order to secure the throne for his grandson Duncan I. But by oversight, negligence, or masculinism, he left one member alive, a woman, Truoch. She later had a son by her first husband, and later still took as her second husband a formidable warrior named Macbeth, son of Findlaech, earl of Moray. Thus, from the standpoint of the eleventh century, Duncan, not Macbeth, was the usurper; and Macbeth was the vindicator of a true line of succession.

How, then, did the righteous Macbeth come to be represented as the abhorred tyrant and dwarfish thief of Scottish monarchy? The answer is, first, that the institution of primogeniture during the twelfth and thirteenth centuries taught people to regard the events of the preceding age in a new light; and second, that Macbeth belonged to the House of Moray, which, being unrelated to the royal stock and controlling a district still largely outside the authority of Scottish kings, played a conspicuous, unsuccessful, and (therefore) disreputable part in the later dynastic struggles that led to the triumph of primogeniture. So, by the end of the thirteenth century, Macbeth was regarded as one of a brood of traitors and would-be usurpers; and being the killer of Duncan I, who was now seen as the rightful heir of Malcolm II, Macbeth already appeared to fill the role of archvillain usurper. Then an event at the end of the following century villainized his character irredeemably. This was the assumption of the throne by a new family, the Stuarts, who, having reached Scotland from Brittainy, via Shropshire, where they received lands from Henry I, stood in need of indigenous Scottish roots. A mythic ancestry was accordingly concocted, with a mythical founder, Banquo, who was added to the ranks of royal victims credited to the House of Moray by means of an imaginary murder committed by the infamous Macbeth, followed by the flight of a mythical son, Fleance, to Wales, from the borders of which the historical Stuarts came. Fleance was said to have married a Welch princess, so the House of Stuart could claim to derive from King Arthur himself, a claim of considerable value to its possessors in fifteenth-, sixteenth-, and seventeenth-century England (Dover Wilson, 1968, pp. viii–x). In *Macbeth*, Shakespeare employs this synthetic mythology, yet seems to have been unable to resist pointing to its fictionality by heavy punning on Fleance's name: "Fly, good Fleance, fly, fly, fly" (3.3.17); and "For Fleance fled" (3.6.7). Moreover, he undermines his own condemnation of Macbeth by giving him the most profound moral imagination of all the characters in the play.

Macbeth refers obscurely to Truoch's first marriage and her kinship with Duncan, in Lady Macbeth's allusion to having nursed a child and in her remark about Duncan's resemblance to her father, yet suppresses the fact that the real-life Malcolm II had killed the family of the real-life Lady Macbeth in order to put Duncan on the throne. From an eleventh-century point of view, when Duncan broke the custom of elective monarchy by proclaiming Malcolm III his heir, even while praising the military prowess of Macbeth, Lady Macbeth was perfectly justified in trying to cut off the rival line from power; one can imagine it might be galling to have the son of one's murderous rival succeed uncustomarily to the throne. Yet far from depicting Lady Macbeth as simply employing her era's customary method of securing the throne and, moreover, avenging on Duncan the crime committed by his grandfather in arranging Duncan's access to power, Shakespeare represents her choice of actions as a matter of demonology, and a distortion of what he supposes are "natural" female functions: "Come, you spirits," she says, "unsex me here . . . take my milk for gall" (1.5.41–48).

In Shakespeare's alterations of the stories that came to him through Scottish legends, we can see the institution of arbitrary differences that Girard describes as essential to the process of mythmaking. First, in fact, though not in legend, the murder of Duncan was in the nature of a revenge. Duncan, not Macbeth, was in the eleventh century the usurper; and Macbeth was the vindicator of a rightful line of succession, the role assigned to Macduff by the chroniclers and later by Shakespeare. In the version of the story we know best, Duncan and Macbeth are set in opposition as a good king-father and a usurping subject-son figure, whereas in Holinshed's *Chronicles*, Duncan is a young man near Macbeth's own age and, upon replacing him, Macbeth reigns for many years as a benevolent monarch. Second, whereas in Holinshed Banquo is an active accomplice to the crime, Shakespeare makes a point of differentiating him from Macbeth. Though Shakespeare's Banquo dreams of power and though he cooperates by complying with Macbeth's accession to the throne, he does not, as does the Banquo in the sources, collaborate in Duncan's murder. Banquo reacts differently from Macbeth to the witches' prophecies. Whereas Macbeth stands "rapt," Banquo realistically tests the presence of the witches: "Were such things here as we do speak about? / Or have we eaten on the insane root / That takes the reason prisoner?" (1.3.82–85). Shakespeare's Banquo warns Macbeth that the witches are "instruments of darkness" who may betray him in "deepest consequence" (1.3.124–126); and he agrees to confer with Macbeth about seeking to augment his own honor provided he will lose none. All these exonerations of Banquo from complicity in Duncan's assassination are Shakespeare's additions to the tale. Third, the playwright compounds Macbeth's villainy as an assassin by having him violate his role as host in murdering Duncan as his guest. This detail of murdering the king while he is sleeping under the murderer's protection Shakespeare interpolated from a separate story, the murder of King Duff by Donwald. These Shakespearean changes continue the mythmaking process the Scottish story tellers had begun 300 years before.

Aside from the allusions to James's mythical roots in the seeds of Banquo, what would have motivated Shakespeare in 1606 to retell the Macbeth story in this new revised form? A brief look at *Macbeth's* other allusions to fears and events in its contemporary political context provides some essential clues. Queen Elizabeth's childlessness, for example, is suggested by Macbeth's "barren sceptre," as Freud

(1916) and others have noticed. When Elizabeth received the news that her cousin Mary had given birth to James, she was said to have declared, "The Queen of Scotland is lighter of a fair son, and I am but a barren stock" (Neale, 1934, pp. 141–142). Macbeth/Elizabeth's lack of issue is contrasted in the play to the long line of kings stretching from the blood-boltered Banquo to King James with "twofold balls and treble sceptres" (4.1.121), an image of genital potency as well as an emblem of coronation referring to the King's titles as monarch of Britain and Scotland. The witches tell Banquo, "Thou shalt get kings, though thou be none" (1.3.67); but Macduff says of Macbeth, "He has no children" (4.3.216). Macbeth fears Banquo because the witches "hail'd him father to a line of kings. / Upon my head they plac'd a fruitless crown, / And put a barren sceptre in my gripe, / Thence to be wrench'd with an unlineal [i.e., from another line] hand, / No son of mind succeeding" (3.1.59–63).

It is a telling historical irony that though Macbeth sees Banquo's issue on the English throne in a line reaching to the "crack of doom," in fact the Stuart line would be broken in the generation following James. His son Charles I was beheaded in 1649; and his grandson James II ended the line with his abdication in 1688. This is hardly the crack of doom, except for absolute monarchists.

One may imagine how the transition from the Tudor to the Stuart dynasty at the beginning of the seventeenth century recapitulated a perennial cultural dilemma and posed a threat of a return to an archaic mode of political authority and succession. Queen Elizabeth's childlessness raised the spectre throughout England of discontinuity and a violent transfer of power upon her demise. Already, during her final years, there had been an attempted usurpation, Essex's abortive rebellion in 1601, which was violently suppressed and punished with decapitation — a fate shared within Shakespeare's play by Cawdor and Macbeth.

It is possible to identify a crisis to which the play responds in the tension in English collective life between potentially violent succession through usurpation, and succession by primogeniture and linear descent. As Dover Wilson (1968) has reminded us, violent transfer of power was the order of the day in Europe during the early Middle Ages; it was not until the thirteenth century that a less destructive custom was instituted. So in staging the double regicides, *Macbeth* dramatizes a tension between orderly succession through inheritance of power by the king's first son ("We will establish our estate upon our eldest, Malcolm" [1.4.37–38]), and succession through assassination and seizure of power, catching "the nearest way."

The play associates the assassins with collapse of hierarchy, as in Lady Macbeth's dismissive order to the thanes at the end of the banquet scene, "Stand not upon the order of your going" (3.4.116), a reversal of Macbeth's opening command in that scene, "You know your own degrees, sit down" (3.4.1). Lady Macbeth's command not only violates the ceremony of hierarchically arranged departure from the Banquet Hall; it is a moment when she, not the King, is in command, a moment of actualized female rule. Such a moment publicly transgresses the principle of "hierarchy," which means "sacred rule" and is linked in our culture to the idea of patriarchy, father-originated power. It thus speaks powerfully to fears raised by the anomaly of female rule and points to the relief Elizabeth's death must have brought to patriarchal thinkers appalled by the idea of female-dominated "sovereign sway and masterdom" (1.5.70).

One significant aspect of the moral distinction in *Macbeth* between succession by assassination (Macbeth's method) and succession by lineal descent (Malcolm's method and, presumably though not clearly, Fleance's) is that it may be regarded as an imposed distinction. It did not exist in the eleventh century; and, from the perspective of psychoanalysis, it does not exist in unconscious, primary process thought, according to which death equals murder. Freud (1913) writes, "In the view of unconscious thinking, a man who has died a natural death is a murdered man: evil wishes have killed him" (p. 62). This points to an important psychological dimension of *Macbeth*: its conflict between the level of mentation psychoanalysis calls the primary process, here associated with assassination and the instant translation of thoughts into deeds, and the transformed level of mentation psychoanalysis identifies as secondary process, rational thought, here associated with linear descent, sequence, consequence, and ordered "measure" and time. Since succession is unconsciously always a matter of assassination insofar as it fulfills the successor's wish to succeed, Macbeth's replacement by Malcolm on the throne is a perfect instance of the transformation of the first process or principle of mentation into the second: Macbeth's acting out of parricidal wishes brings the named heir to the throne without blood on his hands. In this sense, as Harry Berger, Jr.

(1982) has argued, Macbeth and the witches who announce his wishes are scapegoats to the legitimized masculine imagination of the play. Macbeth, acting as the violent medium of succession, embodies the unconscious meaning of historical sequence. He plunges Scotland into a nightmare of violence and rids the kingdom of an old and ineffectual leader who has just been defended from a double rebellion; then Macbeth is expelled from the realm by a magical double, Macduff, thereby allowing Malcolm to succeed his father without committing patricide.

Remarkably enough, the play links Malcolm to Macbeth, for all their differences, through the word "success." In the early scenes, the word attaches to Macbeth. Rosse greets him with, "The King hath receiv'd, Macbeth, the news of thy success" (1.3.89); and when he hears of his additional title, Thane of Cawdor, fulfilling the witches' prophecy, Macbeth comments that the "supernatural soliciting" had given him "earnest of success" (1.3.132); then he writes to Lady Macbeth, "They met me in the day of success" (1.5.1). In his long soliloquy in which he resists the idea of killing Duncan, Macbeth puns on "success" as "succession": "If th' assassination / Could trammel up the consequence, and catch / With his surcease, success" (1.7.2–4). In the scene where Malcolm reports his fantasied vices to Macduff, he says, "Yet my poor country / Shall have more vices than it had before, / More suffer, and more sundry ways than ever, / By him that shall succeed" (4.3.46–49). The differences between Macbeth and his successor are, first, that Malcolm rehearses vices in words but does not act them out; and second, that Macbeth imagines the consequences of assassination and Malcolm profits from it. And Malcolm profits "holily," identifying with the power of the English king, who leaves his healing benediction to the "succeeding royalty" (4.3.155).

A problem of patriarchal culture is how to maintain an ordered system of authority differentiating the role of fathers from that of sons even as sons are in the process of succeeding their fathers, as the differences between them are being superseded. Ludwig Jekels (1943) has analyzed the psychology of this problem in *Macbeth*. For Jekels, the play enacts a cycle in which a bad son becomes a bad father. As Macbeth passes from subject to king, he is in turn punished not only by his conscience, the internalized father or superego, but physically by a bad son figure, the rebellious Macduff, who, as indicated by his name as well as his role as regicide, is Macbeth's double. The prefix "Mac" means "son of." "Macduff" can therefore be seen as the son of King Duff, who in another Scottish legend was said to have been murdered by Donwald. Since King Duff is condensed in *Macbeth* with Duncan, and Donwald with Macbeth and Macdonwald as traitors, Macduff appears to be a son who commits regicide in order to avenge one. Jekels says that it is the father within Macbeth — that is, the never-silenced memories of hatred against his father and of the injury inflicted in his thoughts on that father — that nourishes suspicions of the very same feelings in the son; it is the father surviving in Macbeth who demands the death of the feared son who may visit on Macbeth what he himself had visited on his own symbolic father, Duncan. Jekels (1943) writes, "Macbeth demonstrates the fact that a bad son will make a bad father" (p. 116), and points out that the same close connection of the psychical functions of son and father is revealed in Macduff, who, persecuted by Macbeth, abandons his family to murderous hands, and whose son is stabbed to death before our eyes. Jekels sees Macduff's rebellion against the symbolic father, and the destruction of his own family that results from it, as a duplication of Macbeth's fate. By killing his symbolic father Duncan, Macbeth loses his continuity in the next generation, seeming to forfeit paternity as a punishment for parricide; and "Macduff too, demonstrates that a bad son is also a bad father. . . . Macduff . . . becomes, as it were, the continuation of Macbeth" (Jekels, 1943, pp. 117, 119). But Macduff is not just a son figure subject to Macbeth; he is also a father, the father as progenitor though not as authority. These latter two roles, which were originally united in Duncan, have by Macbeth's parricidal violence been split apart.

The psychoanalytic literary critic David Barron (1960) thinks that it is Macduff who brings Macbeth and the play back into normal reality after its regression and merger with the murky world of maternal malevolence and dream. Barron sees Macduff as a rescuer of Macbeth's masculinity from the preoedipal fluidity that surrounds him as he is overwhelmed by his wife, the witches, and his fantasies. "To be a man requires confrontation with reality," writes Barron (1960), "and a most important component in confronting reality is the opposing male figure — ideally, of course, the father. It is through encountering the strength of the opposing father that one obtains a mastery of reality; for one can then feel the strength of one's own impulses and measure them against a superior force" (p. 273). Accordingly, Barron interprets the play as a contest between the principle of male ascendancy represented by Duncan, Macduff, and Malcolm and the principle of female ascendancy represented by the weird sisters and Lady Macbeth, with Macbeth as their instrument.

This opposition is fundamental to the Shakespearean attitude toward hierarchy in *Macbeth*, in which female ascendancy is linked to disorder in the universe and collapse of the chain of being. On the night the female-dominated Macbeth murders Duncan, "a falcon, tow'ring in her pride of place, / Was by a mousing owl hawk'd at and killed" (2.4.12–13). Barron's brilliant analysis notwithstanding, it is remarkable that this image feminizes Duncan, who is attacked like the falcon in "*her* pride of place" (my italics). This reversal of the ideological image of natural hierarchy is connected to a most primitive fear: mutual devouring, as Duncan's phallic horses break out of their stalls and "eat each other" (2.4.18). In *Macbeth*, female dominance is associated with boundary confusion, as in the broken-down stalls, the witches' beards and female breasts, the witches' ability to melt their corporality into air, and Macbeth's confusion of his outer and inner worlds in the dagger soliloquy and in his vision of Banquo's ghost, the materialization of his guilty conscience. In *Macbeth*, female ascendancy means an ocean of blood, an excess of violence, a loss of "degrees," the death of renown and grace; whereas the male ascendancy associated with Malcolm, who is "Unknown to woman" (4.33.125), means "measure, time, and place" (5.9.38), the realm of ordered differences.

This definition and a confusion of genders is in turn superimposed on the opposition between alternative methods of succession we have already analyzed, producing a psycho-logic that suggests that if the sexes fail to maintain separately defined identities, there can be no procreation, and therefore no orderly patrilineal succession. In screwing Macbeth's courage to the sticking place, Lady Macbeth in effect unmans him as she unsexes herself. Thanks to the woman's insistent assertion of her own powers, she herself is unsexed, grows a beard, exchanges her maternal milk for gall; and the man is rendered impotent, his disappearing dagger leading ultimately to "a barren sceptre." In the beginning of the play, Lady Macbeth is all courage while Macbeth expresses conscience; after

Macbeth's second visit to the witches, he is all courage while she succumbs to guilty fantasies. As Freud (1916) pointed out, these two are a single personality exchanging roles and mingling aspects; and the net result of these blurrings of traditional gender categories and crossings of identification is the construction of a single composite entity simultaneously impotent, mad, and monstrous. Lady Macbeth invokes a stopping up of the "access and passage to remorse" and wills away the "compunctious visitings of nature" in a speech that Alice Fox (1979) reads as a wish for blocked menses. Macbeth imagines Duncan's murder as a stopping of a fount of blood, "the very source . . . is stopp'd" (2.33.98). This image of an emptied source, "The wine of life is drawn" (2.3.95), echoes Lady Macbeth's wish for a stopped passage and is linked to the stopping up or cutting off of issue.

Duncan, however, a King without a Queen, is by contrast a figure of benevolent androgyny, a fertile father and nurturing mother figure who plants his subjects and "will labor" to make them grow, who overflows in "measureless content," and "Wanton with fullness," weeps with gratitude (2.1.17; 1.4.27–28, 34). His generativity in turn contrasts with the "wither'd," sterile witches whose sexual identity is not a fusion but a confusion of male and female, and whose beards suggest the unregenerative old age into which Macbeth's ambition vaults him. A young man looking forward to fathering children in the opening act of the play, after the murder of Duncan and its consequences, Macbeth finds himself in the position of a hibernal king, "ripe for shaking" (4.3.238) in a ritual regeneration of Scotland's wasteland. His life has fallen into "the sear, the yellow leaf" (5.3.23). "The future in the instant" (1.5.58) has left him depleted, an old man before his time.

Kenneth Burke (1941) has explained that assigning a new lineage to one's self, as constructing a new identity requires, must include symbolic matricide as well as symbolic patricide, in spite of the fact that in our culture lineage is traditionally charted after the metaphor of the patriarchal family tree in Western heraldry. So Janet Adelman's (1987) reading of *Macbeth* as dramatized tension between two fantasies, one "of a virtually absolute and destructive maternal power," the other "of absolute escape from this power" (p. 90), is consistent with my structuralist reading of the play as mediating unwelcome contradictions attendant on the transfer of power from the Tudor to the Stuart line. Working along lines quite similar to those I have already traced, Adelman (1987) writes,

> The play enables one version of the fantasy that heroic manhood is exemption from the female even while it punishes that fantasy in Macbeth. The key figure in whom this double movement is vested in the end of the play is Macduff; the unresolved contradictions that surround him are . . . marks of the ambivalence toward the fantasy itself. (pp. 107–108)

In contrast to Macbeth, who does not mourn the death of his Lady and implicitly of his potential heirs, thus exhibiting the lack of human kindness she had claimed essential to manliness, Macduff maintains that being able to feel grief for his slaughtered family is part of being a man. But Macduff's heroic status is allied to the fact that he left his wife behind, dead, as he had previously presumably left his mother, having been "Untimely ripp'd" from her womb, Caesarean births being usually fatal in Shakespeare's time and before. Similarly, the spurious fulfillment of the prophecy that Macbeth would be vanquished by "none of woman born" (4.1.80) both denies and affirms the fantasy of exemption from woman: In affirming that Macduff indeed had a mother, it denies a fantasy of male self-generation; but contradictorily, in attributing his power to having been untimely ripped from his mother, it sustains the sense that violent separation from the mother is the mark of a successful man (see Adelman, 1987).

In contrast to Macduff, whose family we see only in his absence and only to be slaughtered, the mingling of Macbeth and Lady Macbeth into a composite entity carries with it infantile associations that make of man and wife a mother–son pair who have failed to maintain separation. As Barron (1960) writes, in yielding to female influence, Macbeth has become so embedded in the bloody atmosphere diffusing out from wife and witches that he may be said to be mingling with female reproductive capacity but unable to reproduce because the spaces are glutted with foul ingredients strangling the processes of birth (p. 269). This same monstrous construct is reflected in the witches' cauldron, "thick and slab" with poisoned entrails, a foul female brew from which nothing fruitful can emerge — an image that disappears from the stage before the spirits of Banquo and his progeny appear. Throughout the play, in fact, iterative images of choking, of blocked female passages, of being "cribb'd, cabin'd, and confin'd, bound in" are juxtaposed to male-associated images of cutting through, breaking open, ripping, carving out passage. Macbeth, the first we hear of him, is in the midst of a battle in which the two sides "As two spent swimmers . . . do cling together / And choke their art" (1.2.8–9). "Like Valor's minion," he "carv'd out his passage" and "unseamed" his rival "from the nave to th' chops" (1.2.18–22), a weird tailoring image superimposed on a metaphor of a Caesarean birth. Likewise, Macduff, the male violently individuated from woman *via* an actual Caesarean birth, describes the murder of Duncan thus: "Most sacrilegious murder hath broke ope / The Lord's anointed temple" (2.3.67–68).

This metaphor of the body as temple, combined with Duncan's status as an androgynous progenitor, lends associations to the description of his gashed stab wounds: These are said to look like a "breach in nature," a phrase closely followed by the image of the bloody, phallic "daggers . . . breeched [i.e., trousered] with gore" (2.3.116). Alice Fox (1979) says the echo of "breach" here suggests a breach birth. The idea of the murdered Duncan as abnormally giving birth is consistent with Macduff's association of the murder scene with the sight of "a new Gorgon" (2.3.72). Freud (1940) interpreted a Gorgon, in particular the severed head of Medusa, as a displacement upward of male fear of castration: Men fantasize the female genitals as a horrid absence which they fear may be inflicted on themselves.

In effect, by murdering Duncan, Macbeth symbolically castrates himself. Cut off from continuity, he determines to give the edge of the sword to the wife and children of Macduff, all "that trace him in his line" (4.1.153); but Macbeth is unable to free himself from the female environment that engulfs him in a sea of blood — not of lineage but of violence. When Macbeth hears about Macduff's charm, it "cows" his "better part of man" (5.8.18), making him wetter than the cat in the adage, steeped in multitudinous seas. In his psychotic searching out of victims, in killing all Macduff's children, called "young fry" and "egg," and finally killing Lady Macduff, the original carrier of those eggs, Macbeth has performed a profane counterpart to the sacralized rebirth ritual that restores generative cycles when the army of young men cut down the trees of Birnam Wood and come to Dunsinane to break into Macbeth's castle.

If we bring together as an image cluster the killing of Lady

Macduff and her children, the idea of uprooting the forest-as-lineage, and the penetration of Macbeth's castle with the concomitant dispelling of the female charm that surrounds him and makes him the "secret'st man of blood" (3.4.125), we can see them all as symbolic acts of matricide in the service of male birth and regeneration. Moreover, these relatively obvious matricidal acts echo the attack on the feminized Duncan which sets the revenge in motion to begin with. The idea toward which all these actions and image clusters point is that men must get rid of women in order to be reborn. Thus Macduff, the vindicator of the play's rightful line of succession, is from his mother's womb "Untimely ripp'd," and Malcolm, the new king, is "Unknown to woman."

From a feminist perspective these are indeed dire and confused events new hatched to the woeful time. When Frank Kermode (Evans, ed., 1974, p. 1307) remarks on the "pregnancy" of the verse in *Macbeth*, he perhaps speaks more truly than he realizes. The play exploits a male birth fantasy. *Macbeth* transforms the fantasy that being (re)born means separating from woman in violence, leaving her dead. Masculine difference is achieved by cancelling out the feminine. It is instructive to note the oedipal possibilities implicit in the Macbeth stories Shakespeare inherited. In the sources of the play, Macbeth is his Lady's second husband; and though she has had offspring by her first marriage, he generates none with her. It is significant psychoanalytically as well as politically that Shakespeare's Lady Macbeth says she could not murder Duncan herself because he resembled her father as he slept; her reluctance not only makes sense in view of their kinship, but suggests as well primal scene fantasies of nocturnal parental events. Similarly, Macbeth projects Duncan's murder as an impending rape, associating "wither'd Murther" with "Tarquin's ravishing strides" (2.1.52, 55). When he has fulfilled the first of the three early prophecies, Macbeth calls them "happy prologues to the swelling act / Of the imperial theme" (1.3.127–128), an image suggesting phallic erection as well as pregnancy and playwriting. If Macbeth as assassin is identified with Tarquin, then Duncan becomes a feminized victim of murderous male penetration, a notion consistent with Macduff's identification of the King's violated body with a "new Gorgon."

The view of the King as castrated or monstrously feminized connects with the decapitations that occur in the play—Mac-

donwald's and Macbeth's — as well as the apparition of the armed
head of rebellion and the cut trees of Birnam wood. When Macduff
enters in the last scene of the play holding Macbeth's severed head,
the apposite mythological association is to Perseus, especially given
Macduff's earlier invocation of a Gorgon to describe the murder
scene. Perseus conquered dread female magic by decapitating a
woman figure and then appropriating her power, wielding her severed head on his shield to repel his enemies, an action bearing some
similarity to the way in which the young men cut the boughs and
carry them as camouflage in marching against Macbeth, who finds
the sight of the approaching forest terrifying. Medusa was murdered
in her sleep, a fear Malcolm raises the moment before he orders the
cutting of the boughs: "I hope the days are near at hand / That
chambers will be safe" (5.4.1–2), an allusion to Duncan's death.

According to Freud's theory of the castration complex, a little
boy fears that if he fulfills his oedipal wish to supplant his father and
merge with his mother sexually, he will be punished with castration;
and the sight of the female genitals is horrifying to the male child's
imagination because he regards them as having been castrated. The
unconscious logic is, "If she doesn't have one, I could lose mine," a
fearful fantasy complicated by the fact that the boy has come from a
woman's body, and supported by the association of menstrual and
childbirth blood with the mother. The primal scene too is sometimes
understood in association with castration fantasies, since male genitals may seem to disappear in the act of sexual penetration, an idea
perhaps implicit in Macbeth's doubts about whether his air-drawn
dagger is really there or not (see Willbern, 1986, p. 543).

Macduff's role as liberating and punishing hero, then, makes
him a figure of masculine mastery of the fear of women, and links
him to a line of ancient male vindicators such as Dionysus, also
"unborn of woman." Dionysus was responsible for the ritual dismem-
berment of the tyrannical Pentheus, who, like Macbeth, brought
about his own undoing by penetrating into taboo female ritual
space. As Janet Adelman (1987) points out, first Macbeth and then
Macduff is associated with the shared fantasy that secure male community depends on the prowess of the man who slays the "woman's
man" — first Macdonwald, who is "Fortune's man," and then Macbeth himself, who re-embodies and replays Macdonwald's role.

The topical context for this fantasy of male prowess in *Macbeth* is the transitional passage we have already described from female to male power, Elizabeth to James. Already, before James's accession, it is reasonable to assume, the crisis of succession created by Elizabeth's childlessness must have carried with it collective sensitivity to the connections between succession and sexuality. Continuity of patriarchal lineage, after all, depends both on the female capacity for childbirth and upon the future male heir's containment by the primordial sea of fluids within the mother's body. And the principle of hierarchical inheritance and succession, taken to its roots, depends on a blurring of the distinctions it exists to uphold: first, the boundaries between separate persons and between man and woman in the sexual act of generating an heir, and then, the differences between fathers and sons in the son's act of succeeding to his father's role.

These biological and lineal concerns, contradictions, and anxieties all appear in *Macbeth* in the form of distorted, threatening imagery of violence and disruption. Sexuality is violent in the play, as in "Tarquin's ravishing strides"; the son's latent relationship to his father is violent; and the incursion of violence into the shared political domain is mediated by the appearance of female figures who disrupt seasonal cycles of growth by pouring destructively ambitious ideas into the mind of man rather than serving as receivers of male seed. Echoing Seneca's Medea, that avenging child-murderer, Lady Macbeth calls to her husband, "Hie thee hither, / That I may pour my spirits in thine ear. / And chastise with the valour of my tongue / All that impedes thee from the golden round" (1.5.25–28). This image of evil female seduction through the ear reverses the Madonna's conception; here it is Macbeth who will conceive (as in his anticipation of the "swelling act / Of the imperial theme"), and who will then be crowned (crowning being a buried metaphor here for the appearance of the baby's head in birth, as in the final two apparitions: "a bloody Child" and "a Child crowned," a reversal of the order of delivery).

In effect, Lady Macbeth's solicitings breed outward through her husband's mind into the world of the play, culminating in his mad vision tumbling together "the treasure of nature's germains" (4.1.58), a cosmic fantasy of gene pool destruction. To this female-infected primal scene fantasy, *Macbeth* opposes an uprooting and renewal of the life cycle, to be "planted newly with the time" (5.9.31), the founding of an alternative dynasty, all male if we are to believe the witches' final prophecy projecting no queens beside the long line of kings.

III

Girard's claim that the genesis of myth is reciprocal violence is a resonant hypothesis for the study of the revenge play, since revenge is indeed reciprocally violent. But sacralized revenge such as Macbeth's on the betrayers of Duncan and Macduff's on Macbeth is violence with a (mythic) difference. Shakespeare's Macbeth is a figure through whom essential cultural contradictions have been projected. As a son figure, a subject, who becomes a father figure, a king, through violence, Macbeth splits off the negative oedipal dimension of Malcolm's legitimized succession to the throne. Moreover, as Berger (1982) argues so forcefully, Macbeth's role as the evil villain in a morality play is the superficial aspect of his textual role as a scapegoat of the mortified ambitious young men of Scotland. The play both mystifies and develops this scapegoating process by the introduction of the comic and childish weird sisters: figures of evil from the standpoint of the morality play, on a deeper level, "scapegoats of the male imagination" (Berger, 1982, p. 74). Lady Macbeth and Macbeth are both responsive to and responsible for the incursion of the supernatural and unnatural into the political and natural worlds, these two worlds being ideologically identified in the legitimized social order associated with Malcolm. Since mythic thinking involves fusing the cultural with the natural order in one continuous chain of being, Macbeth's hierarchical transgression in regicide — symbolic parricide — is metaphorically linked with "unnatural" images such as women with beards that blur their gender, the killing of a falcon by a mousing owl, and the inversion of normal cycles of growth and decay: "good men's lives / Expire before the flowers in their caps. / Dying or ere they sicken" (4.3.171–173). The witches and Macbeth collapse boundaries between persons as well as binary oppositions in language, thereby demonstrating the Girardian aspect of myth that challenges and then re-establishes differences. Macbeth's opening remark about "foul and fair," for example, echoes the witches' final chant two scenes earlier, although Macbeth has not yet heard the witches. And the rhetoric of the play, with its

repetitions of doubling, antithesis, and paradox in which "nothing is /
But what is not" (1.3.141–142), as well as the symmetrical structure
of revenge and multiple character doublings, all serve to subvert any
official morality-play reading according to which the evil tyrant Macbeth kills the good Duncan and is rightfully punished by the holy
Malcolm and his supporters. As Berger (1982) claims, Macbeth is the
Scottish male community's model, rival, and dark double; he follows
the logic of this community's desire to its ultimate conclusion (p. 73).

The communal revenge on this desire is then Christianized as
holy vengeance, while all the women in the play are eliminated as a
prelude to Macbeth's own death. Macbeth is the cruelest male in the
play; yet as Joel Fineman (1980) has pointed out, a preoccupation
with ideal maleness is female at its source (p. 83). Thus, Macbeth
paradoxically turns out to be the play's most feminized character, as
is symbolized by his emasculating decapitation at the hands of the
womanless Macduff.

The scene of Macduff's victory over Macbeth, of the ultimate
man without a woman holding the severed head of the woman's
man, expresses patriarchal tensions between women and men that
result from women's power over childbirth and early infancy and,
therefore, over succession and continuity. *Macbeth* mediates these
tensions by cosmologizing them as metaphysically induced by unnatural female power. Female powers, along with Macbeth, are scape-
goated as agents of demonic witchcraft. The biological function of
women in sustaining the family tree is either denied mythically, as in
the strange fantasy that there is a man not born of woman, or
uprooted to be replanted by an all male dynasty, as if men (in
Coriolanus's words) were authors of themselves and knew no other
kin. In Shakespeare's play we never see the mothers of Donalbain,
Malcolm, or Fleance; and James's mother, Mary, Queen of Scots, is
conspicuously left out of the long line of kings projected in the
cauldron scene. Lady Macbeth is associated with the androgynous,
sterile witches, and with the infanticidal Medea whose voice echoes
through the "unsex me" speech. *Macbeth* denies women's procreative
power or, at least, cancels it. If Lady Macbeth has had any children,
they are not visible in this play, which splits between Banquo and
Macbeth the dual function of the father as progenitor and as authority figure. Macbeth becomes king; Banquo begets kings though he
never becomes one. The avenging hero Macduff is a father who

never becomes a king; and Malcolm, the new king, is "unknown to woman" and therefore no father. The terrors of sexual violence in genital contact and its issue are expressed and transformed in *Macbeth* through structural strategies which first radically fuse and then radically separate man and woman. By ideologically portraying gender confusion as unnatural, the play mediates this unwelcome masculinist contradiction: Man depends on woman for birth but must get rid of her in order to be (re)born. This fantastical idea mystified and legitimated James I's claim to the English throne, scapegoating Elizabeth for her barreness. By assigning a new (male) lineage to British royalty, *Macbeth* thus provided England with a symbolic passage to a new political identity.

REFERENCES

ADELMAN, J. (1987) "Born of Woman": Fantasies of Maternal Power in *Macbeth*. In M. Garber (Ed.), *Cannibals, Witches, and Divorce: Estranging the Renaissance* (pp. 90–121). Baltimore: Johns Hopkins University Press.

BARRON, D. (1960) The Babe that Milks: An Organic Study of *Macbeth*. In M. D. Faber (Ed.), *The Design Within: Psychoanalytic Approaches to Shakespeare* (pp. 253–279). New York: Science House, 1970.

BERGER, H. JR., (1982) Text against Performance in Shakespeare: The Example of *Macbeth*. *Genre*, 15:49–79.

BURKE, K. (1941) Freud — And the Analysis of Poetry. In *The Philosophy of Literary Form*. New York: Vintage, 1957.

EVANS, G. B. (Ed.). (1974) *The Riverside Shakespeare*. Boston: Houghton Mifflin.

FENICHEL, O. (1945) *The Psychoanalytic Theory of Neurosis*. New York: Norton.

FINEMAN, J. (1980) Fratricide and Cuckoldry: Shakespeare's Doubles. In M. Schwartz & C. Kahn (Eds.), *Representing Shakespeare: New Psychoanalytic Essays* (pp. 70–109). Baltimore: Johns Hopkins University Press.

FOX, A. (1979) Obstetrics and Gynecology in *Macbeth*. *Shakespeare Survey*, 12:127–141.

FREUD, S. (1913) Totem and Taboo. *Standard Edition*, 13:1–161.

———— (1916) Some Character-Types met with in Psycho-Analytic Work, *Standard Edition*, 14:311–333.

———— (1930) Civilization and Its Discontents, *Standard Edition*, 21:64–145.

———— (1940) Medusa's Head, *Standard Edition*, 18:273–274.

GIRARD, R. (1979) Myth and Ritual in Shakespeare: *A Midsummer Night's Dream*. In J. Harari (Ed.), *Textual Strategies: Perspectives in Post-Structuralist Criticism* (pp. 189–122). Ithaca: Cornell University Press.

———— (1986) *The Scapegoat*. Yvonne Freccero (Trans.). Baltimore: Johns Hopkins University Press.

JEKELS, L. (1943) The Riddle of Shakespeare's *Macbeth*. In *Selected Papers*. New York: International Universities Press, 1970.

NEALE, J. E. (1934) *Queen Elizabeth I*. Garden City: Doubleday/Anchor Books, 1957.

SCHOENBAUM, S. (1977) *William Shakespeare: A Compact Documentary Life*. New York: Oxford University Press.

WILLBERN, D. (1978) Rape and Revenge in *Titus Andronicus*. *English Literary Renaissance*, 8:159–182.

———— (1986) Phantasmagoric *Macbeth*. *English Literary Renaissance*, 16:520–549.

WILSON, J. D. (1968) Introduction to *Macbeth*. Cambridge: Cambridge University Press.

Trinity College
Hartford, CT 06106

"HERE ONLY WEAK": SEXUALITY AND THE STRUCTURE OF TRAUMA IN *PARADISE LOST**

Peter L. Rudnytsky

Whether the whole relation be not Allegorical, that is, whether the temptation of the Man by the Woman, be not the seduction of the rational and higher parts by the inferiour and feminine faculties: or whether the Tree in the midst of the Garden, were not that part in the Center of the body, in which afterward was the appointment of Circumcision in Males, we leave it unto the Thalmudist.

         — Sir Thomas Browne, *Pseudodoxia Epidemica*

I

In Book VIII of *Paradise Lost*, near the end of his lengthy colloquy with Raphael beginning in Book V, Adam describes his extreme susceptibility to Eve's beauty. In contrast to the "delight" that he feels in objects of the natural world, but which induce in his mind "no change, / Nor vehement desire," Adam acknowledges the tumult aroused in him by his fair consort:

> but here
> Far otherwise, transported I behold,
> Transported touch; here passion first I felt,
> Commotion strange, in all enjoyments else
> Superior and unmov'd, here only weak
> Against the charm of Beauty's powerful glance. (VIII.524–533)

These lines, together with the remainder of Adam's speech in praise of Eve, are greeted by the angel "with contracted brow"

---

*I am grateful to Margaret W. Ferguson for reading an earlier draft of this paper. Belated thanks to Leslie Brisman for clarifying what I was trying to say about Milton. I am conscious of having assimilated ideas from three of my students at Columbia: Bronwen Jones, Anne Rosen, and Nancy Stade.

(VIII.560) and a reminder of the need for a healthy "self-esteem, grounded on just and right" (VIII.572). In their insistence on Adam's vulnerability in the erotic sphere—the disparity between his "Superior and unmov'd" contemplation of other "enjoyments" and the "commotion strange" with which he is "transported" by Eve—they open the way to a psychoanalytic reading of *Paradise Lost*. For, addressing in Freudian terms the essential issue posed by Adam's declaration, Jean Laplanche (1970) asks, "How is it, *in fact*, that one's sexual life constitutes the only weak point on which repression . . . comes to bear? Why is it our sexuality alone which is repressed?" (p. 30).

Laplanche answers the riddle of why it should be that sexuality forms the "only weak point" in human development by invoking Freud's theory of "deferred action" (*Nachträglichkeit*). This concept, a psychoanalytic model for the structure of trauma, receives its most comprehensive elaboration in Freud's posthumously published *Project for a Scientific Psychology* (1895). Drawing on the case of Emma (as we now know, Emma Eckstein) recounted in the *Project*, Laplanche explains that deferred action results from the interaction of "two scenes linked by associative chains, but also clearly separated from each other by a *temporal barrier which inscribes them in two different spheres of meaning: the moment of puberty*" (p. 40). In Emma's case, puberty intervenes between an occurrence of sexual assault in childhood and a later, innocuous event that reawakens the repressed memory of the earlier, as yet imperfectly comprehended scene. But, as Laplanche notes, puberty retains its conceptual importance even after Freud abandoned his "seduction theory." For it is precisely the *diphasic onset* of human sexuality—coming as it does both "too early" in infancy and "too late" with biological maturity—that causes it to be spontaneously repressed and assures that one's experience of it will necessarily be "after the event" and hence traumatic.

The shared conviction of Milton and Freud that sexuality forms the region of paramount vulnerability in the human psyche suggests the utility of the concept of deferred action to understanding Milton's epic. One of the most disputed problems of interpretation in *Paradise Lost* concerns the relation of unfallen to fallen experience. On the one hand, it is undeniable that the lives of both unfallen Adam and Eve contain a sequence of more or less parallel events that seem to prefigure the Fall (see Stein, 1953, pp. 75–118). For Eve, these are (1) her Narcissus-like attraction to her own "smooth watry image" at the moment of her first creation (IV.449–491); (2) her dream-temptation (V.35–93) in which she imagines partaking of the forbidden fruit; and (3) her argument to Adam in favor of separate gardening (IX.205–375). These three preliminary threats to order, on Eve's part, find their counterpart in Adam when he (1) responds to Eve's creation (VIII.470–480); (2) confesses to Raphael (in the speech from which I have quoted) his continuing undue admiration for Eve (VIII.521–560); and (3) accedes to Eve's request to work separately. Both Adam and Eve, moreover, question the purpose of the stars' shining and the movement of heavenly bodies (IV.657–658; VIII.13–38) in a way that seems dangerously to permit human consciousness to become the measure of God's workings in the universe. Indeed, so pronounced are these anticipations of the Fall in prelapsarian experience that some scholars are driven to argue, as does Millicent Bell (1953), that "there is, in effect, no longer a Fall as the Bible plot presents it. . . . From the first we are after the Fall" (p. 867).[1]

As may be imagined, however, this theory of the "fallacy of the Fall" in *Paradise Lost* has called forth vehement protests from other critics (see Shumaker, 1955; Ogden, 1957) of Milton's poem, particularly those of a theological persuasion. The counter-argument points out that Eve is described by the narrator as "yet sinless" (IX.659) only moments before eating of the forbidden fruit. Most importantly, these critics insist, the connections between the Fall and its ostensible prefigurations are imposed by our consciousness as fallen readers, and in no way render its occurrence inevitable. The Fall, that is, in Stanley Fish's (1967) words, must be "thrown into brilliant relief as an incomprehensible phenomenon" (p. 228), wholly discontinuous with everything that comes before it. As the example of Christ in *Paradise Regained* attests — like Adam and Eve, he is subjected by Satan to a sequence of temptations, but is able to withstand them — if only Adam and Eve had resisted at the crucial moments, their earlier trials would not seem deterministically to anticipate the Fall, but would rather become a series of demonstrations of the dynamic growth and possibilities of human freedom.

Criticism of *Paradise Lost* has imitated the poem itself by exhibiting a tendency to split into opposing "angelic" and "Satanic" camps, and one virtue of the model of deferred action is that it enables us to

subvert the opposition between these seemingly incompatible approaches, taking what is of value in both without being bound by the
limitations of either. If the Fall may be viewed as analogous to a
trauma, Laplanche's account gives due weight to the narrative critics, by recognizing that it can only be formed through the conjunction of two or more "scenes linked by associative chains," as Eve's
downfall is preceded by her creation scene, the dream, and so on.
On the other hand, he endorses the fundamental contention of the
theological critics, by positing the existence of a "temporal barrier"
that divides everything coming before and after it into "different
spheres of meaning," exactly as the Fall intervenes between pre- and
post-lapsarian experience in *Paradise Lost*. As an event, one might
say, which is itself "after the event," the Fall introduces repetition into
human experience and is both continuous and discontinuous with
what comes before it.

Although the tension between theological and narrative readings of the Fall is particularly acute in the case of *Paradise Lost*, it is
latent already in the Genesis story. In his brilliant treatment of these
same issues in *The Rhetoric of Religion* (1961), Kenneth Burke coins the
term "logology" to refer to his attempt to understand the language
used to talk about "God," wholly irrespective of the question of
whether or not God exists. Burke's "logological" point of view is in
essence a more sophisticated version of what would be a narrative
approach to *Paradise Lost*. Despite wishing to regard the theological
and logological interpretations of Genesis as existing in most respects
on "different planes, so that they neither corroborate nor refute one
another," Burke admits that "at one point there does seem to be a
necessary opposition." This is the crucial problem of determinism
versus free will or the avoidability of the Fall. In Burke's summary
formulation:

> Theologically, Adam could have chosen *not* to sin. He could have said
> yes to God's thou-shalt-not. But logologically, Adam *necessarily* sinned.
> For if he had chosen *not* to sin, the whole design of the Bible would
> have been ruined. (p. 252)

Essential to the theological understanding of the Fall, whether
in Genesis or *Paradise Lost*, is the conviction that it could have been
avoided, that disobedience is purely a matter of human choice. In

the famous words of Milton's God, man is created "Sufficient to have stood, though free to fall" (III.99). Burke's unsettling contribution, however, is to point out that the story, as Milton inherited it from the Bible, possesses a foreordained conclusion, and hence from the narrative or logological standpoint this sense of human freedom must be dismissed as an illusion. Although these conflicting assumptions cannot be logically reconciled, much of the imaginative force of *Paradise Lost* resides in the way that Milton remains true to the requirements of theology while yet exploiting the sense of inevitability inherent in the narrative. The epic, that is, demands to be read simultaneously from two incompatible perspectives, one of which "deconstructs" the other.

The need for a dialectical response to *Paradise Lost* is nowhere more evident than in those incidents in the lives of unfallen Adam and Eve that seem to prefigure the Fall. For instance, Eve's abrupt question at the end of her praise of nature in Book IV, "But wherefore all night long shine these [stars], for whom / This glorious sight, when sleep hath shut all eyes?" (657–658), is met by Adam's response that God does not depend on man for approbation of his works: "nor think, though men were none, / That Heav'n would want spectators, God want praise" (675–676). But though he here instructs Eve on the need for order and the proper relation of creature to creator, Adam's own questions to Raphael in Book VIII show that the matter is still unsettled in his own mind: "reasoning I oft admire, / How Nature wise and frugal could commit such disproportions" (25–27). The point is that such doubts may be regarded *either* as the subversive erecting of human consciousness into the measure of God's handiwork *or* as a manifestation of Adam and Eve's excellence, insofar as they lead to a renewed understanding of what lies within the bounds of human nature and a reverent puzzlement about what extends beyond it. Indeed, both readings — doctrinal and narrative, theological and logological — are not merely possible but *mandated* by Milton's poem, depending on the position we wish to adopt on the issue of the inevitability of the Fall.

Similarly, to glance only briefly at analogous examples, Eve's dream in Book V, inspired by Satan "Squat like a toad, close at [her] ear" (IV.800), may with equal plausibility be regarded as evil temptation entering a blameless and innocent mind — as Adam assures her, "Evil into the mind of God or Man / May come and go, so unapprov'd, and leave / No spot or blame behind" (V.117–119)—or as a manifestation of Eve's unconscious desire for forbidden knowledge, especially if Satan's voice is held to be Eve's own, but alienated and made unrecognizable through a process of repression and projection. By the same token, in the debate over separate gardening in Book IX, Eve no longer adheres to her earlier pledge to Adam, "Unargu'd I obey" (IV.636). But are her disputatiousness, and Adam's acceding to her request to depart, the expression of an unhealthy desire for autonomy on her part and an abdication of authority and proper self-regard on his? Or are they, as Diane McColley (1983) has asserted in a recent "regenerative" reading, "the result of a responsible and considered choice whose outcome might have been, though it was not, the greater good of an unfallen race" (p. 141)? Both interpretations, again irreconcilable, may be supported, once more depending on whether we are willing—as McColley is not—to ascribe "the ex post facto appearance of wrongness attached to the separation" to the assumption that "the Fall was inevitable once the separation had taken place" (p. 184).

In one sense, it is the narrative or logological dimension of the poem that predetermines the outcome, and the theological dimension that retains the possibility of freedom of choice for the characters and an alternative plot. C. S. Lewis (1942) has speculated amusingly about what would have happened if Adam had refused Eve's offer of the apple, if he had "scolded or even chastised Eve and then interceded with God on her behalf" (p. 127). But this scenario, although conceivable theologically, is rendered absurd by the exigencies of the story, and is but a more extreme variation of trying to imagine a *Paradise Lost* in which both our first parents remain in a perennial state of innocence. In another sense, however, it is through the very dynamic quality of his narrative, and particularly his use of epic similes, that Milton raises possibilities—including that Eve might refuse to share the forbidden fruit with Adam—that are not explored in the Genesis source.

Within the structure of *Paradise Lost*, it is in the middle books that the most imaginative rewriting of Genesis is to be found. As Arnold Stein (1977) has pointed out, Raphael's mission to Eden follows directly upon the episode of Eve's dream at the outset of Book V, and it concludes in Book VIII "with the sudden disclosure of [Adam's] passion and in the enigmatic revelation of angelic sexuality which quickly return the end of the episode to a narrative mood and tempo resembling the place where the line of action broke off" (p. 109). Eve, that is, had been awakened from her dream of temptation with "glowing Cheek" (V.10), and this pitch of erotic excitement is only reached again at the end of Book VIII, which in turn prepares us for the Fall in Book IX when Eve reports her trespass to Adam: "But in her Cheek distemper flushing glow'd" (887). Thus, the entire cosmic digression provided by Raphael's account of the War in Heaven and the creation has the effect of building the structure of deferred action into the epic, so that the climactic action of the Fall comes as a repetition at a higher level of significance of Eve's dream and the other moments that retroactively foreshadow it.

According to Freud's early theory, it is specifically the advent of puberty that imposes the "temporal barrier" separating experiences before and after it into "different spheres of meaning." Even after the rejection of the seduction theory, as we have seen, puberty retains its importance as defining the inevitably diphasic onset of human sexuality. A scene of sexual seduction in childhood, or even a child's own sexual fantasy, consequently possesses an ambiguous quality, which — following Freud — Laplanche (1970) terms "sexual–presexual" (p. 40). This phrase precisely characterizes the paradoxical prelapsarian sexuality of Adam and Eve, at once innocent yet physical. Only at the Fall do Adam and Eve yield themselves to lust. To underscore that the gaining of forbidden knowledge is tantamount to the loss of mental, if not physical, virginity, Milton refers to Eve after her fall as "Defac'd, deflow'r'd, and now to death devote" (IX.901). Comparable in theoretical terms to the advent of puberty and explicitly equated by Milton with defloration, the Fall indeed provides the necessary line of demarcation between "sexual–presexual" and fully adult sexual experience.

II

As is true of his treatment of the Fall, Milton's attitude toward both women and sexuality in *Paradise Lost* is controversial because it lends itself to interpretation in radically divergent ways. It has long been recognized, for example, that Milton participates in a Puritan tradition that places a high value on the place of physical love in marriage (see Haller and Haller, 1942; Haller, 1946; Frye, 1955). Defenders

of his portrayal of women (see Lewalski, 1974; Webber, 1980), similarly, can point to the companionship and mutuality that obtain
between Adam and Eve, to the richness of his characterization of
Eve, and to his penchant for radical thought generally.[2] Critics of a
more feminist persuasion (see Landy, 1972, 1976; Gilbert and Gubar, 1979, pp. 187–212; Froula, 1983; Nyquist, 1987), on the other
hand, stress the inevitable subjugation of women that results from
Milton's hierarchical conception of the universe. Both Adam and
Eve are subordinate to God, they note, but Adam, unlike Eve,
enjoys an autonomy and mastery in his human realm comparable to
that enjoyed by God in his. While recognizing the force of the
qualifications imposed by those who would defend Milton's views of
women and "wedded love" (IV.750), in what follows I shall align the
insights of feminism and psychoanalysis to argue that sexuality for
Milton is in a fundamental sense equated with femininity, and that
his male sexual anxiety is thus largely expressed through his representation of female characters.

Nowhere is the darker side of Milton's vision of sexual relations
more clearly expressed than in Adam's misogynistic tirade after the
Fall. At his nadir of despair in Book X, when Eve first seeks to make
peace with him, Adam retorts:

> O why did God,
> Creator wise, that peopl'd highest Heav'n
> With Spirits Masculine, create at last
> This novelty on Earth, this fair defect
> Of Nature, and not fill the World at once
> With Men as Angels without Feminine,
> Or find some other way to generate
> Mankind? (888–895)

Spoken in context by a fictional character, these lines cannot be
naively equated with Milton's own beliefs. They have, moreover, a
long literary lineage: Precedents include Euripides's *Hippolytus* and
the soliloquy of Posthumus Leonatus in Act II, scene v of Shakespeare's *Cymbeline*. But just as words uttered in the heat of anger often
disclose feelings normally kept suppressed under the veil of decorum, so — precisely by virtue of being the grimmest indictment of
women in the poem — Adam's diatribe reveals with unparalleled
nakedness the misogyny that is an essential feature of the cosmos of
Paradise Lost.

The counterpart to Adam's view of femininity as "this fair defect / Of nature" occurs in Eve's speech where she contemplates withholding from her husband the knowledge brought by eating the forbidden fruit. It is noteworthy that whereas both in her unfallen state and after her repentance Eve acquiesces in her subordinate position to Adam — going so far as to assert that she enjoys thereby "So far the happier lot" (IV.446; see IV.637–638, X.930–931) — in the brief interval between her own fall and that of Adam she speaks with what twentieth-century readers may recognize as the voice of authentic feminist protest. Eve soliloquizes:

> But to *Adam* in what sort
> Shall I appear? shall I to him make known
> As yet my change, and give him to partake
> Full happiness with me, or rather not
> But keep the odds of Knowledge in my power
> Without Copartner? so to add what wants
> In Female Sex, the more to draw his Love,
> And render me more equal, and perhaps,
> A thing not undesirable, sometime
> Superior: for inferior who is free? (IX.817–825)

A similar note is struck by Eve in the mutual recriminations with Adam at the end of Book IX, and smoldering resentment is likewise expressed in the sequence of episodes that foreshadow her fall: Eve finds her own "smooth wat'ry image" (IV.480) initially more attractive than Adam; during her dream the voice of Satan tells her, "Happier thou may'st be" (V.77), whereas she had previously affirmed that obedience to her husband "Is woman's happiest knowledge and her praise" (IV.637); and in the separate gardening episode Eve likewise invokes Milton's own arguments from *Areopagitica* to secure Adam's permission to work separately. But it is only at the moment of her fall that Eve's incipient feminist consciousness achieves explicit articulation.

From the standpoint of the dominant ideology of *Paradise Lost*, Eve's outburst is subversive and unacceptable; but precisely for that reason it brings out most clearly the female perspective on Milton's patriarchal vision. Both Adam and Eve concur that femininity is constituted by a "defect" or lack, and Eve, who has just paid homage to experience as her "best guide" (IX.808) after the forbidden tree, defines the "odds of Knowledge" she has just acquired in Baconian fashion as the power to achieve not merely equality but even superiority over Adam in the cosmic hierarchy. In psychoanalytic terms, however, it is impossible to resist a more specific inference concerning her allusion to "what wants / In female sex." For Milton, as for Sir Thomas Browne, "the Tree in the midst of the Garden" is indeed "that part in the Center of the body, in which was afterward the appointment of Circumcision in males," and by partaking of its fruit Eve has temporarily usurped possession of the phallus, the absence of which she otherwise may envy but must nonetheless resign herself to accept.

That Eve's pursuit of forbidden knowledge turns on a cosmic case of penis envy—the phallus here representing not merely the male sexual organ but masculine power in all its guises—confirms the fundamentally sexist nature of Milton's portrayal of women in *Paradise Lost*. In Milton's epic, it is emphatically true that "highest Heav'n" is inhabited only by "Spirits Masculine," even though the narrator informs us that "Spirits when they please / Can either Sex assume, or both . . . / Not ti'd or manacl'd with joint or limb" (I.423–424,426). Indeed, one wonders whether Raphael's blushing when Adam asks him about angelic sex (VIII.619) is not due to this absence of women in heaven! Milton's poetic Muse, it is true, is characterized as feminine, and described as playing in the presence of God with "Wisdom thy Sister" (VII.10), but the crucial point is that these celestial female presences are only invoked but not dramatized, just as Milton makes no attempt to give concrete embodiment to his theoretical allowance for angelic sex.

In view of the fact that not only the heavenly Trinity but also all the unfallen angels are male, it becomes especially significant that femininity—and with it sexuality—first enters *Paradise Lost* with the creation of Sin at the moment of Satan's rebellion. Milton's account of the birth of Sin amalgamates the mythological narrative of Athena's springing full-blown from the head of Zeus with the prototypes of female deformity provided by Ovid's Scylla and Spenser's Error. Just as Satan is regularly identified with the values of classical heroism, which are rejected by the standards of Christian epic, so Milton's transformation of the classical goddess of Wisdom into the figure of Sin epitomizes the conflation of the pagan with the demonic throughout *Paradise Lost*. Because of the Hell Hounds perpetually gnawing her womb, Sin possesses a "fair" upper body and "foul" nether parts:

> The one [Sin] seem'd Woman to the waist, and fair
> But ended foul in many a scaly fold
> Voluminous and vast, a Serpent arm'd
> With mortal sting. (II.650–653)

This dichotomy between torso and hips may be understood psycho-analytically as a typical male fantasy resulting from the fact that the nursing infant is permitted to behold the breasts of the mother but not the mysterious genital area (see Thass-Thienemann, 1957, p. 29). The reference to Sin's serpentine "mortal sting," furthermore, suggests the related belief that the mother possesses a penis, as does the Chorus's execration upon the departing Dalila in *Samson Agonistes*: "a manifest Serpent by her sting / Discover'd in the end" (997–998).

Other than Sin, Eve is the only female character in the poem, and Milton contrives in various ways to highlight the association between them. In particular, the grotesque deformity in the lower body of Sin functions as a more extreme version of a telling detail concerning Eve's creation. Upon first awakening into being, she tells Adam, she heard the sound of waters "and laid me down / On the green bank, to look into the clear / Smooth lake, that to me seem'd another sky" (IV.457–459). The importance of this initial impulse to look downward may be measured by Adam's contrasting response to his own creation. Upon finding himself "As new wak'd from soundest sleep," he tells Raphael,

> Straight toward Heav'n my wondering Eyes I turn'd
> And gaz'd a while the ample Sky, till rais'd
> By quick instinctive motion up I sprung
> As thitherward endeavoring, and upright
> Stood on my feet. (VIII.253,257–261)

Whereas Eve only sees "another Sky" as reflected in the "Smooth Lake" below her, Adam looks up at the "ample Sky" forthwith, and likewise springs "upright" by "quick instinctive motion." Although God assures us that humanity is created "Sufficient to have stood," from this contrast between Adam's direct and Eve's mediated first glimpses of the sky it is clear from the beginning that Adam is considerably more "sufficient" than Eve.

The connection between the physical appearance of Sin and

Eve's downward glance at the moment of her creation is made explicit by the Neoplatonic interpretation of Scylla given by George
Sandys in his 1632 translation of Ovid's *Metamorphoses*:

> That the upper part of her body is feigned to retain a human figure
> and the lower to be bestial intimates how man, a divine creature
> endued with wisdom and intelligence, in whose superior parts, as in a
> high tower, that immortal spirit resideth, who only of all that hath life
> erects his look into heaven, can never so degenerate into a beast as
> when he giveth himself over to the low delights of those baser parts of
> the body, dogs and wolves, the blind and savage fury of concupis-
> cence. (Quoted in LeComte, 1978, p. 72)

In Sandys's terms, Adam "erects his look into heaven" because he is
in truth "a divine creature, endued with wisdom and intelligence."
Eve, on the other hand, exhibits a downward pull that shows her to
be less amply endowed with "superior parts," and rather potentially
the embodiment of that "blind and savage fury of concupiscence"
likewise allegorized by Milton in the Hell Hounds gnawing the genitalia of Sin.

After the Fall, moreover, Eve receives her sentence from Christ:
"Thy sorrow I will greatly multiply / By thy conception; Children
shalt thou bring / In sorrow forth" (X.193–195). Her punishment is
harsher than Adam's precisely by virtue of being sexual in nature,
and it reinforces her identification with Sin through its evocation of
the female body in the throes of childbirth. The appropriateness of
using Sandys as a gloss on *Paradise Lost* indicates that Milton's conception of the relations between the sexes, in addition to its individual biographical determinants, is conditioned by his patriarchal cultural milieu; and the same assumptions inhere in Browne's exegesis
of "the temptation of the Man by the Woman" in the Fall as "the
seduction of the rational and higher parts by the inferior and feminine faculties."

Eve's account of her creation contains Milton's most extended
allusion to classical mythology — Ovid's story of Narcissus in the
Metamorphoses (III.402–510). Indeed, Milton compares Eve before
her fall to a series of pagan goddesses, including Proserpina (IV.268–
272), Pandora (IV.714–716), and Aphrodite (V.379–382). In each
case, there is a sinister undertone to the mythological parallel. Such
comparisons are strikingly absent from Milton's portrayal of Adam,
who is never assimilated to a classical hero. The *feminine* is thus a

recurrent third term in Milton's equation between the *classical* and the *demonic*, and together these form an unbreakable chain, the effect of which is to predispose Eve—literally from the moment of her creation—to cast in her lot with the party of Hell.

Eve's attraction to her own image, however, is paralleled by Adam's attraction to her. Indeed, in yielding to his susceptibility to "Beauty's powerful glance," Adam reverses the cosmic hierarchy by making it seem as though he is created in *Eve's* image, rather than she in his (see Stein, 1953, p. 101). As the narrator states, Adam falls "Against his better knowledge, not deceiv'd, / But fondly overcome with Female charm" (IX.998-999), thereby confirming Sandys's warnings against "the low delights of those baser parts of the body." In "On Narcissism" (1914), Freud argues that whereas women tend toward self-love, "which compensates them for the social restrictions that are imposed upon them in their choice of an object," men are characterized by the "sexual overvaluation" attendant upon "complete object-love of the attachment type" (pp. 88-89). Freud's contrast between the types of love prevalent in the two sexes accords precisely with *Paradise Lost*, where the "social restriction" placed upon Eve is represented by the divine voice leading her away from her own reflection toward subordination to Adam, and the efforts of both Eve and Adam to overcome their respective forms of erotic weakness prove equally unsuccessful.

But though love for one's image is variously manifested on Earth in Eve's attraction to herself and in Adam's love for Eve, as well as in Hell, where Sin reminds Satan, "Thyself in me thy perfect image viewing / Becam'st enamour'd" (II.764-765), it is essential to recognize that it is found also in Heaven. Christ is the "radiant image" (III.63) of the Father, and in both our first parents "The image of their glorious Maker shone" (IV.292), though only Adam is said to be created "in the Image of God / Express" (VII.526-527). Milton thus uses the word "image" to bind together the divine, human, and demonic spheres of action in *Paradise Lost*; and in every case, the "image" refers to something that is both part of and physically more attractive than, yet separate from and ontologically inferior to, that which it reflects. Because love for one's image is present in the heavenly relations between Father and Son, it would be erroneous to say that this form of self-love is inherently fallen. The crucial point is that on Earth and in Hell, but *not* in Heaven, the creation of an image is marked by the introduction of genuine otherness through the presence of sexual difference. Christ, Eve, and Sin, that is, all owe their beings to a miraculous feat of male parthenogenesis; but the latter two are not perfect emanations of their respective "authors" as Christ is of his. Thus, it is specifically the "fair defect" of femininity in *Paradise Lost* that renders love for one's own image narcissistic and hence idolatrous.

The equivocal nature of the love between Adam and Eve is especially evident in Adam's conversation with God, recounted to Raphael in Book VIII, in which he requests the creation of a human consort. God teasingly banters with Adam about the reason for his petition, pointing out that he himself is "alone / From all eternity" (405–406), to which Adam fervently replies:

> No need that thou
> Shouldst propagate, already infinite;
> And through all numbers absolute, though One;
> But Man by number is to manifest
> His single imperfection. (419–423)

The word "numbers" is used of God in line 421 with its Latin meaning of "parts," but it bears its ordinary quantitative sense in line 422. The statement that "Man by number is to manifest / His single imperfection" thus becomes especially poignant. "Single imperfection" means "incompleteness when alone" (Latin *perfectus* = "complete"), but also takes on the more insidious implication of "single fault." From this standpoint, man is "In unity defective" (VIII.425), unable to tolerate the single life, precisely because the need for female companionship *stigmatizes him as a sexual being*. Milton's assumptions here are again not peculiar to *Paradise Lost*, but are rather part of a patriarchal tradition in English literature (see Swan, 1985), whose antecedents include the devaluation of women in the poetry of Ben Jonson, and which receives witty expression in Andrew Marvell's praise of the contemplative life in "The Garden": "Two paradises 'twere in one / To live in paradise alone."

Like many other incidents in the prelapsarian state, Adam's desire for an "image multipli'd" (VIII.524) is at once a laudable expression of the nature of his being and—logologically considered—an ineluctable step on the way to the Fall. In accepting Eve's offer of the forbidden fruit, Adam speaks of the "Bond of Nature" (IX.956) that draws him to her; but as their commingling in "carnal

desire" (IX.1014) at the moment of the Fall indicates, it is specifically lust that underlines his need for companionship and ostensibly
altruistic choice to "undergo like doom" (IX.953) with his spouse.
Adam's denunciation of Eve after the Fall, and of God for not creating an entirely masculine world, consequently, is ultimately directed
against what Michael later terms the "effeminate slackness" (XI.634)
within himself.

The contrast between God as "One" and man as constituted "by
number" seems to posit a clear dichotomy between divinity and
humanity with respect to questions of self and other. But, as we have
already noted, the problematic nature of the "image" figures also in
Heaven. Thus, it cannot be overlooked that Milton departs from all
previous literary and theological precedents (see Gilbert, 1942) by
making God's exaltation of the Son as king of the angelic hosts the
occasion for Satan's rebellion. As Mary Nyquist (1985) has compel-
lingly observed, "the deity emerges as, specifically, the Father" by
this elevation of the Son or Logos, and thereby creates "the symbolic
order appropriate to self-presence that is both patriarchal and divine" (p. 188). Satan, however, immediately challenges this order by
his refusal to accept subordination to Christ, and his revolt prompts
the creation of mankind and everything else that happens in the
poem. In Nyquist's formulation, "logos, under attack, gives rise to
mythos. Divine self-presence, magisterially manifesting itself in language and the Word, brings forth the substitutive economy of narrative action" (p. 187).

The effect of this analysis is to show that the implications of
Adam's request for the creation of Eve must be pushed backward to
God's exaltation of the Son in Heaven. The latter, like the former, is
an inherently praiseworthy—the *most* praiseworthy—action. Its consequence, however, is to set in motion the chain of events that leads
immediately to War in Heaven. Satan's rebellion against the patriarchal order, moreover, entails the generation of Sin when he turns
away from God and worships his own "perfect image." Even in Heav-
en, femininity thus intrudes as a representative of mythos or difference: that which cannot be contained within the phallogocentric
ideal of "divine self-presence." Satan's rebellion, seemingly a choice
for which he alone is morally responsible, is in fact made inevitable
by the primordial act of self-division in which God distinguishes
between himself and his "radiant Image" Christ. Because the beget-

ting of the Word gives rise to "the substitutive economy of narrative action," without which *Paradise Lost* could not exist, the logological argument for the necessity of the Fall and our feminist psychoanalytic insights into the sexual thematics of the poem converge here with the deconstructive critique of the metaphysics of presence.

III

In their first recorded conversation, Adam tells Eve that God has enjoined upon them "no other service than to keep / This one, this easy charge" (IV.421–422) not to eat of the Tree of Knowledge. It is, he continues, "The only sign of our obedience left / Among so many signs of power and rule" (428–429). In *The Christian Doctrine*, Milton elaborates discursively on the significance of this prohibition: "It was necessary that something should be forbidden or commanded as a test of fidelity, and that an act in its own nature indifferent, in order that man's obedience might thereby be manifested" (Hughes, ed., 1957, p. 993). Milton's understanding of the Tree of Knowledge is entirely traditional. St. Augustine writes similarly in *The City of God* of "that one tree, which was interdicted not because it was itself bad, but for the sake of commanding a pure and simple obedience" (Bk. XIII, ch. 20). To conclude these psychoanalytic soundings in *Paradise Lost*, I shall explore the implications of the puzzlingly arbitrary or "indifferent" nature of the "test of fidelity" violated by man at the Fall.

For both Milton and St. Augustine, the prohibition against eating of the Tree of Knowledge serves above all as a *marking of limits*, the imposition of a *rule*, which differentiates the creature from the creator. Hence, the tree was not "itself bad," and Adam and Eve's refusal to heed God's commandment entails a *denial of createdness*, a rejection of the existence of a higher power that has preceded them and laid down conditions to which they must adhere. From a theological standpoint, it is God's prerogative to prohibit what he will, and there is no need to look for a further reason why one tree or "sign of obedience" should be specified rather than another.

But this explanation of the Fall may be interrogated further by being transposed into a psychoanalytic framework. Adam and Eve's denial of limits in their disobedience expresses in Freudian terms the oedipal fantasy of taking the father's place and begetting oneself. The force of this interpretation is best seen by juxtaposing Milton's treatment of the falls of man and Satan. In his soliloquy in Eden in Book IV, Satan meditates on his futile rebellion against "Heav'n's matchless king" (41). On the one hand, Satan acknowledges both the justice and the mildness of the duty of obedience imposed upon him: "What could be less than to afford him praise, / The easiest recompense, and pay him thanks, how due!" (46–48); but, on the other hand, he protests against the impossibility of discharging "The debt immense of endless gratitude / So burdensome still paying, still to owe" (52–53). As Thomas Weiskel (1976) has observed, Satan is locked into "a genuine ambivalence, in which identity must at once be ascribed to the Father and won from him" (p. 9). Like Adam and Eve, who find it impossible to keep their single "easy charge," Satan discovers his "easiest recompense" to be intolerably onerous, a "debt immense of endless gratitude" that renders his fall inevitable.

The obverse of the denial of createdness inherent in the Fall is the sin of *idolatry* that occurs when one worships a created being above or independently of its creator. Such an act of idolatry is performed by Eve when, paying obeisance to the "Sovran, virtuous, precious of all Trees" (IX.975), she succumbs to Satan's temptation to see herself as the center of the universe. It is duplicated by Adam when he places his love for Eve — his own image — before his duty to God. According to St. Augustine in *The City of God*, the difference between the earthly and heavenly cities is that the one "is guided and fashioned by love of self, the other by love of God" (Bk. XIV, Ch. 13). But, as Augustine's reference to the "love of self" suggests, the theological concept of idolatry may be apprehended in terms of the psychoanalytic category of narcissism. And since Milton himself links theology and psychology by appropriating the same Ovidian myth that underlies Freud's theory of the ego, the question arises of how the issues of narcissism pivotal to the Fall are related in *Paradise Lost* to those of indebtedness and filial ties emanating from the Oedipus complex.

The problem of the arbitrary nature of the restriction imposed upon the Tree of Knowledge is strikingly illuminated from the standpoint of structuralist anthropology by Lévi-Strauss's (1949) declaration that "*The fact of being a rule*, completely independent of modalities, is indeed the very essence of the incest prohibition" (p. 32). Since the "indifferent" divine interdiction shares with the incest taboo the defining quality of simply *being a rule*, completely independent of modalities" or extrinsic justification, this strongly suggests that the two are identical. Indeed, to bring together psychoanalytic and structuralist lines of my argument, *Paradise Lost* shows that the action of "Man's first disobedience" (I.1) is no more than the "manifest content" of the Fall, the "latent content" of which must be sought in a violation of the incest prohibition.

As we have observed, the repudiation of origins entailed by the Fall, implicit in Adam and Eve's transgression of divinely ordained limits, is most starkly delineated in the predicament of Satan. In his confrontation with Abdiel, contrary to the better knowledge revealed in his soliloquy in Eden in Book IV, Satan goes so far as to assert that he is his own progenitor: "We know no time when we were not as now; / Know none before us, self-begot, self-rais'd / By our own quickening power" (V.859–861). The claim to be "self-begot, self-rais'd" clearly presupposes a defiance of the incest prohibition, since it could only be accomplished through taking the place of one's father. But the full ramifications of Satan's futile oedipal project are dramatized by Milton in the allegory of Satan, Sin, and Death.

This episode has exerted a long-standing fascination over readers of *Paradise Lost*, giving rise since the eighteenth century to a split between those neoclassical, angelic critics (Addison, Dr. Johnson) who condemned it on aesthetic or religious grounds and the demonic, pre-Romantics (Edmund Burke) who hailed it for its sublimity. Part of the controversy elicited by these passages in Books II and X concerns their ontological status, that is, whether they are to be regarded as any less "real" or "historical" than the remainder of the poem because of their overtly allegorical quality (see Gallagher, 1976). But it is not necessary to discount the historicity of the episode, when measured against the remainder of the epic, to grant that its emblematic nature causes it to stand out from the text in such a way as to guide our interpretation of *Paradise Lost* as a whole.

The consequence of the fall of Adam and Eve is the entry of sin and death into the world. By personifying these abstractions as characters in his allegory, Milton gives his most graphic representation of the effects of the Fall. This infernal trinity is conjoined not by a single but by a threefold act of incest (see II.746–815). Satan couples with Sin after she springs from his head; Death, the result of their union, not to be outdone by his father, commits a forcible rape upon his mother; and the Hell Hounds begotten by Death forever gnaw the womb of Sin. When Satan reunites after the Fall with his "Fair Daughter, and thou Son and Grandchild both" (X.384), they meet at a point between Earth, Hell, and Heaven: "three sev'ral ways / In sight, to each of these three places led" (X.324–325). Taken together with the three-generational confusion in the Satanic family, this allusion to a convergence of "three sev'ral ways" cannot fail to evoke the crossroads in the Oedipus myth.

Following her cephalic birth, as Sin recounts to Satan, who initially fails to recognize his progeny upon encountering them in Book II, the heavenly hosts "recoil'd afraid / At first, and called me Sin, and for a Sign / Portentous held me" (759–761). Milton's collocation here of "Sin" and "Sign" anticipates Adam's description of the Tree of Knowledge as "the only sign of our obedience," which in turn becomes the reminder of sin once its limitations have been violated. When Sin tells Satan, "Thyself in me thy perfect image viewing / Becam'st enamor'd" (II.764–765), as we have noted, she connects Satan's rebellion with the theme of self-love throughout the poem, and particularly with Eve's attraction to her own reflection. Satan's copulation with Sin is thus the sexually explicit form of love for one's image, and enables us to conclude that *the fall of Satan is to the fall of man as incest is to narcissism.* As the most radical depiction of the consequences of self-love, moreover, the allegory of Satan, Sin, and Death discloses the "latent content" of the otherwise "indifferent" act of disobedience represented in the Fall.

Before he embarks on his first journey to Earth, Satan cuts short all discussion in Hell of his plans, lest another of the fallen angels volunteer to go in his place, "winning cheap the high repute / Which he through hazard huge must earn" (II.472–473). But when he approaches Hell Gate, Satan encounters the specter of Death wearing "The likeness of a Kingly Crown" (II.673).[3] By proclaiming his own sovereignty over Hell, as Joseph Summers (1962) has remarked, Death makes "the precise challenge which Satan has feared" (p. 47). The sexual dimension to the rivalry between Satan and Death exemplified by their successive acts of incest with Sin is thus augmented by the aggressive struggle for primacy in Hell — a struggle in which Death gains the upper hand. "And reck'n'st thyself with Spirits of Heav'n," he taunts Satan, "Where I reign King, and to enrage thee more, / Thy King and Lord?" (II.696,698–699). In his confrontation with Death, therefore, Satan presents the pitiful spectacle of a rebellious son who attempts to assume the role of a father, an authority which he has undercut by his own actions.

As is consonant with his technique of parallelism throughout the entire poem, Milton unfolds a comparable anatomy of revolution on the human plane. At his bleakest moments in Book X, Adam echoes Satan's protest against the intolerable burden of createdness: "Did I request thee, Maker, from my Clay / To mould me Man, did I solicit thee / From darkness to promote me?" (743–745). (These lines have become famous as the epigraph to Mary Shelley's *Frankenstein*.) But later in the same soliloquy, Adam realizes that the same ingratitude could be turned against him were he to become a father:

> wilt thou enjoy the good
> Then cavil the conditions? and though God
> Made thee without thy leave, what if thy Son
> Prove disobedient, and reprov'd, retort,
> Wherefore didst thou beget me? (758–762)

Adam's forebodings prove justified, as he discovers in Book XI, when Michael informs him that he must leave his "Capital Seat" in the Garden of Eden: "but this preeminence thou hast lost, brought down / To dwell on even ground now with thy sons" (347–348). Adam's loss of "preeminence" and obligation to share "even ground" with his sons is the human equivalent to Satan's enforced acceptance of Death's claim to be his "King and Lord."

For Milton, consequently, the oedipal rebellion entailed in disobedience of God the Father is an ultimately futile, self-destructive gesture. The preferred alternative of filial piety is embodied in the figure of Christ. Milton's theology, verging on Arianism, denies the doctrine of the Trinity and stresses the subordination of the Son to the Father. All human and cosmic history looks forward to the moment when, as Christ says to the Father, "Thou shalt be All in All, and I in thee / For ever, and in me all whom thou lov'st" (VI.732–733). Beatitude, in Milton's view, stems from a voluntary curtailment of the self, which leads in turn to absorption into a paternal deity. Interpreted psychoanalytically, Milton adopts a strategy of symbolic self-castration so as to forestall the threatened punishment at the hands of the Father. As Otto Fenichel (1945) explains the unconscious logic at work in a boy's feminine castration complex: "If

I act as if I had no penis any more they will not cut it off. . . . If castration cannot be avoided anyhow I prefer it actively in anticipation of what is to come, and I shall at least have the advantage of ingratiating myself with the threatening person" (p. 79).[4]

Christ's heroic renunciation culminates at the close of *Paradise Regained*, when he declines on the pinnacle to yield to Satan's temptation to prove his identity as Son of God. As a result, it is not Christ but Satan who falls to the ground; and in a climactic passage Milton compares Satan to the vanquished Sphinx:

> And as that *Theban* monster that propos'd
> Her riddle, and him who solv'd it not, devour'd,
> That once found out and solv'd, for grief and spite
> Cast herself headlong from th' *Ismenian* steep,
> So struck with dread and anguish fell the Fiend. (IV.572–576)

The most important allusion to the Oedipus myth in Renaissance literature, Milton's simile gains particular weight from being placed in a Greek context through the immediately preceding comparison of Satan and Christ to Antaeus and Hercules. But if Satan is the Sphinx, then Christ must be implicitly identified with Oedipus, but an Oedipus who wards off his Oedipus complex by passively refusing to compete with the Father (see Brisman, 1973, pp. 193–194; Kerrigan, 1983, p. 108).

Satan and Christ, the two sides of a son's ambivalent relation to his father, are best seen as enemy brothers, twin aspects of a single autobiographical psyche. One of Milton's recurrent poetic strategies is to fuse these conflicting filial impulses in the same character, who in rebelling against paternal authority on one level bows to it on another. In *Samson Agonistes* — like *Paradise Regained*, a work explicitly concerned with the solving of riddles — Samson spurns the attempts at ransom of his earthly father Manoa in order that he may be released from captivity by his Father in heaven. In *Paradise Lost*, Abdiel likewise blazes contempt against Satan and his fallen crew so as to proclaim his higher obedience to the Almighty. "Among the faithless, faithful only hee" (V.897), Abdiel is Milton's closest approximation to a self-portrait in *Paradise Lost*; but it is in the human characters of the epic, who disobey God but obtain his forgiveness and the promise of ultimate salvation, that Milton offers his most comprehensive synthesis of the impulses of piety and patricide which are polarized in Christ and Satan.

The precursor who most haunts Milton's life and poetry is neither his biological father, the scrivener John Milton, nor the author
of *The Faerie Queene*, but his heavenly Maker. Like Satan, Milton in
Sonnet XIX on his blindness cannot suppress a "murmur" (9)
against the burden of indebtedness imposed on him by "that one
Talent which is death to hide" (3); but, like Christ, he resolves to
learn to "stand and wait" (14). Out of his unceasing quarrel with God
the Father Milton forges one of the most impressive and successful
resolutions of the Oedipus complex in religious and literary history,
and becomes the incarnation of poetic authority for all who come
after him.

NOTES

1. See also Waldock (1947): "It is obvious that Adam and Eve must already have
   contracted human weaknesses before they can start on the course of conduct that
   leads to their fall: to put it another way, they must already be fallen (technically)
   before they can begin to fall" (p. 61). And Tillyard (1951): "the actual eating of
   the apple becomes no more than an emphatic stage in the process already begun"
   (p. 13). For a perceptive study of the contrasts between unfallen and fallen
   experience in *Paradise Lost*, which, however, defines these modalities in purely
   dichotomous terms, see Swaim (1986).
2. In his recent *Feminist Milton* (1987), Joseph Wittreich performs a valuable service
   by documenting the often-sympathetic responses to Milton by seventeenth- and
   eighteenth-century female readers. But Wittreich's larger claim that *Paradise Lost*
   and the other major poems "do not deepen and extend, but rather decry and
   explode, the biblically sanctioned and culturally reinforced traditions of patriarchy and misogyny" (p. 10) fails to carry conviction.
3. Frye (1978) notes that "the only crown in Hell is the crown of Death. Milton
   provides Satan with the most stunningly ornate throne in literature, but he never
   gives fallen Satan the dignity of a crown. In this Milton is at odds with a popular
   element of visual tradition, in which Satan is frequently shown with a crown" (p.
   117).
4. For an analysis of similar mechanisms at work in the poetry of Crashaw, see
   Camden (1983). On Milton's feminine identification as "a private sphere of
   power" and the way his blindness served as an anticipatory punishment enabling
   him to "solicit prophetic vision" in *Paradise Lost*, see Kerrigan (1983, pp. 50, 190).

REFERENCES

AUGUSTINE, ST. (1950) *The City of God*. (Marcus Dods, Trans.). New York: Modern
    Library.
BELL, M. (1953) The Fallacy of the Fall in *Paradise Lost*. *PMLA*, 68:863–883.
BRISMAN, L. (1973) *Milton's Poetry of Choice and Its Romantic Heirs*. Ithaca, NY: Cornell
    University Press.

BURKE, K. (1961) *The Rhetoric of Religion: Studies in Logology.* Boston: Beacon.

CAMDEN, V. J. (1983) Richard Crashaw's Poetry: The Imagery of Bleeding Wounds. *American Imago*, 40:257–279.

FENICHEL, O. (1945) *The Psychoanalytic Theory of Neurosis.* New York: Norton.

FISH, S. E. (1967) *Surprised by Sin: The Reader in* Paradise Lost. Berkeley: University of California Press.

FREUD, S. (1914) On Narcissism: An Introduction. *Standard Edition*, 14:73–102.

FROULA, C. (1983) When Eve Reads Milton: Undoing the Classical Economy. *Critical Inquiry*, 10:321–347.

FRYE, R. M. (1955) The Teachings of Classical Puritanism on Conjugal Love. *Studies in the Renaissance*, 2:148–155.

———— (1978) *Milton's Imagery and the Visual Arts: Iconographic Tradition in the Epic Poems.* Princeton, NJ: Princeton University Press.

GALLAGHER, P. J. (1976) "Real or Allegoric": The Ontology of Sin and Death in *Paradise Lost. English Literary Renaissance*, 6:317–335.

GILBERT, A. H. (1942) The Theological Basis of Satan's Rebellion and the Function of Abdiel in *Paradise Lost. Modern Philology*, 40:19–42.

GILBERT, S. M., & GUBAR, S. (1979) *The Madwoman in the Attic: The Woman Writer and the Nineteenth-Century Literary Imagination.* New Haven, CT: Yale University Press.

HALLER, W. (1946) Hail Wedded Love. *ELH*, 13:79–97.

———— & HALLER, M. (1942) The Puritan Art of Love. *Huntington Library Q.*, 5:235–272.

HUGHES, M. Y. (Ed.). (1957) *John Milton: Complete Poems and Major Prose.* New York: Odyssey.

KERRIGAN, W. W. (1983) *The Sacred Complex: On the Psychogenesis of* Paradise Lost. Cambridge, MA: Harvard University Press.

LANDY, M. (1972) Kinship and the Role of Women in *Paradise Lost. Milton Studies*, 4:3–18.

———— (1976) "A Free and Open Encounter": Milton and the Modern Reader. *Milton Studies*, 9:3–36.

LAPLANCHE, J. (1970) *Life and Death in Psychoanalysis* (Jeffrey Mehlman, Trans.). Baltimore: Johns Hopkins University Press, 1976.

LECOMTE, E. (1978) *Milton and Sex.* New York: Columbia University Press.

LÉVI-STRAUSS, C. (1949) *The Elementary Structures of Kinship.* (James Harle Bell & John Richard von Sturmer Trans.). Boston: Beacon, 1969.

LEWALSKI, B. K. (1974) Milton on Women — Yet Once More. *Milton Studies*, 6:3–20.

LEWIS, C. S. (1942) *A Preface to* Paradise Lost. London: Oxford University Press.

McCOLLEY, D. K. (1983) *Milton's Eve.* Urbana: University of Illinois Press.

NYQUIST, M. (1985) The Father's Word/Satan's Wrath. *PMLA*, 100:187–202.

———— (1987) Gynesis, Genesis, Exegesis, and the Formation of Milton's Eve. In Marjorie Garber (Ed.), *Cannibals, Witches, and Divorce: Estranging the Renaissance* (pp. 147–208). Baltimore: Johns Hopkins University Press.

OGDEN, H. V. S. (1957) The Crisis of *Paradise Lost* Reconsidered. *Philological Q.*, 36:1–19.

SHUMAKER, W. (1955) The Fallacy of the Fall in *Paradise Lost. PMLA*, 70:1185–1187.

STEIN, A. (1953) *Answerable Style: Essays on* Paradise Lost. Seattle: University of Washington Press.

———— (1977) *The Art of Presence: The Poet in* Paradise Lost. Berkeley: University of California Press.

SUMMERS, J. H. (1962) *The Muse's Method: An Introduction to* Paradise Lost. Binghamton: Center for Medieval and Renaissance Studies, 1981.

Swaim, K. M. (1986) *Before and After the Fall: Contrasting Modes in* Paradise Lost. Amherst: University of Massachusetts Press.

Swan, J. (1985) Difference and Silence: John Milton and the Question of Gender. In Shirley Nelson Gardner *et al.* (Eds.), *The (M)other Tongue: Essays in Feminist Psychoanalytic Interpretation* (pp. 142–168). Ithaca: Cornell University Press.

Thass-Thienemann, T. (1957) Oedipus and the Sphinx: The Linguistic Approach to Unconscious Fantasies. *Psychoanal. R.*, 44:10–33.

Tillyard, E. M. W. (1951) *Studies in Milton.* London: Chatto & Windus.

Waldock, A. J. A. (1947) Paradise Lost *and Its Critics.* Cambridge: Cambridge University Press.

Webber, J. M. (1980) The Politics of Poetry: Feminism and *Paradise Lost. Milton Studies,* 14:3–24.

Weiskel, T. (1976) *The Romantic Sublime: Structures in the Structure and Psychology of Transcendence.* Baltimore: Johns Hopkins University Press.

Wittreich, J. (1987) *Feminist Milton.* Ithaca: Cornell University Press.

Department of English and Comparative Literature
Columbia University
New York, NY 10027

NOTES ON CONTRIBUTORS

LOWELL EDMUNDS, PH.D., is Professor of Classics and Chairman of the Department of Classics at The Johns Hopkins University. He is the author of *Oedipus: The Ancient Legend and Its Later Analogues* and has edited, with Alan Dundes, *Oedipus: A Folklore Casebook*.

DIANNE HUNTER, PH.D., is Associate Professor of English at Trinity College in Hartford, CT, where she teaches psychoanalytic and feminist interpretations of literature. Her articles have been published in *American Imago* and other journals.

JOHN KERR is a PH.D. candidate in clinical psychology at New York University and staff psychotherapist at New Hope Guild in Brooklyn. His essay, *"Beyond the Pleasure Principle* and Back Again: Freud, Jung, and Spielrein,"* appears in *Freud Studies*, Vol. 3.

SIR EDMUND LEACH, is a Professor, Fellow, and former Provost of King's College, Cambridge, with a special interest in the iconography of the pictures in the famous windows of that school. He is co-author, with D. Alan Aycock, of *Structuralist Interpretations of Biblical Myth* and other papers and delivered the 1986 Ernest Jones Lecture before the British Psycho-Analytic Society.

THEODORE LIDZ, M.D., is Emeritus Professor and former Chairman, Department of Psychiatry, Yale University School of Medicine. He is the author of *The Person, The Origin and Treatment of Schizopherenic Disorders, Hamlet's Enemy*, and co-author, with Ruth Lidz, of a book based on field work in New Guinea.

DANIEL RUBEY, PH.D., is the Humanities Librarian at Lehman College, CUNY and has published articles on medieval and Renaissance literature, literary theory, and film.

PETER L. RUDNYTSKY, PH.D., is Assistant Professor of English and Comparative Literature at Columbia University. He is the author of *Freud and Oedipus* and has previously served as Guest Editor of *American Imago*.

ELLEN HANDLER SPITZ, PH.D., is Visiting Lecturer of art history at Cornell Medical Center and Adjunct Professor at New York University. She is the author of *Art and Psyche*.